WOMEN OF DISTINCTION

WOMEN OF DISTINCTION:
Remarkable in Works, Invincible in Character

A Series of Biographies

path press
ORIGINAL & REPRINT PUBLISHERS

Published by Path Press, Inc.
Post Office Box 5683
Evanston, Illinois 60204-5683
pathpressinc@aol.com

Printed in the United States of America on acid-free paper

Library of Congress-in-Publication Data
Scruggs, Lawson A. - author
Scruggs Leftwich, Yvonne - editor/compiler
Identifiers: LCCN 2020932167 | ISBN 978-0-910671-22-4 (paperback)
ISBN 978-0-910671-19-4 (hardcover)
Subjects: LCSH: African American women-Biography| African American
Women-History | African American women-Social conditions.

Layout – Aaron Foster (AaronFosternet@gmail.com)
Cover design – Verzell James, JAM Graphics and Publishing, Co.

TABLE OF CONTENTS

My part has been to tell the story of the slave. The narration of the master never wanted for narrators.

Frederick Douglass

WOMEN OF DISTINCTION:
REMARKABLE IN WORKS AND INVINCIBLE
IN CHARACTER: 1892

by

LAWSON ANDREW SCRUGGS - M.D.

FOREWORD BY
Yvonne Scruggs-Leftwich, Ph.D.
Grand-daughter of Author, Lawson Andrew Scruggs, M.D.

My Grandfather, Lawson Andrew Scruggs, M.D, was a remarkable man, especially for his era. He would be remarkable even in this era. Writing in the 1890's – more than a century ago - he was much ahead of his time and also ahead of the gender disempowerment of this nation, as is clearly demonstrated by his focus on the importance of women and their accomplishments. He would easily be certified as a card-carrying feminist consciousness- raiser of this century.

Dr. Scruggs' passionate racial pride and his determination to identify role models for young African-Americans, women *and* men, rival the best efforts of today's civil and women's rights activists. He was, without doubt, a Renaissance Man of great intellectual energy and a compelling sense of history. He was my father's father, a grandfather who died before I was born, but whose legacy has significantly impacted my life.

It is breath-taking to realize that this book, Women of Distinction, was written during such a punitive period in our social and racial odyssey. Women were not yet able to vote, could not participate in many institutional processes in this American democracy – or for that matter- in most of the rest of the world – and frequently had no identity independence from their husbands or fathers. Yet Dr. Scruggs' book celebrates the important contributions of African American women of that era, both to black and white cultures. That he was a fully engaged, practicing physician, a full-time college and University professor, and a man socialized in a largely chauvinistic environment, makes his progressive pre-occupations all the more remarkable.

My grandfather's "Preface" in his book is barren of most details of his life and his own accomplishments. I believe that this is the case largely because when Women of Distinction was published in 1893, Grandfather was 36 years old, just embarking upon his productive medical practice   and entering a new marriage following the death of his first wife. My own father, Leonard Andrew Scruggs, named in part after the Leonard School of Medicine   an affiliate of Shaw University where Grandfather was senior professor of physiology but actually was the Dean. (In that century and well into the next, most African Americans were denied full agency in the leadership of institutions where they would be superior in rank to whites also employed there, as was the case of the Leonard Medical School, in deep-South Raleigh, North Carolina – in the 1900's !)

My grandfather Scruggs sublimated his prolific drive with his work on his intended next book, to share his impressions of the World's Fair, which he attended in Chicago, Illinois.   That book was never completed. His diary of that experience is in my possession and reinforces his constant awe of the human potential and creativity of women. His notes reflect his positive bias for women's station:

"...I next entered the Women's building which,of course, was fine, neatly arranged,well filled and all in good shape. But,of course, I was not so much interested in the special exhibits other than proud to see women do well. The fancy work...etc...was fine, indeed."

Grandfather Scruggs went on in his life to construct and create treatment protocols for the first African American Tuberculosis Sanitarium in the United States, named "Pickfair Sanitarium" located in Southern Pines, North Carolina. Although Dr. Scruggs' personal life is somewhat opaque to us today, we know that his first wife was named Lucy Johnson

Scruggs and that she is profiled in Women of Distinction. She died i
1892 at the age of 28. His second wife and our Dad's mother was Clai
Jane Burroughs,, who Grandfather married in 1895. She also died about
year later at age 27.

When Dr. Scruggs died in Buffalo, New York in 1909,, his medical practice
had flourished,,but the Southern Pines Sanitarium had been destroyed by fire
And,characteristic of many idealists and intellectuals, his material legacy was bu
a trunk full with "accounts receivable" notations from his patients, wh
had been desperately ill and in need of medical treatment, but were equall
desperately impecunious. My father's primary inheritance was th
fond memory of a protected childhood and a keen sense of having live
in the aura of a man of great talent, substance and civility. Leonar
Andrew Scruggs, Sr, also inherited a sharp brain which took hir
through graduation from Ohio State University and into the Mortuary Scienc
field and his own business in St. Louis, Missouri and Niagara Falls, New Yor!
He later became a Master Electrical Engineer in Buffalo, New York.

Copies of the original edition of Women of Distinction remain available, but ar
closely guarded. The book is precious, rare and beautiful to look at and to hold
There were, a few years ago, copies cataloged in the LIBRARY O
CONGRESS in Washington, D.C...but when I gained access to th
Stacks last year, both of these secured copies had been stolen ...fror
scholars and public lovers of rare books *and of social and intellectur*
justice. Some original copies still remain in the libraries of Historicall
Black Colleges and Universities (HBCU's) and in a few private boo
collections. For that reason, Dr. Lawson Andrew Scruggs'

Family is now republishing WOMEN OF DISTINCTION:
REMARKABLE IN WORKS AND INVINCIBLE IN
CHARACTER in collaboration with the Path Press, Inc. of Illinois. Our
inspiration is appropriately found in the prose and poetry of *Dr.
Lawson Andrew Scruggs himself, our gifted Grandfather:*

*"... If in such a short time of greatly abridged citizenship our women have
accomplished so much, and if many of these heroines mentioned did develop
such giant intellects during those dark days of our history,*

may we not be encouraged to make more diligent, protracted efforts in this brighter age?"

Publication by Grandchildren of Dr. Lawson Andrew Scruggs: Leonard Andrew Scruggs, Jr., Dr. Yvonne Scruggs-Leftwich, Harriet A. Scruggs, Roslyn E. Scruggs

February 4, 2020

PREFACE

In launching this little barque, bearing the outlines of a book, the builder (author) is not altogether thought less of the stormy sea over which it may be driven, nor of that far-away. destiny (success) which it may never reach. And yet with hope as an anchor both "sure and steadfast" it has been launched, and out upon life's sea must go.

Who could expect otherwise than as it sails off from the shore that the severe scrutiny of the wise and learned, as well as the keen and rigid criticism of friend and foe, of the interested and the disinterested, the prejudiced and the non-prejudiced, will fall upon it with such activity as may be simply alarming. But, after all, if by chance it is allowed to humbly pursue the journey of its mission, educating public sentiment, stimulating and encouraging the young women and young men of the race who are almost overcome and discouraged by the dashing billows of life's angry sea; if by reading the lives of these noble heroines; if by meditating upon their sacrifices and deeds; if by contrasting the opportunities of those former and darker days with those presented in these brighter days; if from the contents of this volume the young women of our race shall gather a single ray of hope and encouragement which will enable them to stem the tide and become *women of usefulness* and *distinction,* honored of men and blessed of God, then this barque (book) shall have accomplished one of the objects of its mission.

Again, there have been a great many untrue things said by a part of the Southern press that have been against the best interests of the race. The Northern traveler through the South has also quite often gathered information at railway stations and from other unreliable, sources, which has been given to the world through a part of the Northern press, greatly to the detriment of the race. From these sources the womanhood of the race has suffered great and unmerited injustice when taken as a whole. If by reading the contents of this volume contradiction can be justly established and thereby we can reclaim some of the prestige we have been thus caused to lose, then another important object of this mission shall

11

have been accomplished. It is quite evident that the world has not as yet learned to fully appreciate the extent to which *mind* and *character* have been and can be developed in the *women* of this race.

"Great statesmen govern nations,
Kings mould a people's fate
But the unseen hand of velvet
These giants regulate.

The ponderous wheel of fortune
In woman's charms is pearled ;
For the hand that rocks the cradle
Is the hand that rules the world."

If in such a short time of greatly abridged citizenship our women have accomplished so much, and if many of those heroines mentioned did develop such giant intellects during those dark days of our history, may we not be the more encouraged to make more diligent protracted and determined efforts in this brighter age?.

The glorious days that we now enjoy are made the *more sacred* when we remember the sacrifices, the tears, the labors, the prayers and the blood of thousands of our mothers and sisters, most of whom have gone into another world, but some of whose triumphs are here in mentioned To acquaint the world with many of these facts, and to assist in more fully establishing that fundamental principle that under *similar conditions* the, color of the skin nor the quality of the hair can have no bearings whatsoever upon the operations of the human mind, for we believe that in the mental world there is neither Greek nor Jew nor Gentile, neither bound nor free, neither African nor Caucasian, for God "hath made of one blood all nations of men for to dwell on all the face of the earth."

It has also been to the author, who has spent many years in careful observation among the masses, a painful experience to see how little is known of our great women and their works. To assist in giving this information to our young people, that they may be the more proud of their *ancestors* and love more devotedly their *race,* is another part of our mission. And now, in addition to the debt of gratitude lie owes those who have so kindly and ably contributed articles to this book, the author is also grateful to Rev. A. G. Davis, Mr. E. A. Johnson, Mr. George W. Williams Mr. William Still, Mr. I. G. Penn, Mr. E. E. Cooper, Mrs. Christine S. Smith, Mrs. F. W. Titus, Mr. James M. Trotter, Mrs. N. F. Mossell, Mr. W. H. Council and others for valuable assistance rendered by themselves and their writings. While the preparation of this book has been a very arduous task, and might be regarded a presumption, it has nevertheless been a very pleasant duty. We have desired to be just, and as far as possible we have tried to avoid exaggerations. After all, however, we are aware that the book is by no means a perfect one. There are some whose lives should be mentioned herein that are not.

Much of this seeming negligence is due to a failure of some of the parties to respond, while some others we have not been able to reach after repeated trials.

When it is remembered how difficult it is to gather reliable *data* from all parts of this great country, as well as from Africa, we trust that there shall be no reasonable cause of offense, and that no one will have so little charity as to charge that we have been partial or narrow.

If this volume should be accepted to such an extent as to warrant it safe to issue a second edition, and should the author's life and health be preserved, he will gladly record the deeds and achievements of those noble women whose names do not appear herein. We have done the best we could under the circumstances, and therefore send this volume forth with a prayer that God may bless and use the humble effort to the good of mankind.

INTRODUCTION.

by

MRS. JOSEPHINE TURPIN WASHINGTON.

The position accorded the women of a nation is a gauge of that nation's civilization. In one age or clime man's slave and beast of burden, in another his pet and plaything, the hidden adornment of a harem or the inspiration of a chivalry more or less Quixotic, it remained for our own time and country to approach most nearly a recognition of her true place and station.

"God created man in his own image, in the image of God created he him ; male and female created he them."

There need be no trite discussion of the relative superiority or inferiority of the sexes. The claim of equality need not be mistaken for an assertion of perfect likeness.

> "Woman is not undeveloped man,
> But diverse."

The true woman takes her .place by the side of man-as his companion, his co-worker, his help meet, his *equal,* but she never forgets that she is a woman and not a man. Whether in the home as wife and mother, or struggling in the ranks of business or professional life, she retains her womanly dignity and sweetness, which is at once her strength and her shield.

The nineteenth century, " woman's century," as Victor Hugo aptly terms it, marks the acme of her development, but there has been no time when her power was not felt. From the earliest period, when Eve was beguiled of the serpent and in turn tempted Adam, down through the ages when Sappho sang and Hypatia showed what genius repressed could yet accomplish, woman's influence has been potent. That influence, however, is greatly enhanced, both in the quiet walks of life, where fate and preference retain the majority, and in the more public ways, where duty calls an increasing number, by the recognition of woman's equality with man. This belief has steadily made its growth among nations in proportion as they advanced from savagery and the butchery and brutality by which it is attended. As war waned and the arts of peace prevailed, as the necessity for more bodily strength decreased, and more attention was paid to the cultivation of the mind, woman's claim for recognition grew in popular favor and esteem.

Even in this age, however, there are some who refuse to see any good in what is sometimes termed the emancipation of woman. Because many noble and lovable -women have been content to abide beneath the shadow of the home-roof, and have never sought to extend their influence beyond the domestic circle, they deny the fitness of any woman's doing so, regardless of the difference in the nature and circumstances of different individuals, and even of the fact that many women have no roof-tree under which to abide. The "progressive woman" is caricatured and held up as a horror and a warning to that portion of the feminine world who might be tempted into like forbidden paths. "She is out of her sphere, she ought to be in her home, she is trying to be a man, she is losing the tender consideration and the reverence once accorded womanhood." All these things are said, and, as might be expected, are applicable to individual cases. They do not, however, portray the true type of the "progressive woman" of to-day. She is modest and womanly, with a reverence for the high and holy duties of wife and mother. She does not advocate the abandonment of any real duties near at hand for fancied ones afar off. She would not have women neglect home and husband and children to enter professional life, or to further any public cause, however worthy. She only claims the right to admission in the varied fields of employment and usefulness of those who either have no domestic ties, or, having them, are forced, despite this fact, to enter the arena of life in the struggle for bread, or those who, without a disregard of existing claims, yet have leisure and inclination for interests outside of the home.

The woman is a human being as well as a woman. It is within the range of possibility that sometimes she may be endowed with great gifts which it is fortunate for all minds if she can find opportunity to exercise. What would we not have missed had Patti never sung, Rose Bonheur never painted, or Mrs. Stowe never written? Besides, contact with the outer world, a little rubbing against other minds, an occasional directing of the energies into new channels, refreshes and invigorates the tired wife and mother and enables her to give of her best to the dear ones at home. The various gatherings of women throughout the land, in clubs and societies and combinations for the progress of the temperance movement and other reforms, are to be applauded, even if they accomplish no other good than this drawing away, for a time at least, of wives and mothers from the treadmill of a routine house-life.

The fruits of woman's work are not, however, to be so limited. Organized she has advanced countless humanitarian causes, while individually she has risen to eminence in the varied fields of her choice. Will any one sneer at the life-work of Hannah More, Harriet Martineau, Caroline Herschel ? Can any be found, even among those who oppose the public life of women, to do otherwise than commend the character and achievements of such women as Florence Nightingale, Frances Willard, Clara Barton and Mary Livermore ?

This widening of woman's sphere of thought and action is a thing to be encouraged rather than denounced, even by those who reverence most highly the home-life and believe that woman finds there her truest element and highest usefulness. In the "good old days" marriage was deemed a necessity to woman, the end of her being, while only an incident, albeit an important one, in the career of man. Women shrank from the title of "old maid," and to avoid that and an aimless, purposeless existence, or to secure a home and the means of support, were tempted often into loveless, unsuitable marriages. Is it so, to the same extent, in our day? The term "old maid," even when used, is not uttered with the contempt of former times. Think of the many noble single women of your acquaintance who are bravely fighting the battle of life alone, winning for themselves a competency and fair renown, and at the same time doing good service for humanity. The prince has not come to them. Some have grown old in life's struggle and will go through the remainder of their years without the halo of love, without tender home ties of their own; but they will have fought a good fight, and in many cases they have given of their strength and courage to some weak wife or mother, bowed down with the burdens and responsibilities of a position too often lightly and thoughtlessly assumed. Some of these brave and earnest working women are young and blooming. For them the prince may come, he may not. They are content to wait, not idly, not with folded hands and the feeling that if he come not all hope is lost and life not worth the living, but working sturdily and blithely, developing the energies of mind and body, proving themselves worthy of their womanhood and fit mates for strong and manly men. So the car of progress moves onward, rapidly in favored localities, more slowly in sections less tolerant of innovation; but always towards that perfect solution of the "woman question" so happily pictured in Edward Bellamy's "Looking Backward."

What of Afro-American womanhood? What of our wives and mothers and sisters and daughters? Are they, too, included in these movements of progress, in this marvelous advance of womankind? Much have they wrought, yet much remains for future work. It is not just to rate them according to the status they occupy in comparison with Anglo-American womanhood. Not alone should be considered the height to which they have ascended, but also the depth from which they have arisen. Alas, that it must be written! Afro-American women, like Afro-American men, in this "laud of the free and home of the brave," are shut out from much which is helpful to a higher development; they are pursued by a monster prejudice whose voracious appetite is appeased only when they have been reduced to abject servitude and are content to remain "hewers of wood and drawers of water." All the disabilities which affect the race in this country our women have to contend against, with the added disability of sex. These disabilities, while artificial and transitory in character, must affect our expectation and our estimate of the work hitherto accomplished. That work, while marvelous in view of the obstacles which have beset the path of Afro-American womanhood, is to be considered rather as a promise than as a fulfillment. If it sometimes fails to be impressive, like the child in whom we watch the dawning of the man, it never fails to be interesting. The sky is

> Bright with flashes which forerun
>
> The glories of a yet unrisen sun."

What has been accomplished by our women has been despite many obstacles and discouragements. The Afro-American is no anomaly in that at one stage of his development he failed to recognize the importance of cultivating his women. All peoples, in their progress toward civilization and while yet afar off, have been in the dark on this point. Even the benefactors of the race, the philanthropists who so generously aided the cause of education among us, by their own example fostered this idea of the comparative unimportance of educating the women of the race. The mistake was in not measuring the negro by the same standard applied to other peoples. Our only educational need was thought to be that of educated ministers, and even they were educated often in theology at the expense of spelling and grammar.

For a long time the idea held sway among us that it did not "pay" to spend much time and money in schooling the girls. "They made no use of their education," was affirmed, unless, indeed, they taught for a year ,or two, after which they resigned to marry. So the woman who might have become the mother of a Bacon or a Newton, or who might have blossomed into a George Eliot or a Mrs. Browning, was left with dormant intellect and unexpanded energies to grope her way in darkness, unwitting even of all she had missed.

Our poverty, too, has been, and even is, a strong force to repress ambition and to thwart the desire for a broad and liberal culture. Woman's role has ever been that of self-sacrifice. It has seemed to her right and natural that all the available funds of the family should be lavished on the son in college, even though some of it was spent in useless little extravagances, while the sisters at home received but scant culture from the village pedagogue, or none at all, spending their time, instead, bending over the wash-tub or the sewing-machine, striving by their industry to add to the comforts or to the advantages of the idolized brother in school. Gray-haired mothers, from whose youth every ray of learning was rigorously excluded, have suffered untold toil and privation in the effort to give to their children the blessings of an education. All honor to them, and to the patient, self-sacrificing wives who have struggled under the burden of the family maintenance, while the husband pursued the course in school from which he was debarred in earlier life, and which was essential to his usefulness and success in his chosen calling.

Everywhere the Afro-American woman is educated and is unopposed by any prejudice against the exercise of her talents, by reason of lack of leisure and freedom from household cares, in most cases she is hindered in mental effort and in the production of any work which might take definite shape before the world.

In view of all these facts it is surprising that we have as many women among us who have to so considerable an extent, worked out their own salvation and that of the race. Let us not use extravagant words of commendation, lest we have left no fit terms of praise for the woman of our future who is hopefully prophesied by the achievements of her progenitors, toiling today amid varied disadvantages; but let us chronicle their deeds in fitting phrase that those who come after may be inspired by the record of what has been wrought to make the most of their more liberal opportunities, and so hasten the time when our work may be criticized as that of human beings, and neither as that of colored women nor as that of women.

The day is coming when we shall not

> "Be satisfied with praise.
> Which men give women when they judge a book—
> Not as mere work, but as mere woman's work,
> Expressing the comparative respect.
> Which means the absolute scorn."

Even now we have some among us for whom it is not meet to intimate an apology, women whose work speaks for itself and has neither sex nor complexion.

It is necessary only to mention Edmonia Lewis, in whose veins courses the blood of the despised race, and whose genius and triumphant career are universally conceded, to instance the possibilities of Afro-American womanhood. Many others there are, also, whose successes in educational, professional, industrial and literary pursuits have been chronicled by our author, and still others, no doubt, whose achievements, though equally praiseworthy, have been unintentionally omitted.

It is most fitting that one whose early struggles for education and a higher development were nobly supplemented by the self-sacrificing efforts of a loving mother should himself become the champion of that mother's sex, and especially of the numbers just entering the light studiously shut out from her longing eyes.

Such a son of such a mother is Lawson Andrew Scruggs, born in Bedford county, Virginia, January 15, 1857, of slave parentage. Like many another of our able and successful men his early educational advantages were extremely limited. When he reached the age of twenty years he could do scarcely more than read and write. Even this scant knowledge was gained under great difficulties. His days were usually spent in arduous labor on the farm. At night, when not too worn-out from physical toil, he would pore over his books by a torch-light fire. When the weather did not admit of work on the farm he was allowed the privilege of attending the common school, if the one in his neighborhood chanced to be in session. Probably the whole time spent in school in this manner did not aggregate eight months in as many years.

After leaving the farm he was employed as a laborer on the telegraph lines in the South. He still tried to pursue his studies, though now without any assistance whatever, even learning a little of English grammar by carrying a page or two in his pocket and committing it at odd moments. It was while on a telegraph inspecting tour that, in company with some fellow-workmen, he visited the Richmond Institute, at Richmond, Virginia, one of the Baptist Home Mission Society schools. He was at once impressed with the desirability of "going to college," mostly on account of the name and prestige it would give him among his youthful companions in the old home neighborhood. Inflated with a " little learning," he had no true conception either of what he knew or of what he lacked of knowing. Despite his scanty schooling he was already acknowledged the brightest lad in the country round about, and by common consent was accorded the honor of letter-writer for all his love lorn. In October, 1877, he entered the Richmond Institute with the intention of staying one session. He stayed five, though unable to complete any session but the last. It was in this institution that the writer became acquainted with him, and then began that friendship which, unlike many school intimacies, has stood the test of time.

Young Scruggs was quite a favorite with both professors and fellow-pupils. He was live, earnest and genial, a hard-working and conscientious student, and a merry comrade on the play-ground. In May, 1882, he was graduated, taking the school prize in oratory and delivering the salutatory of his class.

His views of what he knew had changed somewhat since the days when he wrote love-letters for the youthful swains of Bedford county. In the fall of 1882 he entered Shaw University, at Raleigh, North Carolina. Here he pursued, at the same time, the literary and the medical courses, being graduated in 1886 and 1887 respectively from the literary and medical departments. In each case he was the valedictorian of his class, and he was, in addition, the recipient of the prize in surgery from the medical department, having previously taken a prize in anatomy. He was at once appointed resident physician and instructor in hygiene and physiology at Shaw University and resident physician at Leonard Hospital. After having served acceptably in these capacities for four years he resigned to give himself more completely to private practice, which, during this *interim,* had engaged his hours of leisure. He has since accepted the position of Visiting Physician and Lecturer on Physiology and Hygiene at St. Augustine Normal and Collegiate Institute, which position he now holds.

It is a noteworthy fact that Dr. Scruggs was the first colored man to hold these appointments in either Shaw University or St. Augustine Institute. He has also the distinction of having organized the Medical Association among Afro-American physicians of North Carolina. As an earnest and effective race worker he has won a high reputation. For five years he has been the regular North Carolina correspondent of the *National Baptist* of Philadelphia, a paper having probably the largest circulation of any Baptist organ in the country. His letters deal mainly with race interests, and he never fails to present the negro's case in equity. One communication of especial importance is a reply to Mr. Thomas Nelson Page, who had published in the *North American Review* an arraignment of the colored people of the country for what he considered a lack of progress during the year of their freedom.

Dr. Scruggs is a hard-working physician, but he finds time amid arduous duties of a most exacting profession, to keep in touch with the living issues of the day, and especially with those which concern us as Afro-Americans. Honor to all such young men among us! "May their tribe increase!" Afro-American womanhood may be congratulated upon entrance into the lists on her behalf of so worthy and zealous a knight as Lawson Andrew Scruggs.

JOSEPHINE TURPIN WASHINGTON

PHILLIS WHEATLEY

CHAPTER I

PHILLIS WHEATLEY

In 1761, when the inhabitants of Africa were stolen by cruel hands and brought to America, the "sweet land of liberty," and sold, as so many cat-tle, under the protection of the flag of this "land of the pilgrim's pride," among the cargo of this human freight that watt put upon the market at Boston, Mass., was a collection of little children, one of whom was the afterwards famous Phillis Wheatley.

A lady of some prominence, Mrs. John Wheatley, desiring to purchase a bright little girl whom she might train for a suitable staff upon which to depend for service in old age, went to this market and of all the any she saw none so attracted her admiration as a delicate, meek, intelligent-looking little girl about seven years old, whose nakedness was covered only by a piece of dirty carpet drawn about her loins. Mrs. Wheatley made the purchase with the intention of making a faithful domestic of her, but the wholesome effects of clothing, along with general cleanliness, were so marked that the good lady arranged at once to have her daughter give the girl such instruction as might appear necessary

Anxious to learn and quick to acquire at this very early age of seven or eight years, she astonished her teacher and mistress beyond measure, in that she was able in one year and a half to read and write with much accuracy; and at the end of four years from the time she was purchased in the slave-pen she could extensively and intelligently converse and write upon quite a large number of difficult subjects. Her wonderful intellectual powers,,keen insight and general scholarship became a matter of such admiration among the educated Bostonians that her society was in great demand by a large part of the aristocracy of that city. Some of the best citizens were kind to her in lending her books and pushing her forward whenever possible.

Having made considerable advancement in the English branches, she began the study of Latin, in which she succeeded to such an extent that she made a translation of "Ovid's Tales," which was published in Boston, also in England, and was regarded by the best critics as an excellent rendering.

At the age of sixteen she became a Christian and (although an exception to the rule of a slave's relations to the Church) was baptized into full membership into the "OLD SOUTH MEETING HOUSE" with the noted Dr. Sewall as pastor. Her Christian life added much to the quality and effect of her writings. In public or in private she was noted for the emanations of gratitude from a thankful heart in appreciation of any kindness rendered her. She was a great lover of her race, although remembering but little of her former home and surroundings in Africa. Being of a very delicate constitution, and having applied herself rigidly to study, along with the effects of a severe northern climate, all combined told very much on her physical strength.

It is, however, pleasant to note that her mother, by adoption, Mrs. Wheatley, from whom she derived her name, was very prompt in securing for her the best medical aid. After all it was thought advisable for Phillis to take a trip over the ocean and having been previously made free by her owner at the age of twenty, she could easily determine her own course of action. Subsequently she accompanied the son of Mrs. Wheatley to Europe. Phillis had already had some correspondence with prominent parties in England and had become quite well known there, as a poet, by reputation.

She was well received and greatly honored by the nobility and moved in the highest social life. To her the doors of some of the best families were opened and tables spread. The newspapers told the story of her excellence in glowing language, describing her as a poet of African birth, the most remarkable upon the continent. She swayed England as by magic. At the earnest solicitations of many friends she allowed her poems to be published to the world in 1773, appearing in London in a volume of about 120 pages, consisting of thirty-nine pieces. So excellent were these poems in all respects that the publishers, suspecting that some critic would doubt that Phillis was the real author, prepared a certificate and obtained the underwriting of the names of the Governor and Lieutenant Governor along with the names of sixteen others of the most prominent and most competent white citizens all of whom certified that there was no reasonable grounds for any doubt whatsoever but that Phillis Wheatley was the original author of the poems.

Her glory and fame had been sounded far and wide, but now comes a dark day. Mrs. Wheatley, while Phillis was in the height of her glory in Europe, became quite sick and much desired to see her Phillis, although the photo of this girl hanging upon the wall was some comfort. She finally grew worse and kindly asked Philllis to come home at once. This summons the grateful and loving-hearted girl obeyed, immediately sailing direct for Boston. She arrived in time to see but little of her former mistress—mother—before death came and called the sick away. Not very long afterwards Mr. Wheatley and daughter followed Mrs. Wheatley to the grave. The son married and took up his abode in England. Phillis, now, left to look out entirely for herself, accepted a proposal to marry a colored gentleman of respectability named John Peters.

The noble woman,, being quite popular and much beloved, caused John Peters to become jealous, which jealousy grew into cruelty. Their only child had died at an early age—all of which bore so heavily upon the already feeble woman that she, after spending a very short married life, died on the 5th day of December 1784, at the age of thirty-one. Thus, passed away the brightest and most generally beloved Afro-American woman of her day. This Afro-American, coming in a slave-ship, a heathen child of seven years, from the jungles of Africa, and although at once putting on the galling yoke of slavery, nevertheless she grew and developed such traits of character and displayed the genius of such a powerful intellect that in less than twenty years from the time she was purchased at the slave-pen in Boston she became the admiration and wonder of the best minds in Europe and in America. She especially addressed one of her poems to General George Washington, which so pleased the great conqueror that the following complimentary letter flowed from his stately pen to her.

CAMBRIDGE, 28th February, 1776.

MISS PHILLIS:—Your favor of the 26th of October did not reach my hands till the middle of December. Time enough, you will say, to have given an answer ere this. Granted. But a variety of important occurrences continually interposing to distract the mind and withdraw the attention I hope will apologize for the delay, and plead my excuse for the seeming but not real neglect. I thank you most sincerely for your polite notice of me, in the elegant lines you enclosed; and however undeserving I may be of such encomium and panegyric, the style and manner exhibit a striking proof of your poetical talents; in honor of which, and as a tribute justly due to you, I would have published the poem, had I not been apprehensive that, while I only meant to give the world this new instance of your genius, I might have incurred the imputation of vanity. This, and nothing else, determined me not to give it place in the public prints. If you should ever come to Cambridge, or near headquarters, I shall be happy to see a person so favored by the Muse, and to whom Nature has been so liberal and beneficent in her dispensations.

I am with great respect, your obedient, humble servant,

GEORGE WASHINGTON

The whole life of Phillis Wheatley, while rising to the highest point of sublime grandeur in her day, also constitutes one of the large number of witnesses that we are ready to place upon the stand in defense of Afro-American capabilities and success with which we challenge the civilized world to produce a parallel.

Frances E. W. Harper.

CHAPTER II.

MRS. FRANCES ELLEN WATKINS HARPER.

In presenting this very condensed narrative of the life and works of Mrs. Frances Ellen Watkins Harper the writer makes no pretensions to a development of any new facts not already known to the reading public, but simply tells the old, old facts that seem each time that they are told more " wonderfully sweet " because of the underlying forces of real inspiration which the simple story of her life contains. This wonderful woman was horn in the city of Baltimore, Md., in 1825. Her parents were not 'slaves, and yet she was subjected to the inconveniences and ill influences of the slave law, which held within its grasp both bond and free. Before her third year the dearest of all friends—mother—had been taken from her by death; being the only child, she came under the watch-care of an aunt who cared for her during her earlier years and sent her to school to an uncle, Rev. William Watkins, until she was thirteen years old. After this the burden of earning her own bread was laid upon her own shoulders; certainly, a very heavy burden for a motherless girl of thirteen, and yet heavy burdens are sometimes great tutors and incentives that we in after-life appreciate more fully.

While earning her bread she chanced to be in a family that taught her some of the domestic arts and at the same time gave her a chance to satiate her great and growing thirst for books. She was notably never idle, and ere she had reached womanhood her first volume, "Forest Leaves," was written, consisting of both prose and poetry, which was afterwards published. So creditable were her early writings that some critics doubted that she was the author.

About 1851, desiring to be in a free State, she moved from Baltimore to Ohio, where she engaged in school-teaching for awhile, but soon found her way into Pennsylvania, where she again taught school at Little York.

Still, not satisfied because of her profound love for her people who were in the cruel bonds of slavery, she often of the condition of affairs in Baltimore, and upon one occasion said, "Homeless in the land of our birth and worse off than strangers in the home of our nativity." While yet in doubt as to whether she might be more useful to her race as a school-teacher or otherwise she wrote as follows to a friend for advice: "What would you do if you were in my place? Would you give up and go back and work at your trade (dressmaking)?) There are no people that need all the benefits resulting from a well-directed education more than we do. The condition of our people, the wants of our children and the welfare of our race demand the aid of every helping hand, the God-speed of every Christian heart. It is a work of time, a labor of patience to become an effective school-teacher, and it should be a work of love in which they who engage should not abate heart or hope until it is done. And after all, it is one of woman's most sacred rights to have the privilege of forming the symmetry and rightly adjusting the mental balance of an immortal mind."

Mrs. Harper was in full accord with everything that tended towards the freedom of the slaves from a bondage of both soul and body. She was a real missionary, a Christian missionary, in all her works.

For about one year and a half she lectured and traveled through Eastern States, creating a sensation wherever she spoke. The Portland Daily Press, in speaking of a lecture which she had delivered upon the invitation of the Mayor of the town, said: "She spoke for nearly an hour and a half, her subject being 'The Mission of the War, and the Demands of the Colored Race in the Work of Reconstruction,' and we have seldom seen an audience more attentive, better pleased, or more enthusiastic. Mrs. Harper has a splendid articulation, uses chaste, pure language, has a pleasant voice and allows no one to tire of hearing her. We shall attempt no abstract of her address; none that we could make would do her justice. It was one of which any lecturer might feel proud, and her reception by a Portland audience was all that could be desired. We have seen no praises of her that were overdrawn. We have heard Miss Dickinson, and do not hesitate to award the palm to her darker colored sister."

She then went to Canada to see the fugitives, and expressed her delight as follows: "Well, I have gazed for the first time upon *Free Land,* and, would you believe it, tears sprang to my eyes, and I wept. Oh, it was a glorious sight to gaze for the first time on a land where a poor slave, flying from our glorious land of liberty would in a moment find his fetters broken, his shackles loosed, and whatever he was in the land of Washington, beneath the shadow of Bunker Hill Monument or even Plymouth Rock, here he becomes a man and a brother. I have gazed on Harper's Ferry, or rather the rock at the Ferry; I have seen it towering up in simple grandeur, with the gentle Potomac gliding peacefully at its feet, and felt that that was God's masonry, and my soul had expanded in gazing on its sublimity. I have seen the ocean singing its wild chorus of sounding waves, and ecstasy has thrilled upon the living chords of my heart. I have since then seen the rainbow-crowned Niagara chanting the choral hymn of Omnipotence, girdled with grandeur and robed with glory; but none of these things have melted me as *the first sight of Free Land.* Towering mountains lifting their hoary summits to catch the first faint flush of day when the sunbeams kiss the shadows from morning's drowsy face may expand and exalt your soul. The first view of the ocean may fill you with strange delight; Niagara—the great, the glorious Niagara—may hush your spirit with its ceaseless thunder, it may charm you with its robe of crested spray and rainbow crown, but the land of *Freedom* was a lesson of *deeper significance* than foaming waves or towering mounts."

While in Ohio, in autumn, 1860, the subject of our sketch was married to Mr. Fenton Harper, a resident of that State. She had laid by some means, with which she purchased a farm and soon went into her own home after marriage. She still remained a strong anti-slavery advocate, and despite domestic duties she continued her literary pursuits at times, and during this period produced some of her best works.

May 23, 1864, death came as a swift messenger and called from her side her husband. Still she was undaunted,, and like a warrior continued to fight the great enemy of her country—Slavery; she fought him to the end.

She had full confidence in God as intending to bring about just such results from the war as would free the bonded slaves. She watched every step the great and bloody struggle made, and once in a letter to a friend said: " And yet I am not uneasy about the results of this war. We may look upon it as God's controversy with the nation, His arising to plead by fire and blood the cause of His poor needy people. Some time since Breckinridge, in writing to Sumner, asks, if I rightly remember, 'What is the fate of a few negroes to me or mine?'

Bound up in one great bundle of humanity, our fates seem linked together, our destiny entwined with theirs, and our rights are interwoven together."

She still trusted, for she had, by long experience, learned to "labor and to wait." She labored, she prayed, she trusted, and sure, as God always does on the side of the right, the war ended and the slaves were free, for Lincoln's proclamation had sounded the death knell to the cursed institution at the door of every slave-holder. The door had opened and the light had shone in. Who can tell the millions of hearts that leaped for joy? Praise God, the war ended, the slaves are free, and now the burdens of education and justice before the law fall upon the shoulders of this great and good woman.

How shall I best elevate them and how shall they get their rights? seemed to have been two of the questions that now confronted Mrs. Harper. She set out and for a good part of several years traveled through the South, visited them in their homes and speaking to them from the public rostrum, and never, through fear of any consequence whatever, allowed herself to disappoint an audience.

In joke a friend wrote her from Philadelphia as to her being bought out by the Rebels. She replied as follows: "Now in reference to being bought by Rebels and becoming a Johnsonite, I hold that between the white people and the colored there is a community of interests, and the sooner they find it out the better it will be for both parties; but that community of interests does not consist in increasing the privileges of one class and curtailing the rights of the other, but in getting every citizen interested in the welfare, progress and durability of the State. I do not, in lecturing, confine myself to the political side of the question. While I am in favor of universal suffrage, yet I know that the colored man needs something more than a vote in his hand; he needs to know the value of a home-life; to rightly appreciate and value the marriage relation; to know how and to be incited to leave behind him the old shards and shells of slavery and to rise in the scale of character, wealth and influence; like Nautilus, outgrowing his home to build for himself more stately temples of social condition. A man landless, ignorant and poor may use the vote against his interests, but with intelligence and land he holds in his hand the basis of power and elements of strength."

During this long journey through the South Mrs. Harper was ever mindful of the virtue and character of our women. She well knew the abuses they had suffered, the wrongs that they had endured, the advantages that had been •taken of them when they were not allowed, under the cursed and cruel lash, to utter a murmuring word in self-defense. Now it was just and proper for some strong friend to remind them that they had rights which all men should respect; that as free people they could be a moral people only when the women were respected and treated as moral beings. This she seems to have been anxious to have them do; hence she wrote as follows from Georgia: "But really my hands are almost constantly full of work; sometimes I speak twice a day. Part of my lectures are given privately to women, and for them I never make any charge, or take up any collection. But this part of the country reminds me of heathen ground, and though my work may not be recognized as part of it used to be in the North, yet never, perhaps, were my services more needed; and, according to their intelligence and means, perhaps never better appreciated than here among these lowly people. I am now going to have a private meeting with the women of this place if they will come out. I am going to talk with them about their daughters, and about things connected with the welfare of the race. Now is the time for our women to begin to try to lift up their heads and plant the roots of progress under the hearthstone."

Up to the time she returned to Philadelphia, Mrs. Harper continued to write and discuss the condition of the ex-slave. She worked in home, in church-, in Sunday-schools and on the public rostrum North and South; she was the constant advocate of the rights of an oppressed people.

Mrs. Harper has been one of our most energetic temperance workers, and has held sway with the Woman's Christian Temperance Union as no other Afro-American woman has ever done. Her work in this respect has given the race great prestige before the world.

A great and profound writer in both prose and poetry, a lecturer of no ordinary tact and ability, a master-hand at whatever she applies herself, she still lives at the time of this writing. Her pen is ever at work; her writings are many and varied.

CHAPTER III.

MISS HALLIE QUINN BROWN.

In the onward march of Christianity, with its civilizing influence as well as its saving power, we know of no better index to its real effect on man than the high esteem in which he holds *woman,* and the estimation he places upon her as an agency in *purifying and preserving human society.* As he rates her, just so the world rates him, and as she is appreciated and encouraged, so he is elevated and strengthened.

What is true in this respect of a man as a part of a race may also, to an extent, be true of the whole race.

The Afro-American is moving in the line of march with other civilized races in that he is placing upon the women of the race their merited worth. Among the class of highly distinguished women is the subject of this sketch, Hallie Q. Brown, who was formerly of Pittsburg, Pa., but while quite young her parents made their abode upon a farm near Chatham, Canada. While still very young, in 1868, she began a course of study in Wilberforce College, State of Ohio, the present residence of her parents, "Homewood Cottage," from which she graduated in 1873 with the degree of B. S.

I quote below a very unique description of her early life on the memorable old farm near Chatham, Canada:

A traveler passing by a country farmhouse, a few miles from Chatham, Canada, a few years ago, might have seen a little girl of eight or nine summers mounted upon colt without bridle or girth, hair given to the winds to be tossed, dashing up a lane to the pasture. There he would have seen her dismount and hastily perform the duties of dairy maid, first calling each cow by name, and inquiring the health of each or making some playful remark. The milking finished,, she now goes through the programme that absorbs her whole attention, having risen before any other one of the household so that she could not be seen

She jumps upon a stump or log and delivers an address to the audience of cows, sheep, birds, etc. Neither knowing nor caring what she says, she goes through her harangue, earnestly emphasizing by arm gesture and occasionally by a stamp of the foot. She has a separate speech for the larger animals, and special addresses to the lambs, ducklings and any other juvenile auditors that happen to be near. Having exhausted her vocabulary, she begins a conversation in the language of the horse, cow, sheep, goose, rooster, or bird, until each is imitated; then bidding adieu to her pet auditors, she remounts her prancing steed and canters back to the house. This is her daily morning programme. She supposed all along that her secret was locked in her own breast. But a farm hand saw her one morn by chance, himself unobserved, and 'twas a secret no longer. Nor did she realize her "ridiculous capers," as she has called it since, until she had grown to young woman- hood. Who can say but that propitious Fate had her then in drill in order to develop the powers of her soul so that she might make a portion of mankind happier by the instruction and amusement she should furnish? "Who was this little girl," ask you? The subject of this sketch—Miss Hallie Q. Brown.

In full sympathy with her brethren in the South in those dark days, she could not be happy in the comfortable home which she left to take charge of the work that rested most heavily upon her as a duty. She first taught a country school in South Carolina and at the same time a class of old people, whom she greatly aided in the study of the Bible; after this she went to Mississippi, where she also had charge of a school. The house in which she taught was built of logs, cracks all open, window-glass all out. In cold, windy weather comfort was a stranger. After fruitless appeals for repairs she determined to try her own hand. "She secured the willing service of two of her larger boys. She mounted one mule and the two boys another, and thus they rode to the gin-mill. They got cotton seed, returned, mixed it with earth, which formed a plastic mortar, and with her own hands she pasted up the chinks, and ever after smiled at the unavailing attacks of wind and weather."

After much success here she was employed as teacher at Yazoo City, where she remained a while and then, on account of the condition of the South at that time, returned North. She was then secured as teacher in Dayton, Ohio, where she served four years, but on account of bad health had to resign, and afterwards traveled in the interest of Wilberforce University, lecturing with marked success, and was particularly welcomed at Hampton Normal School in Virginia. Now, having been engaged in school-teaching North and South in which there was much of the missionary spirit, and having also completed a course in elocution, she served several years as an important factor in "The Wilberforce Grand Concert Company," which also traveled in the interest of that well-known institution.

From the day of graduation at the famous Wilberforce University she has continued to grow in public favor and popularity as one greatly eminent in her chosen profession; entering so fully into the real spirit of the author, and making such vivid descriptions, that she renders perfectly the idea of the writer, as the following will show:

The greatest compliment ever paid to. Miss Brown, at least the one she doubtless appreciates the most, was received under the following circumstances: While at Appleton, Wis., she recited, among other selections, "How He Saved St. Michaels." After the concert a lady came forward, requesting to he introduced to the elocutionist. The Rev. F. S. Stein then introduced to Miss Brown Mrs. Dr. Stansbury, the author of "How He Saved St. Michaels." Madam Stansbury grasped the hand of the elocutionist and exclaimed, "Miss Brown, I have never heard that piece so rendered before." This notwithstanding a famous reader, a few weeks before, had given the same selection there, and advertised by announcing that she would render Mrs. Stansbury's famous poem. Miss Brown was confused. She did not even know the lady lived in the State, and did not dream of her presence in the house, hence she was taken completely by surprise, nor would she have attempted to give it had she heard of the presence of the authoress. The compliment was all the more appreciated because every elocutionist who visits that section renders "St. Michaels."

She is a prominent member of the A. M. E. Church; also, a member of the "King's Daughters," " Human Rights League," and the "Isabella Association."

She has served as lady-principal at Allen University and traveled extensively soliciting aid for the same. While on this tour the *Chicago Bee* said of her:

Miss Hallie Q. Brown delivered a soul-stirring lecture at the Bethesda Baptist Church last Sunday evening to a large audience. She is without doubt a fine speaker. The audience was held spellbound from beginning to end, and her able, forcible and earnest remarks provoked frequent applause. Miss. Brown is a graduate of Wilberforce University, and has been engaged in educational work for sixteen years. She is now giving a series of lectures throughout the North in aid of the Allen University at Columbia, S. C., in helping to erect a new building for that institution.

She was elected as instructor in elocution and literature at Wilberforce University, but declined in order to accept a position at Tuskegee.

In 1886 she graduated from Chautauqua, N. Y., and in 1887 received the degree of M. S. from her Alma Mater, being the first female thus honored.

Wherever she has gone there her impress has been left as a pleasant reminder. The honors that have been heaped on her, a knowledge of her own influence and ability, her excellence as a speaker before the public and as an elocutionist at large, the encomiums of the public press and the voice of the people, *have not turned her head.*

Meek as a lamb, gentle, kind, sociable and pure, yet eloquent, proficient, popular and progressive, Miss Brown is not only a public speaker and an elocutionist of great note, but possesses poetical ability of rare excellence as well. Her poem of fifteen verses, "At Eventide it Shall be Light,",composed in one hour, from 12:30 to 1:30 A. M., at the time of her father's death, is indeed very excellent and would do credit, due credit, to any American poet. The poem closes with the following two verses in a most pathetic manner:

> He left that tenement, that house of clay,
> He took that spirit, bright and fair as day.
> The one we bore to yonder "city of the dead,"
> The other, clothed immortal, dwells with Christ our head.
>
> 0 when that " Day of God" shall come,
> When we shall hear the happy sound, " Well done,"
> In joy we'll sweep through gates of light,
> With souls all pure and garments white.

The following are a few of the many press notices of ability and popularity:

Miss Hallie Q. Brown, the elocutionist, who has always been a great favorite with Xenia audiences, was cheered to the echo, and in some of her pieces was really interrupted by the continuous applause. She certainly excels in her character delineations and varied modulations of tone three-fourths of the elocutionists on stage. —*Daily Gazette, Xenia, O.*

 Miss Hallie Q. Brown, the elocutionist with the company, was loudly applauded... Many credit Miss Brown with being one of the best elocutionist before the public.—*Indianapolis Times.*

Miss Brown the elocutionist, is a phenomenon, and deserves the highest praise. She is a talented lady, and deserves all the encomiums that she receives.— *The Daily Sun, Vincennes, Ind.*

The select reading of Miss Hallie Q. Brown was very fine. From grave to gay, from tragic to comic, with a great variation of themes and humors, she seemed to succeed in all, and her renderings were the spice of the night's performance.—*Monitor, Marion, Illinois.*

We must say the capacity of Miss Hallie Q. Brown to entertain an audience is wonderful.— *Tri-County Reporter, Gosport, Ind.*

Miss Brown's recitals will compare favorably with many of the female elocutionists who are classed with Mrs. Scott Siddons and others of lesser note.— *Vincennes Daily Commercial.*

Never in the history of Birmingham have the colored people displayed more intelligence and showed such appreciation for literary ability by the coming together of the best element of the race at St. John's Methodist Church last night, to hear and do honor to Miss Hallie Quinn Brown, the noted elocutionist. Miss Brown has few equals in her chosen art. Her manner of delivery is very charming and graceful, while her gestures are perfect. Fully eight hundred people were present. Miss Brown may well consider this one of the greatest testimonials ever tendered her in the South.—*Age-Herald, Birmingham, Ala.*

The greeting received by Miss Brown was very enthusiastic. The famous elocutionist recited with the greatest power and pathos "The Gypsy Girl," which was received with the liveliest demonstrations of approval. As an encore she upset the equanimity of the audience by her inimitable lecture on "Apples." Miss Brown acquitted herself in two other recitations in a manner that showed her elocutionary powers in the highest degree.—*Savannah, Ga.*

Miss Hallie Q. Brown is, without exception, the finest elocutionist that ever appeared in this city.—*News and Courier, Charleston, S. C.*

Miss Hallie Q. Brown has a fine voice well cultivated; a pleasing stage presence, and the freshest repertoire of any reader we have had here.—*Niles, Mich.*

Miss H. Q. Brown, the elocutionist, ranks as one of the finest in the country. —*Daily News, Urbana, O.*

The select reading of Miss H. Q. Brown is done to perfection. She has an excellent voice and has good control of it. She wakes every piece sound as if it were the author speaking, and in many of them doubtless she excels the one she imitates.—*Neoga, Ill.*

Miss Hallie Q. Brown, a general favorite at Island Park, rendered in her inimitable style "The Creed of the Bells." A prolonged encore followed.—*Island Park "Assembly."*

Her style is pure and correct; her selections excellent. The "Fifty Miles an Hour" made me thrill, it was very impressive - *Long Branch (N.J.) News.*

Miss Brown displayed remarkable powers of pathos and dramatic elocution.*** Her excellent dramatic talent was displayed to the best advantage in the selection entitled "The Sioux Chief's Daughter." The audience was the largest ever gathered at a public entertainment in that place.- *Newport (R.I) News.*

The readings of Miss H. Q. Brown confer a histrionic glow upon the colored race She is superior of nine out of ten elocutionists before the public.-Her description of "The Bells"" is a masterpiece of elocutionary art which will withstand the severest and most cultivated criticism. Her prolongation of the tones of the bells is a wonderful representation of the poet's lines. Miss Brown's selections were all of a difficult order, and exhibited great versatility and ability to reach in most of them a still better execution - *Daily Republican, Emporia, Kans.*

Of the recitations of Miss Hallie Q. Brown too much cannot be said. As a reader she is the peer of any professional in the land.—*Richmond (Ind) Palladium.*

Miss Brown in her elocution is unquestionably brilliant. Her "Fifty Miles an Hour," descriptive of Mrs. Garfield's ride to Washington when her husband was shot, was given with that generous touch of womanly feeling that made it the gem of the entertainment. --*Miama Helmet, Pigua, 0.*

But the crowning feature of the company is the elocutionist, Miss Hallie Q. Brown. Nothing finer in elocution has been heard in this city, with no exception or reservation in favor of other eminent elocutionists who have appeared in this city. She is capable of touching every chord of emotion, equally effective in pathos and humor. The intonations of her voice are as exquisite as those of an aeolian harp, and as melodious as music itself, and in dramatic fervor and power of dramatic expression Miss Brown is inimitable. What, for instance, can be more melodious and touching than her recitation of the Church Bells, or what more genuinely humorous than the recitation of the original piece called The Apple. Miss Brown cannot fail of establishing for herself a national reputation at no distant day.—*Republican, Xenia, Ohio.*

WILBERFORCE, OHIO.-- To whom it may concern: This is to certify that Miss Hallie Quinn Brown, as a graduate from Wilberforce University, has excelled as an elocutionist, and in our judgment she has no equal in the West. If she has we have never seen nor heard of the person. We all honor and love her upright conduct ever since she left the halls of Wilberforce. We commend her to the esteem and patronage of all who know her.

(BISHOP) DANIEL ALEXANDER PAYNE

WASHINGTON, D.C. -- I heartily concur in the above, and wish Miss Brown success in our community and elsewhere.

(BISHOP) JOHN M. BROWN

WILBERFORCE, OHIO, October 8, 1888 - To whom it may concern: I take great pleasure in bearing testimony to the moral, religious and professional character of Miss Hallie Q. Brown. She is an elocutionist, an excellent teacher of the art of expression and bears the reputation of always improving her pupils

Any one who follows her instruction will speak with ease, energy, elegance and variety of pitch and rate of the voice. Whatever you may do to assist her will be considered a personal favor.

I am yours for God and the race,

(BISHOP) BENJ. W. ARNETT

Miss Hallie Q. Brown, elocutionist of the Wilberforce Concert Company, has the distinguished honor of being the teacher of the department of elocution at the Monona Lake Assembly, and is meeting with great success.-- *Correspondence Cleveland Gazette*

**** Miss Hallie Q. Brown was decidedly entertaining in has efforts of elocution. She "brought down the house" on various occasions, and had to respond repeatedly to the spontaneous calls of the vast audience--"*Monona Lake Assembly," Madison, (Wis.) Daily Democrat*

Miss Hallie Q. Brown, teacher of elocution, was tendered a handsome benefit at Masonic Temple by members of her class. The entertainment consisted of music, recitations and tableaux. and was witnessed by an audience that not only filled the house from parquette to the gallery, but was as enthusiastic as it was large in numbers. The various parts of the programme were rendered in a manner somewhat surprising to those who have taken little note of the progress of the colored people in Louisville, and the talent displayed is most worthy of mention.

****

At the conclusion of the programme President Simmons, of the State Baptist University, appeared on the stage and offered the following resolution, whihc was put to vote of the audience and unanimously adopted:

"Resolved, That we, the citizens of Louisville, in concert assembled, hereby express our heartfelt appreciation of the high order of talent displayed by Miss Hallie Q. Brown, our distinguished guest and eminent teacher in elocution, and hereby thank her for the rich and rare treat furnished by the pupils of her training" -- *Courier Journal, Louisville, Ky.*

Prof. W.F. Sherwin, of New England Conservatory, Boston, Mass., says: "Miss Hallie Q. Brown has few superiors as a refined reader and a careful trainer in the art of elocution and oratory."

CHAPTER IV.

MRS. N. F. MOSSELL.

A heart true as steel; a manner without affectation of reserve; at once sincere and direct; a plump, compactly built body, five feet high; a symmetrical head and speaking countenance; eyes which dance with fun, or are eloquent with tender feeling; a musical laugh, a bright, cheery personality that looks determined on the bright side of life; a keen sense of the humorous and ridiculous, yet a nature bubbling over with the milk of human kindness; a shrewd business woman, yet counting no labor too arduous for the comfort of those she loves; a woman who is intensely interested in her race and sex and who has done more varied newspaper work than any other woman of her race in the country. This, gentle reader, is Mrs. N. F. Mossell, of Philadelphia, Pa. The ancestors of Mrs. Mossell, for three generations, were Philadelphians. Her parents, Charles and Emily Bustell, were raised in the faith of the Society of Friends, but they afterward joined the Presbyterian Church.

Her mother dying when she was an infant, Gertrude and her sister were reared without the tender knowledge of a mother's care. She attended the schools established by the Friends, also public schools, especially the Robert Vaux Grammar School, of which the noted Jacob C. White was teacher. While a pupil at this school she read an essay on "Influence" at commencement exercises which attracted the attention of Hon. Isaiah Wears and Bishop, then Doctor, B. T. Tanner. This essay was published in the Christian Recorder, of which Bishop Tanner was then editor. Leaving school at seventeen, she taught the Terry Road School, Camden, N. J. for one year; then the Wilmot School at Frankford, a suburb of Philadelphia, for seven years. This work she gave up to marry Dr. N. F. Mossell, of Lockport, N.. Y. During this time she contributed essays, stories and poems to the Recorder, the publication of which stamped them of unusual merit, as Dr. Tanner's literary standard was well known to be the most critical of all the Afro-American editors. Four years after marriage she assumed charge of the Woman's Department of the *New York Age,* and *Philadelphia Echo.*

She has written for the *Alumni Magazine* and *the A. M. E. Review* of her native city, the *Indianapolis World,* and other race journals. For seven years she wrote specials and reported for the *Press, Times and Inquirer,* the three most influential dailies of Philadelphia.

The past two years have brought increasing household cares. Her two growing daughters and her husband's large office practice leave her little time for literary or newspaper work. Yet, even now, she finds time to edit the Woman's Department of the *Indianapolis World.* So great is her love for the work I predict she will yet find time to give the literary world something- more substantial and tangible than it has yet had from her pen. She has a rare collection of race literature, among which are two of the oldest books published concerning the race. They are, "An Inquiry Concerning the Intellectual and Moral Faculties and Literature of Negroes," by Abbe Gregorie, and "A Narrative of Gustavus Vassa, by Himself." She has also a copy of the original edition of Phillis Wheatley's poems.

Most of Mrs. Mossell's literary work having been done since her marriage and with the care of home and children, what an inspiration and incentive her life should be to the young woman of literary tastes and aspirations! The race needs more of forceful, earnest, able workers like Mrs. Mossell in the literary field. The harvest truly is great, but the laborers are few. How many will forsake indolence, ease and pleasure, and gathering inspiration from the work of such pioneers will answer the call to work and go gleaning in the literary field?

" IOLA. "

CHAPTER V.

MADAM FLORA BATSON BERGEN
("QUEEN OF SONG")

Flora Batson was born in Washington, D. C., in 1865. While but a babe her father died from wounds received in the war. When three years of age, with her mother, she went to Providence, R. I., where she attended school and, also, studied music until she was thirteen. At this very early age she entered upon her professional career, traveling extensively and singing two years for Stoerer's College at Harper's Ferry, W. Va.; three years for the People's Church of Boston; one year in Redpath's Lecture and Lyceum Bureau of Boston; two years in the temperance work under the management. of Thomas Doutney. It was at this time, during a great temperance revival in New York, that Miss Batson sang "Six Feet of Earth Make Us All One Size " NINETY SUCCESSIVE NIGHTS in the great hall of the Masonic Temple.

Thousands whom argument and eloquence failed to reach were transfixed and moved to tears (signing the pledge) by the magic sweetness and the irresistible pathos with which she clothed sermons in song. Manager J. G. Bergen,,of Star Concert fame, went to hear her and was at once infatuated with her voice. The result was that one year later he succeeded in engaging her services for one year. At the expiration of that year admiration for a great voice had grown into love for a noble woman, and Miss Flora Batson was married to Mr. J. G. Bergen, at the Sumner House in New York, December 13, 1887. *The New York World*, in a half-column sensational article, spoke of the marriage of the successful concert manager to the famous colored prima donna, and hundreds of papers in America and Europe commented on the bold defiance given to that almost universal American sentiment that says the races shall not intermarry.

One week after the marriage, in the presence of a large audience in Philadelphia, she was crowned 'QUEEN OF SONG," and was presented with a magnificent crown and diadem, set with precious stones.

A month later, at Steinway Hall, in the presence of over three thousand people, she was presented with a superb diamond cut bead necklace by the citizens of New York City. In the fall of 1888, under her husband's management, she commenced a tour of the continent which covered nearly three years, singing with unparalleled success in nearly every city between the two oceans.

Flora Batson Bergen is a lady of medium size, beautiful form, modest, free from affectation; and it can be truthfully said of her, "Success has not turned her head."

She cuts, fits and makes all of her magnificent costumes, not from necessity, but because there is no dress-maker in New York City who can do it as well.

The following are some of her many splendid press notices:

The colored Jenny Lind. -- (New York World).

The Patti of her race -- (Chicago Inter Ocean).

The peerless mezzo-soprano--(New York Sun).

The unrivaled favorite of the masses-- (N. Y. Age).

A mezzo-soprano of wonderful range-- (San Francisco Examiner).

A mezzo-soprano of wonderful range-- *(San Francisco Examiner)*.

A sparkling diamond in the golden realm of song -- *(San Jose Californian)*.

Worthy to rank among the great singers of the world. -- *(Portland Oregonian)*.

Her progress through the country has been one continuous triumph. --*(Denver Rocky Mountain News)*.

All her numbers were sung without effort--as the birds sing. -- *(Mobile, Ala. Register)*.

A voice of great range and of remarkable depth and purity. -- (*Louisville KY Courier Journal*).

She will never lack for an audience in the "City of Seven Hills." -- (*Richmond Va. Planet*).

The sweetest voice that ever charmed a Virginia audience. -- *(Lynchburg Va. Advance)*.

Has earned the fame of being the greatest colored singer in the world. -- (*Vicksburg Miss. Post*).

Her articulation is so perfect her renditions scent like recitations set to music.—*Kansas City Dispatch.*

The indescribable pathos of her voice in dramatic and pathetic selections wrought a wondrous effect.-- *The Colonist (Victoria), British Columbia.*

She scored a complete success as a vocalist of high ability, and fully justified the favorable criticisms of the Eastern press. --*San Francisco Examiner.*

A highly cultivated mezzo-soprano, of great sweetness, power and compass, and of dramatic quality. --*Charleston (S. C.) News and Courier.*

She electrified the vast audience of 12,000 people at the Mormon Tabernacle service on Sunday by her marvelous rendition of the 27th Psalm. --*Deseret Evening News (Salt Lake), Utah.*

In response to an encore, she gave a selection from "Il Trovatore" in baritone, showing the extraordinary range of her voice, and producing a melody like the low tones of a pipe organ under a master's touch. --*San Diego (California) Sun.*

She wore a crown heavily jeweled and diamonds flashed upon her hands and from her ears. Her singing at once established her claim of being in the front rank of star artists, and there is a greater fortune than that already accumulated in store for her. --*Providence (R. I.) Dispatch.*

Flora Batson, known as the greatest colored singer in the world, created such a furore in Old City Hall last evening that before the programmer was half through the excitement became so intense that cries of "Bravo!" were heard from all parts of the house. Many people arose to their feet and the applause was uproarious and deafening in its intensity, and not only rounded out the conclusion of selections but broke in spontaneously at every interlude. The singer was certainly a marvel. Her voice showed a compass of three octaves, from the purest, clear-cut soprano, sweet and full, to the rich, round notes of the baritone register. --*Pittsburg (Pa.) Commercial Gazette.*

MRS W. E. Mathews

CHAPTER V I.

MRS. W. E. MATHEWS.

("Victoria Earle")

This very gifted writer was born May 27th, 1861, in Fort Valley, Ga., just prior to "the breaking out of the war" of the rebellion, being the youngest of nine children, all of whom were slaves.

It did not then appear to what extent the world would feel the influence of *her pen* and *her strong moral* and *mental power*s in after-years.   Those dark days of solicitude, filled with the gravest uncertainty as to the results of the then much talked of war, furnished but a very few bright hopes of a brilliant future to this then little girl and her associates. However, the world was open to her and Providence in the lead, to support her feeble, honest, childish efforts.

She left Georgia in 1869, spending about three years in Virginia, reaching New York in 1872, where she entered the public schools, in which she remained four years only, being compelled by necessity to leave and go to work for the support of a widowed mother and herself. This must have been a great trial to one so young and so intensely fond of study. She did not stop, however, because of obstacles or discouragement, but pushed her way onward, hewing out a pathway for herself; and in this way she has applied her powers as a thinker and writer.   Ten years ago she began to write stories and has also edited the ''Household Columns" in several journals, and has from time to time contributed to most if not all of our leading Afro-American journals and magazines.

She has worked on many of the New York leading dailies for years as a "sub", namely, *The Times, Herald, Mail and Express, The Earth, Sunday Mercury* and *The Phonographic World,* and she is now writing some able articles for *Ringwood's Journal of Fashion.*

Among her stories are "Aunt Lindy," "Little Things," "Well," "Under the Elm," "The Underground Way," "Steadfast and True," ''Nettie Mills," "Eugenia's Mistake," "Zelika," and others of peculiar interest.

She is now preparing for publication in book form an illustrated story which will be followed by an historical story.

She was married in 1879 to W. E. Mathews, of Petersburg, Va., and is the mother of one child, a boy of twelve years. To say that "Victoria Earle" has already succeeded and stands shoulder to shoulder with most of her white sisters is only to tell a part of the truth. She indeed has but few equals, and when chances or opportunities and environments are compared, she may safely be said to be the peer of her more favored sisters.

She stands as a *living example* to the very large number of our young women who are so well acquainted with the trials and discouragements of a dependent life; and still more an example is she because by *energy, courage* and *self-reliance* she has steadily developed from a *slave-born child of dependence* to a *woman* of *national character* with *recognized worth* and *ability*. The world has truly felt her impress. She is in demand wherever she is known and is honored by the intelligent of all classes whose fortune it is to become acquainted with her noble womanly and scholarly qualities.

The excellence of her writings is simply grand and encouraging.

CHAPTER VII.

IDA B. WELLS, A. M.

O ne of the marvels of modern society is the honorable position which woman has secured in the affairs of mankind. She is no longer a cipher; she is a positive force. Regnant in the home, a co-ordinate force in the movements which make for human happiness, she must reckon in every accurate estimate of contention or achievement. In what manner she has arisen from the thralldom of ancient times is answered by the grasp which Christianity has secured upon a large portion of mankind. Only in Christian countries has woman secured a measure of equality with the forceful agents that make the world's history. In pagan countries she is still the idol of the harem or the beast of burden for the peasant.

It is a notable fact that in the anti-slavery struggle women contributed almost as largely as men to the moulding of public opinion necessary to the manumission of the slave. Women such as Lucretia Mott, Harriet Beecher Stowe, Sojourner Truth, Lydia Maria Childs, Anna Dickinson and others were towers of strength as well as inspiration. The work before the Afro-American, comprehending the intricate problems of his relation as a man and citizen, I feel safe in saying will never be performed as it should be until we have a race of women competent to do more than bear a brood of negative men. That such a womanhood, untainted by the horrible moral malformation and obliquity of slave masters, is already a possibility we have sufficient evidence.

Ida B. Wells, the oldest issue of James and Elizabeth Wells, the subject of this sketch, was born at the beautiful town of Holly Springs, Miss. in the midst of a fateful epoch. Great moral questions were uppermost in the public mind and discussion. In the forum of public prints, in the homes of the slave-holding oligarchy, in the cabins of the haunted and oppressed slave, the one question uppermost in the minds of all was that of abolition of slavery. The immortal Lincoln had issued the most momentous proclamation ever promulgated by the chief executive of a great nation. The alarms of internecine strife were dying away in subdued echoes, in which the sorrows of a great people were commingled with abounding joy. It was a period in which it was well to be born, if a man is a product in the development of his character of contemporaneous as well as prenatal influences.

The subject of this sketch was precocious in the acquisition of useful knowledge. When the Freedmen's School was established at Holly Springs, she attended it until the building of what was then known as Shaw, but was subsequently Rust University. In consequence of the death of both parents of yellow fever, within a day of each other in 1878, she was under the necessity of leaving school for the purpose of undertaking the support and education of the five children, younger than herself, who had been so suddenly committed to her care. A greater responsibility could not have fallen upon shoulders so young and upon one less experienced as a bread-winner, for she had had indulgent parents, whose chief delight was to give their children all the advantages of school which had been denied them through a cruel and barbarous institution. How hard the task was and how well performed need not be dwelt upon here, further than to say that the two sisters are given every. advantage possible in the way of education.

For three years she taught in the Marshall and Tate county public schools of Mississippi, attending Rust between the terms. She then went to Arkansas and taught six months in Cleveland county; then returned to Memphis and taught two years in the Shelby county public schools, resigning to take a position in the Memphis city schools in the fall of 1884, which she held for seven years.

It was while teaching in Memphis that she began to write for the public press, appearing- first in the Memphis *Living Way,* for which she wrote some time under the *nom de plume* of "Iola." She dealt mostly with some one or other of the phases of the race problem, and her views were widely quoted by other newspapers of the country. She became a regular contributor for the Kansas City *Gate City Press,* the *Detroit Plain Dealer,* the *American Baptist,* the *Christian Index, a*nd other race papers. In June, 1889, she secured a one-third interest in the Memphis *Free Speech* and became its editor. Messrs. Nightengale and Fleming, the former owners of the paper, continued the partnership until January 1, 1892 when Rev. Nightengale sold out to Mr. Fleming and Miss Wells.

Because of utterances of the *Free Speech* regarding the management of the public schools in 1891 the School Board decided that they could not employ so severe a critic; hence she was not re-elected to her position for the ensuing session of 1891— '92. She then gave her entire time to the paper, not at all deterred by the usual fate of race newspapers. She firmly believed that such a venture could be made to pay by first putting something in her paper worth reading, then taking steps to see that it was read by placing it in the homes of the people. She traveled extensively in the Mississippi Valley, from which she wrote graphic letters descriptive of the country and condition of the people. She went into their homes and not only learned of them but endeared herself to them as well. Her paper became a household visitor throughout the valley.

Few persons have brought more enthusiasm to their work than Miss Wells. She properly estimated the work of the race newspaper in educating the people to a proper conception of their rights and duties as citizens, and labored with an eye single to this object. The people seemed to feel the unselfish nobility and sustained it as they had never before sustained a newspaper. Of course it was natural that Miss Wells should take a strong stand against mob law. Many a sturdy blow she dealt upon the head of the gigantic monster. She felt that her life-work was in the South, where the vast majority of her people reside, and here she once expected they would always reside. At the highest point of her enthusiasm in the work, with prosperity crowning her labors on all hands, there came a rude awakening, a terrible shock, and the foundation of her confidence was destroyed forever. On March 9, 1892, there occurred in Memphis a tragedy which threw the whole city into a ferment of the wildest excitement and despair. Three reputable members of the race had been confined in the county jail for defending themselves and property from an attack by white ruffians masquerading in citizens clothes as officers of the law. Several of these ruffians had been wounded. A mob of white ruffians proceeded to the jail and securing the three Afro-Americans did them to death. Panic seized upon the people. Confidence in the legal machinery of county and State was undermined and many began to move away from the mob-infected city, encouraged thereto by the *Free Speech* and the ministers of the gospel.

After these brutal murders the white papers of Memphis, in the mad effort to placate the mob sentiment, teemed with the vilest utterances that ever disgraced the freedom of speech. They wrought the white masses to a state of absolute frenzy. It was in this state of the public temper that a paragraph in the *Free Speech* was taken by a daily paper and distorted into an excuse for calling on the white citizens to mob the proprietors of *Free Speech*. To this end a meeting was held. The business manager of the paper fled for his life, and Miss Wells, the editor,, who was in Philadelphia at the time, was warned that she could not return to the city without danger to her life.

As in the old days at Alton, Ill., her splendid business was destroyed, the voice of a brave champion of right, justice and law was silenced in the home of oppression, and free speech, which John Milton has made the heritage of Anglo-Saxon-speaking races, was strangled to death. The concerted attempt of many Southern white men to put a padlock on the lips of freedom. of speech will prevail no more in the case of Miss Wells than in the case of Elijah Lovejoy at Alton, and of William Lloyd Garrison in Baltimore. The *Genius of Universal Emancipation* is the voice of God, and cannot be stifled. The suppression of Miss Wells' newspaper at Memphis possibly marked a well-defined period in the contention upon which we have entered to wrest from wicked men the justice denied us as men and citizens, and she should consider it an honor that such a calamity came upon her in the prosecution of a cause so sacred. No history of the Afro-American of the future will be complete in which this woman's work has not a place. From the vantage ground of New York, and associated with the *Age,* the splendid work she began in the South Miss Wells hopes to continue until the victory is won. The extensive statement made by her in the *New York Age* of June 25, 1892 of the reasons which led to the suspension of her newspaper, and as an exhaustive statement of the true causes of lynch and mob law, was one of the clearest, most convincing and most pathetic expositions of fact made in recent times to the voluminous discussion of the race problem. It created a veritable sensation and was referred to and discussed in hundreds of newspapers and thousands of homes. It is a historic document, full of the pathos of awful truth.

Although not a graduate, because of reasons previously stated, Rust University conferred upon Miss Wells the degree of Master of Arts at the commencement exercises of 1892.

As a writer Miss Wells lacks in the beauties and graces affected by academicians. Her style is one of great strength and directness. She is so much in earnest that there is almost an entire absence of the witty and humorous in what she writes. She handles her subjects more as a man than as a woman; indeed, she has so tong had the management of a large home and business interests that the sharpness of wit and self-possession which characterize men of affairs are hers in a large measure.

Few women have a higher conception of the responsibilities and the possibilities of her sex than Miss Wells. She has all of a woman's tenderness in all that affects our common humanity, but she has also the courage of the great women of the past who believed that they could still be womanly while being more than ciphers in "the world's broad field of battle."

There is scarcely any reason why this woman, young in years and old in experience, shall not be found in the forefront of the great intellectual fight in which the race is now engaged for absolute right and justice under the Constitution. No other woman of the race occupies today a better position to do good work, or is more generously endowed to perform it. Strong in her devotion to race, strong in the affections of her people, and strong in the estimation of influential men, co-workers with her in the cause, with all the future hers, if she fails to impress her personality upon the time in which she lives, whose fault will it be?

T. THOMAS FORTUNE.

CHAPTER VIII.

JOSEPHINE A. SILONE—YATES.

Mrs. Josephine Yates, youngest daughter of Alexander and Parthenia Reeve-Silone, was born in 1859, in Mattituck, Suffolk county, New York, where her parents, grandparents and great-grandparents were long and favorably known as individuals of sterling worth, morally, intellectually and physically speaking. On the maternal side Mrs. Yates is a niece of the Rev. J. B. Reeve, D. D., of Philadelphia, a sketch of whose life appears in "Men of Mark."

Mrs. Silone, a woman of whose noble, self-sacrificing life of piety from early youth to her latest hours volumes might be written, began the work of educating her daughter Josephine in her quiet Christian home, consecrating her to the Lord in infancy, and earnestly praying that above all else the life of her child might be a useful one. Possessed herself of a fair education, she well knew the value of intellectual development, and spared no pains to surround her daughter with all possible means of improvement; the latter, now grown to woman hood, delights to relate that the earliest event of which she has any distinct remembrance is of that sainted mother's taking her upon her knee and teaching her to read from the Bible, by requiring her to call the words after her as she pointed them out.

Josephine was sent to school at an early age and had already been so well advanced by her mother in reading, writing and arithmetic that she was at once admitted to one of the higher classes of the district school, and because of her eagerness and readiness to learn soon became a favorite with her teachers, although the only colored pupil in the school. She possessed an excellent memory, good reasoning powers, and at the age of nine was studying physiology and physics and was well advanced in mathematics.

Through the kindness of a Mrs. Horton, her Sunday-school teacher, she had access to a large and well-selected library for young people, and in all probability thus acquired an additional taste for literature, which was undoubtedly, primarily, a natural inheritance from her ancestors; be this as it may, an ambition to write, and a corresponding love for the best things in literature, began to assert itself at an early period. Her school-girl efforts at composition were favorably commented on by her teachers; and while yet in her ninth year she wrote a story which she sent to one of the prominent New York weeklies. The manuscript was returned, it is true, but was accompanied by a letter of such kind encouragement and suggestion that it served to increase rather than to diminish her ambition.

At the age of eleven the Rev. Dr. Reeve, feeling that her desire for knowledge should have better opportunities for fulfillment than could be obtained in a district school, very kindly invited her to his home in Philadelphia that she might attend the institute conducted by Mrs. Fannie Jackson-Coppin. Here, for the first time, brought in contact with a large number of cultured persons of her own race in the home, church and school, she received a new and stronger inspiration for the acquisition of knowledge. Rapid progress was made during this school year. Mrs. Coppin, who has ever since been deeply interested in her welfare, still often refers to her as a brilliant example of what a girl may do.

The year following the Rev. Dr. Reeve was called to Washington to accept the chair of theology in Howard University, and Miss. Silone returned to her home, but did not give up studying. A year later Mrs. Francis L. Girard, of Newport, Rhode Island, her maternal aunt, a lady well known for moral and intellectual strength of character, and revered by many students because of her hospitality and benevolence, made her a proposition which was accepted; and in her fourteenth year she went to Newport and became a resident of that beautiful "City by the Sea." Here she entered the highest grade of the grammar school, and maintaining her usual scholarship, the only colored pupil in the school at the time, she attracted the attention of Colonel T. W. Higginson, then a citizen of Newport and a prominent member of the School Board; of the Hon. George T. Downing, through whose untiring efforts the doors of the public schools of Rhode Island were thrown open to all without regard to race or color; of Thomas Coggeshall, Chairman of the School Board; of Rev. Dr. Thayer and wife, and many other persons of distinction.

The year following, she entered the Rogers High School, of Newport, an institution which takes foremost rank among the schools of the land. Taking the four years' course in three, she graduated in the class of 1877, delivering the valedictory address and receiving the Norman Medal for scholarship. She had the honor to be the first colored graduate of the above mentioned school,and here,as in the other schools which she attended, gained the love and admiration of her teachers by her demeanor and devotion to her studies. Her instructor in science considered her his brightest pupil, and especially commended her for her work in chemistry, a study in which she was particularly interested (although, if it were not paradoxical, it might be said that she was particularly interested in each study), and by doing additional laboratory work at odd hours under the guidance of her instructors became quite an efficient and practical chemist.

On graduating from the Rogers High School she was urged to take a university course. All of her own purely personal desires and inclinations led her that way, but from the beginning it had been her purpose to fit herself for teaching, and, if possible, to be not an artisan, but an artist in the profession; therefore, after reflecting calmly on the matter,taking the advice of Colonel Higginson and other staunch friends, she decided to take a full course in the Rhode Island State Normal School. She was already well known in the capacity of an earnest student to the principal, Professor James. C. Greenough and found him and his able corps of teachers very willing to assist her to gain what she needed in the line of preparation for her professional career. In 1879, the only colored scholar in a large class, she graduated with honor from the Normal School. While attending this institution she entered a teachers' examination in Newport with sixteen Anglo-Saxon candidates, and came out of it with a general average of 94.33 per cent. This, while not exceptionally high, was, according to official statement, the highest average that had, up to date, been gained in that city in a teachers' examination. A regulation certificate duly signed was given her, the first time that anything of this kind had occurred in the history of Rhode Island.

In the fall of 1879 she began her life-work as a teacher, and ten consecutive years were thus spent in an enthusiastic and self-sacrificing manner. Eight of these years were spent in Lincoln Institute, Jefferson City, Missouri to which institution she was called by Professor Inman E. Page soon after he became its official head. He had been made acquainted with her success as a student through her former instructors. She was at once put in charge of chemistry and succeeded so well with this and other scientific branches assigned her that eventually the entire department of natural science was turned over to her. At the time of her resignation she was Professor of Natural Science in the before mentioned institution, at a salary of one thousand dollars per school year, and was, at that time, probably the only colored lady in the country to hold such a position.

During this entire period her summers were invariably spent in the East, where seizing every opportunity offered by teachers' associations, summer schools and individual effort, she endeavored to find out the best methods which to present the subjects she taught. It was not long before her work as teacher and author became well known to the public. It attracted, among others, the attention of such well-known educators as President Mitchell, of Wilberforce, Booker T. Washington, of Tuskegee, and the late Miss Briggs, of Washington. In 1886, Mr. Washington, feeling that she was just the one needed for the work in Tuskegee, urged her to become lady-principal of that institution, but, after giving the matter careful thought, she decided to remain at Lincoln Institute.

In 1889 she resigned her position in this institution to become the wife of Professor W. U. Yates, Principal of Wendell Phillips School, Kansas City, Missouri. Mrs. Yates carried with her the love of the pupils and patrons, the best wishes of President Page and the Board of Regents, and all felt that in parting with her they were losing the services of an able and enthusiastic educator.

Mrs. Yates has many friends among the colored and white citizens of Kansas City, where she was well known in educational circles before her marriage. Previous to this event she had, on request, read a paper before the general section of the "Kansas City Teachers' Institute," a highly educated body, consisting of about three hundred white and thirty colored teachers. During the first winter of her stay in Kansas City she was invited by Superintendent Greenwood to read a paper before the "Greenwood Scientific Club," a circle composed of the leading educators and literary lights of Kansas. Her doors and heart are always open to young people, for whom she has an intense sympathy and love, as many students in various State will testify.

In the midst of social, household and maternal duties she finds time to pursue a regular line of study and of literary work; in this she has the full sympathy of her genial husband. He is very proud of his wife's attainments, and she feels that his searching criticism aids her not a little in her efforts. Besides the work already referred to she has during a portion of the time since her marriage, taught in Lincoln High School of Kansas City, performing the work assigned her to the entire satisfaction of all parties concerned.

Reading French and German with ease, she has made quite a study of the literature of both these languages and a few years ago wrote a series of articles upon German literature which was very well received by the press.

Russian life and literature possess for her a particular fascination, possibly because of the large class of persons in Russia which, in some respect like the negro in America, is struggling for a more complete independence. Gogol, Turgenief, Tolstoi, Stepniak, and other Russian writers who set forth the cause of the people, find in her an appreciative admirer.

She has great pride of race, and fully believes in the bright future of the negro, provided the young people for the next quarter of a century are fully alive to the great responsibilities resting upon them. For years she has been a close observer of human nature and of the great problems of the age. As a writer her articles are characterized by a clear, vigorous, incisive style, and have embraced a wide range of thought, from the purely literary to the more practical, social, economic and scientific questions now confronting us. These have appeared in various periodicals, usually under the signature "R.K. Potter," a *nom the plume* which she selected while yet a student and has ever since retained.

In some moods the poetic strain of her nature asserts itself, and several little gems have thus found their way into print. Among these may be mentioned "Isles of Peace," "The Zephyr," and "Royal To-day." During the early years of her work in teaching she made quite a name as a lecturer, and by many friends was urged to give uputeaching and enter the field as a lecturer,,but feeling that the class-room was the place where her effort would result in the greatest good to the greatest number, she decided to remain there. Mrs. Silone used to relate that before Josephine could talk plainly when asked what she wanted to be when grown, the answer would invariably be, "I want to be a *tool-teacher.*

Mrs. Yates is the mother of one child, a little daughter, and in the line of special study much of her work is done with the hope of being the better prepared to wisely direct the education of this child.

CHAPTER IX.

SOJOURNER TRUTH.
(" ISABELLA ").

Sometimes historians review the lives and recount the deeds of certain members of their peculiar race with much timidity and regret. At other times some of them unfold and even magnify the mistakes and inefficiencies of certain other less favored races to the entire neglect and exclusion of any of their more important accomplishments.

It is in this light that the inhabitants of Africa, as well as Afro-Americans and all their direct relatives, have been held up to the world by some historians who are more zealous to draw a veil over our good deeds than they are ready to give credit for what the race has accomplished.

It is therefore a real pleasure, as well as a privilege, even at this late period of our country's history, to present in this short sketch a few of the important facts contained in the life of "Isabella," a once slave woman, of whom many of our women, both young and old, have never heard.

To hear of her trials, her difficulties, her embarrassments and her triumphs will be inspiring and encouraging to many of our young women.

She was possibly born sometime between 1797 and 1800. Her parents were "James"and "Betsy", the slaves of a man of possibly Dutch descent, by the name of Ardinburgh, residing in Ulster county, N. Y. Isabella was one of many human chattels owned by this family; and although it seems that she was somewhat a favorite slave, yet she in after years *vividly remembered the cold, wet, dark, sloppy cellar-room in which all the slaves of both sexes slept,* having a little straw and a poor excuse for a blanket as their entire bed outfit.

She also remembered the auction-block upon which she, at nine years of age, was sold to a John Nealy of Ulster county, N.Y. for $100; the cruelty of her new owners; the frozen feet in winter with which she suffered, and, as Mrs. F.W. Titus puts it, "They gave her a plentytoeat and also a plenty of whippings."

She had been taught by her mother to repeat the Lord's Prayer and to trust in God for all things and especially in times of trouble. This instruction she strictly adhered to and sought to be honest in all things.

However, she became the third lawful wife of a fellow slave, Thomas, and was in after years the mother of five children. Often, when in the fields at work, she would place her babe in a basket suspended by a rope from the bough of a tree and let other little ones swing it to sleep. Sometime in 1817 the State made a law that all slaves forty years old and above should be free; others under were kept in slavery till 1827. Her master promised Isabella that if she would be real good and, obedient he would give her free papers one year sooner, July 4, 1826.

When this long-looked-for day came he refused to keep his promise, and when the same date came in 1827, he also refused, to comply with the law; so early one morning, as by "underground railroad," she left.

Some friends took her in; she was pursued and found. Rather than have her go back into slavery a friend paid twenty dollars for her services and five dollars for her child the remainder of that year, after which she was indeed free. Now homeless and friendless, in search of a child that had been, in this time, stolen bu cruel hands and sold, night came on and she, a traveling stranger, was taken in by a Quaker family. As Mrs. Titus says, "They gave her lodgings for the night; and it is very amusing to hear her tell of the 'nice, high, clean, white, beautiful bed' assigned her to sleep in, which contrasted so strangely with her former pallets that she sat down and contemplated it, perfectly absorbed in wonder that such a bed should have been appropriated to one like herself. For some time she thought that she would lie down beneath it, on her usual bedstead, the floor. "I did, indeed," says she, laughing heartily at her former self. However ,she finally concluded to make use of the bed, for fear that not to do so might injure the feelings of her "good hostess." She subsequently moved to New York City, and having already become a Christian, she united with the John Street Methodist Church and afterwards joined the Zion's Church in Church Street, in which was a large number of colored people. She entered heartily into the cause of amoral reformation which was being carried on among the degraded classes of women. In this she did much earnest work, even entering dens of wicked women where her comrades were rather too timid to enter. She, by strict economy, had deposited some of her earnings in the savings bank: but being urged to invest it otherwise, she did so, losing all she had saved. Again, she tried, but failing to accumulate on account of losses one way and another, she said, "The rich rob the poor and the poor rob each other." Upon deciding to leave New York on a lecturing tour through the East, she made ready a small bundle as her baggage and when about to leave informed her hostess that her name was no longer Isabella, but Sojourner. So, she pursued her journey, speaking and lecturing to the people wherever she found them assembled. On one occasion, when at a camp-meeting, some young rowdies came in and broke up the meeting. It seemed as if a mob was threatened. She hid herself in one corner of the tent, but on thinking the matter over she said, "Shall I run away from the Devil—me, a servant of the living God? Have I not faith enough to go out and quell that mob, when it is written, "One shall chase a thousand and two put ten thousand to flight'? I know there are not a thousand here, and I know I am a servant of the living God. I'll go to the rescue, and the Lord shall go with me and protect me." She drew herself a few rods to a little hill and began to sing:

It was early in the morning; it was early in the morning,
Just at the break of day,
When He rose, when He rose, when He rose,
And went to heaven on a cloud.

The rioters left the camp and came to hear her sing. She asked them why they surrounded her with such clubs in their hands. When told that they only wished to hear her sing, she made them pledge. that if she would sing one more song they would not pester the meeting any more that night, So she began to sing:

I bless the Lord I've got my seal--to-day and to-day--
To slay Goliath in the field--to-day and to-day.
The good old way is a righteous way;
I mean to take the kingdom in the good old way

Before she had finished this song the mob crowd fled in a mass. In this she showed more tact and courage and real generalship than all the preachers in the camp could muster up. That she was a woman of power of speech there can be no question when one reads the many testimonials of the newspapers and friends of those days, when men possibly spoke the truth more at ease than now.

The Rochester papers spoke of her while lecturing in the State of New York *as* follows:

She was forty years a slave in the State of New York. Wholly uneducated, her eloquence is that of Nature, inspired by earnest zeal in her Heaven-appointed mission. She speaks to crowded houses everywhere. Let Rochester give her a cordial reception.

The lecturer is a child of Nature, gifted beyond the common measure, witty, shrewd, sarcastic, with an open, broad honesty of heart and unbounded kindness. Wholly untaught in the schools, she is herself a study for the philosopher, and wonder to all. *** She is always sensible, always suggestive, always original, earnest a practical, often eloquent and profound.

She often asked visitors, "Don't you want to write your name in the Book of Life?" She delighted to have her distinguished friends write their names in this "Book of Life." Among those who wrote their names were Lucretia Mott (who calls herself a "co-laborer in the cause of our race."), Senators Revel, Morrill, Pomeroy, H. Wilson, Patterson, and also Abraham Lincoln and U. S. Grant. She received communications from Gerrit Smith, William Lloyd Garrison, Vice-President Colfax, Theodore Tilton and a *host* of other distinguished white men and women. She received calls from hundreds of the best Christian people of the North, and has been entertained in many of the aristocratic homes of the whites in this country. She sought to have the United States government set apart certain lands for the homes of ex-slaves. She was well prepared to do this work, having spent much time in the anti-slavery cause. A Northern paper said of her:

That old colored woman was so earnest, so fearless and untiring a laborer for her race during the long contest between freedom and slavery that she is known and loved by thousands in every State in the Union. Very black and without much education, she has remarkable faith in God, wonderfully clear perception of moral right and wrong, the most devoted love for the poor and needy, and the most untiring determination to carry forward plans for the amelioration of the condition of her race.

A Detroit paper said of her, among other things:

Those who have before heard her lectures will doubtless remember well the strong and yet well-modulated voice and the characteristic expressions in which she delivers her addresses, as well as the pith and point of her spicy sentences. Sojourner proposes to solicit government aid, in the way of having some portion of the as yet unoccupied lands of the West donated for the purpose as set forth in the petition first mentioned, and there to have suitable buildings erected and schools established, where the now dependent thousands of colored people may go, and not only attain an independence for themselves, but become educated and respectable citizens.

Harriet Beecher Stowe says of her:

I never knew a person who possessed so much of that subtle, controlling personal power, called presence, as she.

The following are samples of her poetical productions:

THE VALIANT SOLDIERS.
(Tune—"John Brown").

The following song, written for the First Michigan Regiment of colored soldiers, was composed by SOJOURNER TRUTH during the war,and was sung by her in Detroit and Washington. **F. W. TITUS.**

We are the valiant soldiers who've 'listed for the war;
We are fighting for the Union, we are fighting for the law;
We can shoot a rebel farther than a white man ever saw,
As we go marching on.

CHORUS:

Glory, glory, hallelujah! Glory, glory, hallelujah!
Glory, glory, hallelujah,!as we go marching on.

Look there above the center,where the flag is waving bright;
We are going out of slavery, we are bound for freedom's light;
We mean to show Jeff Davis how the Africans can fight,
As we go marching on.—*Cho.*

We are done with hoeing cotton, we are done with hoeing corn;
We are colored Yankee soldiers as sure as you are born;
When massa hears us shouting he will think 'tis Gabriel's horn,
As we go marching on. —*Cho.*

They will have to pay us wages, the wages of their sin;
They will have to bow their foreheads to their colored kith and kin, They
will have to give us house-room, or the roof will tumble in,
As we go marching on.—*Cho.*

We hear the proclamation, massa, hush it as you will;
The birds will sing it to us, hopping on the cotton hill;
The 'possum up the gum-tree couldn't keep it still,
As he went climbing on.—*Cho.*

Father Abraham has spoken, and the message has been sent;
The prison doors have opened, and out the prisoners went,
To join the sable army of African descent,
As we go marching on.--*Cho.*

The following original poem was sung at the close of a meeting, in which
American slavery was discussed, at New Lisbon, Ohio:

I am pleading for my people—
A poor, down-trodden race,
Who dwell in freedom's boasted land,
With no abiding place.

I am pleading that my people
May have their rights astored [restored],
For they have long been toiling,

And yet had no reward.
But not for them they yield,
They are forced the crops to culture,

Although both late and early

They labor in the field

Whilst I bear upon my body
The scars of many a gash,
I am pleading for my people
Who groan beneath the lash.

I am pleading for the mother.
Who gaze in wild despair
Upon the hated auction-block,
And see their children there.

I feel for those in bondage—
Well may I feel for them;
I know how fiendish hearts can be
That sell their fellow-men.

Yet those oppressors steeped in guilt—
I still would have them live;
For I have learned of Jesus
To suffer and forgive.

I want no carnal weapons,
No enginery of death,
For I love not to hear the sound
Of war's tempestuous breath.

I do not ask you to engage
In death and bloody strife,
I do not dare insult my God
By asking for their life.

But while your kindest sympathies
To foreign lands do roam,
I would ask you to remember
Your own oppressed at home

I plead with you to sympathize
With sighs and groans and scars,
And note how base the tyranny
Beneath the stripes and stars.

How she received her name: "And the Lord gave me Sojourner because I was to travel up an' down the land showin' the people their sins an' bein' a sign unto them. Afterwards I told the Lord I wanted another name, 'cause everybody else had two names, and the Lord gave me Truth, because I was to declare the truth to the people."

Although deprived of the advantages of even a common school education, that once slave girl became the most remarkable woman this century has produced; a wonder to the philosopher, the philanthropist and sage. A bold Defender of the rights of men, a powerful temperance advocate, lecturer, preacher, reformer, and a most profound thinker and reasoner; a poet of no small merit, and in fact a sojourner wherever she found opportunity to do good. The world has indeed had but one Sojourner Truth.

While her bones lie lifeless in the dust she still lives on earth and in heaven. With grateful appreciation of a great woman we utter our final farewell to her dust:

Sleep peacefully silent, "Sojourner," in thy dust,
None hath labored more faithful than thou;
The work of life-time in the cause of the just
Is remembered by us, even now.

AMANDA SMITH

THE COLORED
EVANGELIST

CHAPTER X.

MRS. AMANDA SMITH.
("THE FAMOUS NEGRO MISSIONARY EVANGELIST")

F ew, if any, Afro-American women have done more real work that has gained for them a world-wide reputation than this faithful member of one race. However, at the time of this writing we are informed that Mrs. Smith is preparing for publication a history of her life. Therefore, out of *our very great respect for* her and her writings,

we withhold all recent fact concerning her life, and simply make a few brief extracts from "The Life and Mission of a Slave Girl," by Rev. M. W. Taylor, D. D., *which, we trust, will not in the least affect the sale of her book.*

As our apology for the course we pursue attention is called to her letter to us, which we take e liberty to publish without consulting her:

No. 64 PARK ST., NEWARK, N. J., October 13, 1892.

DR. L. A. SCRUGGS:

Your very kind letter of October 8th I got on my return from Boston yesterday, and I hasten to reply. I should be glad to respond to your wish, but I am in the act of writing a little sketch of my life and work, which I hope to get in the hands of the publisher by December.

Wishing you much success, I am yours in great haste,

AMANDA SMITH.

Amanda Berry was born March 17, 1836, according to her best information, at Long Green, Maryland. Among her earliest recollections is the kind face and gentle voice of her grandmother, who, she remembers hearing, was married three times. Her first husband's name was Mathews and the last Burgess. The name of the second is not remembered. They lived near Monkton, in the State of Maryland, and there her grandmother died. Her father died in Philadelphia, July1868, and her mother at York, Pennsylvania, but the year we do not know.

The deed of Mr. Berry's and his family's freedom is recorded in the Baltimore court-house. He had a copy of it, with the county seal attached in due form, which he often showed to his children, but his copy was lost after his death.

Her grandmother, father and mother were all truly pious people. Her grandmother was mighty in prayer, and her mother and father often said that to her grandmother's prayers they owed their freedom. Her mother, inheriting the spirit of her grandmother, was a woman of great faith and strong moral courage. And this faith and courage, in the third generation, has given to the world Amanda Smith.

SOJOURNING AMONG THE FRIENDS.

The sweet, mild manner, unadorned costume, sturdy integrity, deep piety and all-embracing philanthropy characteristic of the Friends had charms for Sister Berry. So, about March 1856, she went to reside with a family of Friends at Columbia, Pennsylvania, Robert Mifflin being the head of the family. Here her situation was conducive to piety. She returned to the Lord, and after struggling in ignorance, darkness and doubt for three months, it pleased the Lord to scatter the darkness of unbelief and set her soul at liberty. Speaking of that occurrence Sister Smith says: "Oh what joy and real peace swept through my soul like a flood of light and love! I obtained a clear and distinct witness of the Spirit that God for Christ's sake had pardoned all my sins. And though I have had many storms and conflicts from Satan, yet, glory to God! I have never had a doubt from that hour. From then until this time I have had no spiritual trouble."

* * * * * * * *

Mrs. Smith has been twice married and is the mother of five children. The name of her first husband was Calvin M. Devine, of Columbia, Pennsylvania. He died in July 1856. She next married Rev. James H. Smith, of Philadelphia, Pennsylvania, a local deacon in the African Methodist Episcopal Church. Mr. Smith died November 1869 in the State of New York.

* * * * * * * *

In 1879, Mrs. Smith left America and sailed for England. She was all alone—yet not alone; for the Lord bade her go and promised to go with her.

While holding a meeting in old Sands Street Church, Brooklyn, she chanced to meet Miss Price, an English lady who was visiting Mrs. Parker, a friend of hers. Mrs. Smith was at the time very much debilitated from overwork. Miss Price, observing this, seemingly in a casual manner, remarked to Mrs. Smith that a trip to Europe would be nice and she thought beneficial to her. She said, "I intend to go to Europe in April myself, and I think a trip would do you good." Says Mrs. Smith, "I supposed only well folks went to Europe for a change, but such as me, never, no, never."

The matter then passed out of Mrs. Smith's mind and was forgotten; but after a few days Miss Price mentioned it again, when Mrs. Smith replied, "Of gold and silver have I none; but it takes money to go to England." This was precisely what Miss Price knew, and to this point she had been directing her conversation from the first. So, she promptly advised Mrs. Smith to take the matter to the Lord in prayer, saying, " And if you decide to go, *I will see that the money is all right.*"

* * * * * * * * * *

Mrs Smith has been made to realize, by substantial and practical testimony, that her friends were many and resided in many lands. Touching this she says: "Some of the kind friends that helped me I have never seen. They have heard of the work and of me as an humble instrument in God's hands, and He has moved them to remember me. Praise His name!"

" We thank thee, O Father, For all
things bright and good,
The seed-time and the harvest,
Our life, our health, our food."

IN THE LAND OF BRAHMA AND BUDDHA.

The journey from London to Bombay gave Mrs. Smith a glance at Egypt; the land where her forefathers wrought splendidly, and whence many a grimy monument of theirs peers down with awe-inspiring ken upon the sweeping centuries.

Almost every object was full of interest, and served to enrich her store of illustrations for future use.

AT THE ECUMENICAL CONFERENCE IN LONDON.

In July, 1881, Sister Smith found herself again in London, and also found London the seat of one of the greatest religious gatherings of the nineteenth century. World-wide Methodism was convening there by its representatives for the purpose of a' great "Ecumenical Conference."

IN LIBERIA.

On the 24th of December 1881, Sister Smith sailed from Liverpool for Liberia, and arrived at Monrovia, west coast of Africa, the 18th of January 1882. The Lord was with her then, as He had been at other times and in other lands.

She had her first attack of fever three weeks after landing. During her prostration she was the guest of Miss May Sharp, a zealous and devout missionary then at service in Liberia. She was tenderly cared for, and was speedily restored. The mercy of the Lord was with her, and led her out into His work.

*   *   *   *   *   *   *   *

HER SPECIAL MISSION TO AFRICA.

Says Sister Smith: "I believe God's leading me to Africa was that I might call the attention of the Church, both here and at home, more definitely to the subject of holiness and Gospel temperance. There never was a time when the attention of the Church in all lands was so clearly called to consider these subjects as in the past ten years, more or less, and why should not Africa wheel into line? May God help her."

Sister Smith, putting her faith into words and showing it by her works, says: "I have organized Bands of Hope and Gospel Temperance Societies in all the country and towns I have visited here, except Cape Palmas and Cape Mount. I have not visited Cape Mount, and expect to organize here in Cape Palmas this week." (First week in June, 1886).

*   *   *   *   *   *   *   *   *   *   *   *

As an enlightened, thoroughly consecrated Christian evangelist among negro women, Mrs. Amanda Smith takes the first place in American history.

CHAPTER XI

MRS. H. M. GARNET BARBOZA.

Mrs. Barboza was born to Henry Highland Garnet and his wife, February 11, 1845, at Troy, N. Y., and graduated from Hopedale, Mass., 1861. We have not been able to learn much as to her early life. She was an educated, consecrated woman who ever thought out the best possible means of lifting up her down-trodden race.

In 1881 her father, Dr. Garnet, was appointed Minister to Liberia by the United States government; the document of his appointment was the last official document signed by the lamented President Garfield. Dr. Garnet arrived in Africa in December and died in a few weeks thereafter of African fever. Then came up the question of erecting for him some fitting monument to be dedicated as a permanent memorial of this noble, race-loving man. This memorial was to be erected in Liberia. It was also decided to make it a training school for girls. This school was to reach four classes of Liberians : the Americo-Liberians, the Veys, the Mandingoes, and the Galahs. The next thing to do was to find someone who could make the project a success. That one was found in the person of our subject. To this work she joyfully consecrated her life, sailing from America in November, 1880, having married in 1866. The project was endorsed in this country by the New York State Colonization Society and by the National Afro-American Union for Home and Foreign Missions, and in Africa by the State Legislature of Liberia; in England by the British and Foreign Anti-Slavery Society, the Ladies' Negro Friend Society, the British Women's Temperance Association. As societies they took great interest in the memorial. And many prominent individuals, such as Sir John J. Howard, Oliver Haywood, Joseph Mabins, and the Dowager Lady Kinnaird, gave also material aid to the project.

The institution was called "The Garnet Memorial School," followed by this inscription: "For the Domestic, Scholastic, Artistic and Christian Training for Girls. Founded in Memory of the late Rev. Henry Highland Garnet, D. D.; a. Negro Clergyman, appointed by the late President Garfield United States Minister Resident and Consul-General to the Negro Republic of Liberia."

The Legislature of Liberia, upon application, at once chartered the institution, and endowed it with a hundred acres of land at Brewerville, where it was situated, as well as an annual grant of three hundred dollars to assist in the operations. When our noble sister had gotten the work well on footing she returned to this country, leaving a hundred and twenty five students in charge of Mrs. C. L. Parsons, wife of the Chief Justice. Here she solicited aid to make the institution all it was meant to be. On leaving America to return to her work she purposed visiting England also to solicit aid. On hearing this some of her prominent American friends gave her recommendations to Julia Colman, Secretary of the Afro-American Union, and said of her: We commend our sister, Mrs. M. H. Barboza, who is to visit you on the way to Africa, where she has established the Garnet Memorial School at Brewerville. *This is a school with industrial training*—just what Africa needs so much." Her visit in England excited a great deal of interest. Here is what some of the newspapers said about her:

Mrs. Garnet Barboza is not only the daughter of a negro who achieved distinction, Dr. Henry Highland Garnet, but is herself an educated, fluent and graceful speaker. Naturally she is interested in the education of women and seeks the aid of philanthropists in Europe to help her in that work. TheThe education of women has l agged behind that of men in Liberia.-- *(Manchester Guardian, August 21), 1888.*

We trust that the appeal made by Mrs. Garnet Barboza, in the Manchester Town Hall yesterday, for English sympathy on behalf of her educational work in the African Republic of Liberia, will not remain without response. Mrs. Barboza, who is herself a lady of color, succeeded in thoroughly carrying with her a most influential and intelligent audience. Her work seems to be of a thorough and satisfactory character, and is carried on at an expense which may be regarded as almost insignificant when compared with the substantial advantages which it promises to confer upon the native women of Liberia.— *Manchester Courier, August 21,1888.*

AN ILLUSTRIOUS VISITOR FROM LIBERIA.—An interesting visit has just been paid to Birmingham by a talented and highly educated negro lady, Mrs. M. H. Garnet Barboza, an ardent worker in the cause of educational training among colored people of the negro Republic of Liberia. A large circle of friends in Birmingham was invited to meet her and take tea at the Garden Restaurant, Paradise Street, on Monday evening last-- *Birmingham Daily Post, September 5, 1888*

On reaching her home in Liberia this noble educator had fresh courage for the work, and carried forward not only educational work, but also that of soul-winning. In seeking a special fitness for the latter service Mrs. Barboza saw the truth of baptism, and applied to the Baptist Church, of which Rev. J. O. Hays, of North Carolina, was pastor, for baptism. The faithful missionary administered the sacred ordinance and became pastor to this great woman.

Not long was this star to shine as a blessing to dark Africa, for in 1890 the death angel was commissioned from Heaven to take her from labor to reward. She fell at her post and with her father rests from her labor, awaiting in Africa to hear the sound of the first trumpet when she shall be forever with the Lord.

May the works of her hand be established among the children of men in Africa "until He comes"!

L. C. FLEMMINGS.

CHAPTER XII.

HARRIET, THE MODERN MOSES.

I n those dark days of our history when the negro for the most part was only so much property in the hands of his owner rather than a human being or an American citizen, God condescended to use some of that despised and oppressed people as His agencies of love and mercy. Among these agencies was one "Harriet" who was born a slave in the eastern part of Maryland.

Finally deciding that she would no longer be the chattel of a slave owner, she, with her brothers, resolved to escape to the North. When the journey was a little more than begun her brothers turned back, leaving Harriet to pursue the journey alone. This she did bravely, sometimes without food, without shelter or without friends. Still determined she went on, and after many days traveling alone she found herself beyond the bounds of slavery. But not satisfied with freedom for herself only, she returned as best she could as many as nineteen times and carried other slaves to the then land of the free, until, besides herself, she had been the guiding star of the east to as many as four hundred human beings from the then land of oppression to the then land of freedom. Was not this remarkable for an uneducated slave to out-general all the intelligence of the South in her locality? One very friendly and seemingly truthful lady, "Emma P. Telford," in the October number of the Household (I think of 1891 or '92), speaks of the deeds of this wonderful woman Moses as follows:

Just outside of the limits of the city of Auburn, N. Y., stands an unpretentious little house surrounded by a motley yet picturesque collection of tiny cabins, sheds, pens and kennels. This modest home shelters a varying crowd of lame and halt and blind widows, orphans and wayfarers, all dependent for care and support upon an old black woman, whose heroic deeds in plague-stricken camps and on bloody battle-fields as scout and spy, as deliverer of her people, and defender of the oppressed, have made for her a name as worthy of being handed down to posterity as Grace Darling's, Florence Nightingale's or Jean D'Arc's.

This woman, a full-blooded African, thick-lipped and heavy-eyed, with the signs of her seventy years set fast in deep wrinkles and stooping shoulders, has, perhaps, done more than any single individual to free her nation and hasten the "crash of slavery's broken locks." After making her own escape by almost superhuman efforts from slavery, taking her life in her own hands, she returned to the South nineteen times, bringing hack with her nearly four hundred slaves to the land of liberty. At the beginning of the war she was sent to the South by Governor Andrew of Massachusetts to act as scout and spy for our own armies. She was a trusted friend and confidante of John Brown, who drew up his constitution at her house, and who used to refer to her as General Tubman.

This woman was a personal friend of Thomas Garrett, Garrett Smith, Wendell Phillips, Fred. Douglass, and William Lloyd Garrison, who delighted to introduce her to a cultured Boston audience as his foster-sister, Moses. When in Concord she resided with the Emersons, Alcotts, Whitneys, Matins, and other well-known families, who respected and admired her as one of the most extraordinary persons of her race. "Harriet" encountered great trial and vexation while guiding fugitives to the land of freedom. Once she went into the town where she had lived a slave and bought some fowls. While carrying these along the street in her native town, she saw coming just ahead of her her former master, who, with others, had offered a liberal reward for her head. What to do Now was the question of the moment. She disturbed her fowls so as to make them flutter, and with her sun-bonnet pulled over her face and she half bent as if trying to control her fowls, the master passed by, not once thinking he had come into touch with the one he desired to punish for stealing away so many of his slaves. At another time, while going North with a band of fleeing, trembling followers, she came at early morning to the residence of a colored man whose doors had ever been open to "underground railroad" passengers. The rain was falling heavily and thickly. Leaving her crowd, Harriet stepped to the door and knocked. Behold! a white man's face was seen, who informed her that the colored man had been forced to abandon the house because of "harboring runaway niggers." The rain still falling, yet Harriet was equal to the emergency. Daylight had come; she must not travel longer. After a prayer she thought of a thick swamp just out of town. To this, she and her crowd went in great haste, having two babes in a basket well drenched with an opiate. While they thus lay all day in the swamp, wet and cold and hungry, a strange figure at evening appeared; dressed as a Quaker, and drawing near, talking as if to himself, saying, "My wagon stands in the barn-yard of the next farm across the way. The horse is in the stable; the harness hangs on a nail."

After this he disappeared. In obedience to this message Harriet moved after dark and found it just as she supposed, wagon, horse and food for her use. Again, she was off on a safe journey for the night with these helps.

We might gather much more of interest from the writings of Emma P. Telford, to whom we are very thankful for much of the above, but space being limited we must stop here, after giving one of Harriet's songs. When leaving for the North the first time she sang as follows:

> I am gwine away to leab you,
> We'll sing and shout ag'in ;
> Dere's a better day a comin',
> We'll sing and shout ag'in.
> When we git ober Jordan,
> We'll sing and shout again;
> Makes me sorry for to leab you,
> We'll sing and shout ag'in.
> A partin' time is comin',
> We'll sing and shout ag'in;
> I'll meet you in de mawnin',
> We'll sing and shout ag'in.

CHAPTER 13

EDMONIA LEWIS.

To develop along all the diverging and converging lines that take their beginning in the comprehensive word "education" it becomes nec-essary for us to sometimes turn aside, as others have done, from the ordinary school-room to the workshop, where we may train the eye and the hand to a skillful use of the implements of industry and thrift; and at the same time broaden and sharpen the intellect in original thought and de-scription by the use of the chisel and the brush.

The Afro-American sculptress is an infallible proof of the possibilities of the race along this line. Think of her as of humble birth and left a helpless girl without the guiding counsel and tender care of a mother.

Although without an education; she was determined to make her mark and stamp her impress upon the world. She chanced to get to Boston, and, possibly while looking upon the statue of the great Benjamin Franklin, she became inspired with the thought that some hand had wrought that upon which she was gazing with emotion that stirred her very soul.

She exclaimed, "I too can make a stone man." The liberty-loving William Lloyd Garrison, whose advice she sought, gave her introduction to a Mr. Brockett, a professional sculptor, whose kind and sympathetic heart could appreciate holy am-bition even in a poor girl to become a great woman.

He presented to her the pattern of a human foot and some simple materials with which to try her hand, saying, "Go home and make that; if there is anything in you it will come out." She tried once and had to " try again," but after all succeeded admirably. Encouraged by this victory, she pushed her way on and on until she has been recognized and honored throughout a large part of the civilized world by those who admire the beauties of the work of an artful hand. Some of her works are "Hagar in the Wilderness," "Madonna with the Infant Christ and Two Adoring Angels," " Forever Free," " Hiawatha's Wooings," "Longfellow, the Poet," "John Brown," "Wendell Phillips." These, with her honored reception in Rome and the attractions which her studio had for the travelers from all parts of the world, all speak in no uncertain tones of her real merits as an artist and sculptress.

CHAPTER XIV.

MRS. SARAH J. W. EARLY.

Sarah J., the fifth daughter of Thomas and Jemima Woodson, was born near the city of Chillicothe, Ohio, November 15, 1825. Early in life she exhibited remarkable intelligence for a child and a peculiar aptness to learn whatever came within her observation. Her parents were not only devoted Christians, but zealous members of the A. M. E. Church. Their house was always a home for ministers and a sanctuary for devout Christians. Thus, she was early brought under the best moral and religious influences while her heart was susceptible to the unction of the divine spirit. Thomas Woodson, being an intelligent man, had an intense desire that his children should be well educated, and as colored children were not admitted into the public schools he, with others, made peculiar efforts to supply them with the best instructors in the sciences. These they obtained from Oneida College, in New York, and Oberlin, Ohio. They were abolitionists and mostly of the best families, who brought with them their piety, their intelligence and their culture, and diffused them in the communities in which they labored. These schools she attended until she reached her fifteenth year, when the anti-slavery question was agitated with such vigor and the hostility became so great on the part of the pro-slavery element of society that the schools were closed and the young colored people had no other resources to improve their minds but from the reading of the best selected books and the exercises of good literary societies, which they never failed to form for that purpose.

In the year 1837 she made a profession of religion and became a member of the A. M. E. Church, and from thenceforward became a zealous worker, both in church and Sabbath-school. The frivolous amusements of youth had no charms for her. Her pleasures arose from the practice of Christian virtues and diligence in the cultivation of her mind. Her desire for better educational privileges increased with her years, and in 1851 she entered Albany Academy, in Athens county, Ohio, and began a course of study. After passing through the preparatory department she repaired to Oberlin, Ohio, in the year 1852 and on the 3d of May entered a regular course of study, which continued without intermission for four years. In August of 1856 she graduated with an honorable degree of scholarship and entered immediately upon the duties of teaching public schools for colored youths, opened about this time in Ohio, and as there were but few teachers among them then she had a fair opportunity to show her ability as a scholar and teacher. After teaching intensely for three years in different cities of the State with remarkable success she was elected to hold a professorship in Wilberforce University, being the first colored teacher to fill such a position; this was in the year 1859. In the year 1861 the war commenced, and the hostility being so great between the North and the South, and as the students were from the South, and could not pass the lines, the school was stopped. Miss Woodson was appointed principal of the colored public school of Xenia, Ohio. In 1865 Wilberforce University re-opened and she was elected to the position of female principal. She filled this position with much acceptance for two years. She was then called by the Freedman's Aid Society to be principal of the colored school of Hillsboro, North Carolina, for it was impossible then to keep male teachers there. Her labors were very successful, though attended with danger and difficulties. In September 1868, she was married to Rev. J. W. Early and removed to the State of Tennessee and was principal of one of the public schools of Memphis. She continued the work of teaching in Tennessee for eighteen years, having taught in all thirty-six years. During that time she instructed more than six thousand scholars, being principal of very large schools in four different cities. In the year 1886 she was elected superintendent of the temperance work among the colored people of the Southern States by the National Women's Christian Temperance Union. In the year 1890 she was appointed by the National Temperance Missionary Society to travel and lecture among the colored people of the Southern States in the capacity of superintendent and also of missionary. In four years she has traveled in seven States, accomplishing many thousand miles, and has lectured more than one thousand times to very large audiences; has visited and talked to more than five hundred schools and conferences of religious bodies; has visited two hundred prisons and talked to the inmates, besides doing an immense amount of writing and other work in which she is now actively engaged.

The facts of this life of usefulness are very strong evidence of the very remarkable ability of this noble woman. She was a woman in the field when it cost something to be a woman, and when *only* such brave and invincible characters as she could stay in the field. In the midst of threats and suspected bodily harm by night and by day, in those dark days of our history, Ms Early stood like a granite wall in the defense of right and truth.

CHAPTER XV

MRS. FANNIE M, JACKSON COPPIN.

A giant intellect and powerful force of character, with keen insight to duty and duty and a wise zealousness in the discharge of the same well-developed business capacity of unusual proportions, supported by strong executive and financial abilities, are not as a rule the genereal combined possessions of the women of any race. Indeed, they are the sacred combined endowments of the few. Such a woman of such rare qualifications is Mrs. Fannie M. Jackson Coppin, who was born a slave in Washington, D. C., and was purchased by her aunt, Mrs. Sarah Clark. She was then sent to Newport, R. I., where she lived at service with the well-known Calverts family, who sent her to school. She afterwards, through the kindness of this family, entered the High School, from which she graduated; thence to Oberlin College, in Ohio, where she took the men's course, because in the course laid down for the women there certain studies were omitted. Feeling as she did that she must take all the Studies of the highest course in the institution accounts for her departure from the general rules under which the female students were governed as to departments. She proved herself equal to the task and stood side by side and shoulder to shoulder with the men in whose department she had so wisely entered.

She has the honor of being the first colored person to teach a class at Oberlin College, which she taught with marvelous success for two years.

Now, well prepared for the arduous duties of life's work; she went to Philadelphia in 1865 and took a position in the Institute for Colored Youth. In 1869 the principalship was made vacant, to which she was at once called. Accepting this important position, she has wisely and acceptably managed this school until now (1892).

As a successful teacher and a fluent and attractive public speaker, she needs no words of comment from us. Her record in this direction is far more eloquent in praise of her accomplishments than anything we can possibly say.

About 1886—'88 she began a movement to have an industrial school opened so that colored young men and women could learn trades that would be useful to them in after-life. This idea possibly grew out of the fact that the trades-unions closed their doors against young men and young women of this peculiar people. A lot of land was purchased at a cost of $17,000 and brick buildings erected thereon, and now over three hundred persons are learning trades.

The men learn stone-masonry, plastering, brick-laying, carpentry, shoe-making, tailoring and type-writing; in all seven useful trades. The women learn dress-making, millinery and cooking. So that all the members of the race receive instruction in and complete ten different trades in this industrial school without any additional cost.

The managers of the Institute have become the managers of the industrial department.

This immense undertaking has been from its beginning the work of Mrs. Coppin, who has successfully carried it to completion, raising by her own personal efforts every cent of the enormous cost of this industrial department.

That she is a truly great woman no one who knows of her work can deny. Her work at this school will stand for centuries as an imperishable monument to her memory and an inestimable blessing to her race long after the monuments of granite erected to the memory of the great men of this country shall have crumbled to the dust.

Mr. George W. Williams, the negro historian, has this to say of her:

Without doubt she is the most thoroughly competent and successful of the colored women teachers of her time, and her example of race pride, industry, enthusiasm and nobility of character will remain the inheritance and inspiration of the pupils of the school she helped make the pride of the colored people of Pennsylvania.

She has traveled extensively in this country and also in foreign countries and is admired by all whom she meets. To know her is to simply admire her noble qualities of spirit and character.

CHAPTER XVI.

ELIZABETH TAYLOR GREENFIELD.

(" BLACK SWAN ")

This most noted lady of song, so often called the "Queen of Song," was born in Natchez, Miss., in 1809, and was early taken to Philadelphia and cared for by a Quaker lady, who loved her as fondly as if the two were mother and daughter; and in keeping with this the good lady, who died in 1844, left in her will a legacy to our subject; but somehow Miss Greenfield was deprived of the gift by some decision of the courts. The name (Greenfield) affixed to her name was derived from her faithful friend and guardian. She was always ambitious and apt. She began to receive instructions in music in a family in the neighborhood of Mrs. Greenfield's residence. This was quite astonishing to her guardian, who, however, learning that it was a fact, was well pleased. We quote the following from "Some Highly Musical People," by James M. Trotter;

Previous to the death of this lady, Elizabeth had become distinguished in the limited circle in which she was known for her remarkable powers of voice. Its tender, thrilling tones often lightened the weight of age in one who was, by her, beloved as a mother. By indomitable perseverance she surmounted difficulties almost invincible. At first she taught herself crude accompaniments to her songs and, intuitively perceiving the agreement or disagreement of them, improvised and repeated until there was heard floating upon the air a very lovely song of one that had a pleasant voice, and could play well upon a guitar. In October 1851, she sang before the Buffalo Musical Association, and her performances were received with marks of approbation from the best musical talent in the city that established her reputation as a songstress. "Give the ' Black Swan,' " said they, "the cultivation and experience of the fair Swede, or Mlle. Parodi, and she will rank favorably with those popular singers who have carried the nation into captivity by their rare musical abilities."

In Rochester, N. Y., in December, 1851, she was extended the following invitation by a large number of the best citizens:

The undersigned, having heard of the musical ability of Miss Elizabeth, T. Greenfield, of the city of Buffalo, and being desirous of having her sing in Rochester, request that she will give a public concert in this city at an early day, and we feel confident that it will afford a satisfactory entertainment to our citizens.(Signed by a large number of the most respected citizens of Rochester).

The following quotations were taken from the various papers by Mr. Trotter:

The Rochester American had this to say of her singing:

Corinthian Hall contained a large and fashionable audience on the occasion of the concert by this new candidate for popular favor on Thursday evening. We had never seen an audience more curiously expectant than this was for the debut of this new vocalist. Hardly had her first note fallen upon their ears, however, before their wonder and astonishment were manifest in an interchange of glances and words of approval, and the hearty applause that responded to the first verse she sang was good evidence of the satisfaction she afforded. The aria, "0 Native Scenes," was loudly encored, and in response she gave the pretty Ballad " When the Stars Are in the Quiet Sky."

The Buffalo *Commercial Advertiser* says:

Miss Greenfield is about twenty-five years of age, and has received what musical education she has in the city of Philadelphia; she is, however, eminently self-taught, possessing fine taste and a nice appreciation, with a voice of wonderful compass, clearness and flexibility. She renders the compositions of some of the best masters in a style which would he perfectly satisfactory to the authors themselves. Her low or properly bass notes are wonderful, especially for a female voice, and in these she far excels any singing we have ever heard.

The Daily State Register, of Albany, N. Y., speaks as follows:

THE "BLACK SWAN'S" CONCERT — Miss Greenfield made her debut in this city on Saturday evening before a large and brilliant audience in the lecture-room of the Young Men's Association. The concert was a complete triumph for her; won, too, from a discriminating auditory not likely to he caught with chaff, and none too willing to suffer admiration to get the better of prejudice. Her singing more than met the expectations of her hearers, and elicited the heartiest applause and frequent encores. She possesses a truly wonderful voice, and, considering the poverty of her advantages, she uses it with surprising taste and effect. In sweetness, power, compass and flexibility it nearly equals any of. the foreign vocalists who have visited our country, and it needs only the training and education theirs have received to outstrip them all. The compass of her marvelous voice embraces twenty-seven notes, reaching from the sonorous bass of a baritone to a few notes above even Jenny Lind's highest.

A New York paper speaks of her thus:

MISS GREENFIELD'S SINGING — We, yesterday, had the pleasure of hearing the singer who is advertised in our columns as the "Black Swan." She is a person of lady-like manners, elegant form and not unpleasing though decidedly African features. Of her marvelous powers she owes none to any tincture of European blood. Her voice is truly wonderful, both in its compass and truth. A more correct intonation, so far as our ear can decide, there could not be. She strikes every note on the exact center with unhesitating decision. She is a nondescript, an original. We cannot think any common destiny awaits her.

The Globe, Toronto, May 12-15, 1852, said:

Anyone who went to the concert of Miss Greenfield on Thursday last expecting to find that he had been deceived by the puff of the American newspapers must have found himself most agreeably disappointed.

A Brattleboro, Vt., paper, in January 1852, said of her:

"The Black Swan," or Miss Greenfield, sang in Mr. Fisk's beautiful new hall on Wednesday evening last to a large audience. We had seen frequent notices in our exchanges and were already prepossessed in favor of the abilities and life purposes of our sable sister, but after all we must say that our expectations of her success are greater than before we had heard her sing and conversed with her in her own private room. She is not pretty, but plain. *** Still she is gifted with a beauty of soul which makes her countenance agreeable in conversation; and in singing, especially when her social nature is called into activity, there is a grace and beauty in her manner which soon make those unaccustomed to her race forget all but the melody. * * * Nature has done more for Miss Greenfield than any musical prodigy we have ever met, and art has marred her execution less.

From triumph in America she sailed to Europe, where the *London Morning Post* said of her:

A large assemblage of fashionable and distinguished personages assembled by invitation at the Stafford House to hear and decide upon the merits of a phenomenon in the musical world. Miss Elizabeth Greenfield, better known in America as the "Black Swan," under which sobriquet she is about to be presented to the British public. This lady is said to possess a voice embracing the extraordinary compass of nearly three octaves, and her performances on this occasion elicited the unmistakable evidence of gratification.

The *London Times* also said of her:

Miss Greenfield sings "I Know that My Redeemer Liveth " with as much pathos, power and effect as does the " Swedish Nightingale," Jenny Lind.

The *London Observer* also said of her:

Her voice was at once declared to be one of extraordinary compass. Both her high and low notes were heard with wonder by the assembled amateurs and her ears were pronounced to be excellent.

CHAPTER XVII.

MISS NELLIE E. BROWN.

After all it would seem that rare musical talent is like the rare and gifted poet—" born and not made." Certainly there is in the musical being, as there is in the poetical being, something that is rather more natural than it is artificial, however much training and pruning it may require to develop it.

The subject of these lines evidently possessed natural ability, peculiar and rare, before she received the strong support and help of that special training that has added so much to the complete development and roundness of her most remarkable gift.

Miss Nellie E. Brown, of Dover, N. H., early began the onward march to eminence with such zeal and earnestness that she was soon the pride of all men who knew her enough to appreciate her ability and worth

In speaking of her Mr. James M. Trotter uses the following:

A few years ago, while attending a private school in Dover, Miss Caroline Bracket, a teacher in the same, noticing that Miss Brown possessed a naturally superior voice, earnestly advised its fullest cultivation. This lady became her first music teacher. Diligently pursuing her studies, she made rapid progress. Being induced to take part in occasional school and other concerts, our subject soon became quite prominent in Dover as a vocalist, and was engaged in 1865 to sing in the choir of the Free-will Baptist Church of that city. Here she remained until November 1872, at which time, having learned of Miss Brown's fine vocal powers, the members of Grace Church, Haverhill, Mass., earnestly invited her to become the leading soprano in their choir, offering her a liberal salary, besides the payment of her traveling expenses twice each week between Dover and Haverhill. This very complimentary invitation she accepted, and for four years her fine singing and engaging manners rendered her deservedly popular with the Members and attendants of the church mentioned—people of fine Christian and general culture, before whom, in the public halls, she sang on several occasions.

In writing to a friend once she said, "My motto is 'Excelsior.' I am resolved to give myself up wholly to the study of music and endeavor, in spite of obstacles, to become an accomplished artist."

In keeping with this view she applied herself assiduously and soon entered the New England Conservatory of Music, and was soon invited by the manager to take part in the quarterly concert. Mr. Trotter says:

Here on two occasions, before large and highly cultivated audiences, with beautiful voice, correct method of expression, and ease, and grace of stage deportment—singing in Italian, music of a high order—Miss Brown won the most enthusiastic applause. Predictions of her complete success as a lyric artist were freely made by many connoisseurs. But these have not been her only appearances in Boston. She has many times sung at concerts in the finest music halls of the city before critical audiences, her charming rendition of the numerous English, Italian, French, Scotch and Irish songs in her rich repertoire making her one of Boston's favorite cantatrices.

The *Boston Traveller,* April 1874, said:

Miss Nellie E. Brown has for some months been the leading soprano at Grace Church, Haverhill, Mass., which position she has filled with eminent acceptance, and with marked exhibition of artistic powers.

The *Gazette,* of New York City, said, November 4, 1874:

Miss Nellie Brown, born and bred from the hills of New Hampshire, possesses a voice of rare power and beauty, which she has diligently labored to cultivate and improve by close and unremitting study. She has also a rare charm of manner, which, united with her exquisite singing, won for her an enthusiastic reception. The great popularity of this very excellent lady is not by any means due alone to musical ability. It is quite possible for one to have all the abilities of this woman, and yet someone else with much less ability could be more popular. Miss Brown possessed *politeness, kindness* and *expression.* She was *sociable, not arrogant,* but *positive,* and yet carried a *winning sweetness of temper* and *disposition.*

No ability alone does not always bring success or popularity, but it is one of the essential elements to success, and is, possibly, regarded by some as being of more importance than any other one element; yet, since it costs no more to possess all the necessary qualities than it does to possess a part, and since it pays far better to have them all, why not imitate Miss Brown and succeed as she has?

There is much more which might, with profiit, be said of her more recent days and achievements, and certainly many more testimonials of later date, but want of space forbids at this late day, having failed until very recently to get such facts as we desired.

HENRIETTA VINTON DAVIS

CHAPTER XVIII.

MISS HENRIETTA VINTON DAVIS.
(ELOCUTIONIST)

The subject of this sketch, Miss Henrietta Vinton Davis, was born in the city of Baltimore, Maryland. Her father, Mansfield Vinton Davis, was a distinguished musician, and from him she inherited a natural taste for music. Shortly after her birth her father died, leaving a young and beautiful widow and the subject of this sketch. In the course of a few years her mother contracted a second marriage with Captain George A. Hackett who during his whole life was devoted to the best interests of his race and was their recognized leader in Baltimore up to the time of his death. He was a man of ample means and generous heart and gave to his little stepdaughter all the advantages which such conditions allow. He, like her own father, died while she was quite young.

Her mother, a year after the death of Captain Hackett, removed to and became a permanent resident of the city of Washington, D. C. This good mother devoted herself to the training of her only child, and as she early displayed a fondness for books and an eagerness for knowledge, she was given every advantage of the excellent schools of Washington. She soon made rapid progress in her studies, and by her studious habits and genial manners became at once a favorite of her teachers. Her elocutionary power was early displayed, and each year at the closing of school she was the bright, particular star in oratory. Miss Mary Bozeman, Miss Emma Brown and Miss Addie Howard, her teachers, all aided Miss Davis by their admirable training, and to them she returns thanks for encouragement.

At the early age of fifteen she passed the necessary examination and was awarded a position as teacher in one of the public schools of her native State. While holding this position she attracted the attention of the Board of Education of the State of Louisiana, who tendered her a higher position to teach, which she accepted. She remained there some time until called home by the illness of her mother. Miss Davis left Louisiana amidst the regrets of many friends. She also bore the certificate of the Board of Education testifying to the efficiency and ability with which she had discharged her arduous duties.

Miss Davis, in 1878, entered the office of Recorder of Deeds at Washington, as copyist, where she remained until 1884, when she resigned to follow her chosen profession. It was while holding this position that she decided to carry out a long-cherished desire to study for the dramatic stage. She had in the meantime, by a wide and thorough study of the best masters in classic and dramatic literature, laid the foundation for a promising career.

Miss Davis became the pupil of Miss Marguerite E. Saxton, a lady of undisputed ability and a most conscientious teacher—a lady who knows no one by their color. Under the tuition and guidance of this lady she made her debut April 25, 1883 at Washington, before an audience that was cultured, critical and large. She was introduced by the Hon. Frederick Douglass, who takes a deep interest in her success.

On this, her first appearance, her success was instantaneous and she received a veritable ovation. The Associated Press flashed the news throughout the world, and Miss Davis at once took her place among the professional women of the age.

A few weeks after her first appearance she made a tour of the principal cities of the East under the able management of Lieutenant James M. Trotter and Mr. William H. Dupree. At Boston, Hartford, New Haven and other places she was received with every mark of approval by both press and public.

In April 1884, Mr. Thomas T. Symmons became her manager. Mr. Symmons is one of the few gentlemen of our race who possess the ability and spirit of enterprise calculated to secure success. He formed a dramatic and concert company to support his star, and by novel and liberal advertising brought her to the notice of new audiences. At Buffalo, N. Y., she received most flattering newspaper notices and was the recipient of much social attention from both white and colored admirers.

Again, at Pittsburgh, Pa., Cincinnati, Ohio, and Chicago, Ill., and in fact wherever she has appeared, her genial manners and modest deportment attract to her many friends.

Miss Davis has received numerous presents from individuals and from the public; a massive gold star presented to her by the citizens of Chicago, two magnificent necklaces, a basket of flowers two feet high, made of tiny shells from Key West, Florida, presented by the leading ladies of that city, and many other testimonials of appreciation too numerous to mention.

Miss Davis is one of the pioneers of her race in the legitimate drama, and by her success has been the means of stimulating and encouraging others to emulate her example. While she has many imitators she has few, if any, superiors, and stands unique in being one of the few representatives the race has in the tragic art.

She is entirely devoted to the upbuilding of her race and believes the solution of the vexed problem lies in the hands of the Negro. She believes that the education of the *hand,* the *head* and the *heart* is the prime necessity of the hour. She has invented a dress-cutting chart and has done much in the rural districts, where sewing seems to be one of the lost arts, to instill a love for this useful occupation.

MRS. JOSEPHINE TURPIN WASHINGTON

CHAPTER XIX.

MRS. JOSEPHINE TURPIN WASHINGTON.

It is a noted historical fact that man becomes great, refined and powerful, either as an individual or as a nation, only in proportion as woman, his immediate companion and associate in society, is elevated to her natural sphere in the affairs of life that contribute to the highest good and happiness of both. Her place is fast proving to be not a secondary one, but an important one, at his side. As he succeeds and conquers, she also succeeds and conquers. As he fails and goes down in the struggle, she also goes down with him. The interests of the two are inseparably linked together by a golden chain that makes his destiny her destiny, and certainly his glory should be her glory.

In this condensed presentation of the life and works of Mrs. Josephine Turpin Washington the writer has no occasion for any exaggerated description of her. A simple statement of the facts is amply sufficient to tell of her greatness, and especially so when we remember that she has become noted long before reaching the age when scholarship usually ripens into golden fruit.

She was born in Goochland county, Va., July 31, 1861, being the daughter of Augustus A. and Maria V. Turpin. She was always a brilliant little creature, and learned to read quite early under the instruction of a friend of the family. Her parents moved to Richmond when she was yet young, where she entered the public schools and was an attractive pupil, learning readily. She soon entered the High and Normal School, from which she graduated in 1876. From this time up to 1879 or 1880 she was engaged in teaching school, when she entered Richmond Institute, both as a teacher and student. Here she filled her twofold position with credit to herself and satisfaction to all concerned, remaining for three years, during which time she was a faithful, hardworking student. It was here that the writer first came into contact with her in a practical way, as school-mate in the class-room. Her zeal, keen intellect, kind disposition and general scholarship, all combined, did much to stimulate the writer during those three memorable years to greater effort in study, for *it was then* that he often had to burn midnight oil in order *to come out even* with her *in the next day classes.* She was a student from whom the writer could always, when discouraged, catch new inspiration a real genius in the class-room, yet gentle, never arrogant, always wearing a pleasant smile, occasionally interrupted by a blush passing over her face. She did not remain to graduate, though only lacking one or two studies of completing the course, these not having been made on account of the class reciting at an hour when she was engaged in teaching (a class). Although offered a diploma at any time she felt disposed to come up for examination, she declined; preferring to take a more extended course of study elsewhere, resigned as teacher and entered Howard University in the fall of 1883, from which she graduated in 1886.

During her vacations she served as copyist in the office of Hon. Fred. Douglass, Recorder of the District. During and since graduation she has held responsible positions at Howard University, which she resigned for the consummation of that affection which had been steadily growing between herself and Dr. Samuel H. H. Washington, to whom she was married, and who is now a busy, practicing physician in Mobile, Ala. She may be truthfully called a brainy woman, of strong Christian character—a refined lady of no small heart. Besides scholarship Mrs. Washington became quite into prominence as a writer, during her maiden days. Her first article appeared in the *Virginia Star,* of Richmond, in 1877.. It was a good thrust at intemperance, against selling wine at entertainments for church benefit. She has since written many articles for the *Virginia Star, Planet, New York Globe, Industrial Herald, New York Freeman, Christian Recorder and the A. M. E. Church Review.*

The following are some of her subjects: "Paul's Trade and the Use He Made of It," "Notes to Girls," "Higher Education of Women," "The Hero of Harper's Ferry," "The Remedy for War," "Teaching as a Profession," and quite a number of other articles. Her writings have been published in the leading Afro-American journals of the country. Her writings have consisted of both prose and poetry. "Thoughts for Decoration Day" is one of her choice poetical writings, into which she seems to have put her whole soul. The following are only a few verses selected from this poem:

Throughout our country's broad domain,
In North and East and South and West,
In city street and village lane,
The nation pauses and takes rest.

Yet honor we the men who gave
Their lives and all that makes life dear,
To save our land and free the slave
From cruel fate than death more drear.

For women who, like Spartans brave,
Had tied the sash round soldiers gay,
And sent them forth a land to save,
And cheered them as they marched away.

We are not one; an alien race,
Distinct, the negro dwells apart;
The crime of color his disgrace,
What matters brain, or brawn, or heart?

Through ages dark in bondage held,
And freed by accident of state,
Deemed strangers where our fathers dwelled,
The strife of party feud and hate.

Arouse, awake, bend to your oars!
Much work remains yet to be done;
Till opened wide all closed doors,
Rest not, nor think the battle won.

Unite to build the race in wealth,
For money is a magic key;
Seek power frankly, not by stealth,
And use it wisely as may be.

With all thy getting, wisdom get;
Acquaint thyself with minds that soared;
Tis knowledge makes the distance set
Twixt cultured men and savage horde.

No cloud of doubt disturbs my mind,
This nation's destined to be one,
And future ages sure must find
The night dispelled by risen sun.

Hence, let us pass with hopes renewed,
Fresh courage for the daily care;
Forget past wrongs, avoid all feud,
And only what is noble dare.

The brave men we have honored here
Knew how to die like heroes true;
Who questions we will be their peer,
If we like heroes learn to do?

CHAPTER XX.

LOUISA DEMORTIE.

Down on the lower part of the James, in the proud little city of Norfolk, Va., was born in 1833, of free parents, Louisa DeMortie. She, like the children of other free parents, was denied the advantages of education. She found her way to Boston, Mass., in 1853. Here she seized every opportunity for gaining instruction. It is said that she was a girl of much beauty and sweetness of manner and appearance. She was a remarkable winner of friends wherever she went; high-toned but not arrogant. In 1862 she became a center of attraction as a public reader, a natural and refined elocutionist. To her acquired ability she added her natural wit and most attractive manner, which placed her high in her chosen sphere. About the time she came very prominently into public favor she heard of the needs and cries of colored children in the city of New Orleans. With a brave and sympathetic heart full of desire to help them, and like a disciple of Jesus Christ, she started for the spot. It seemed to be her chief object to do good and serve Him whom she loved because He first loved her. There she labored in the interest of the orphans with a zeal of earnestness and devotion that gained the admiration of all who knew of her work.

In 1867 she had raised sufficient money to be ready to build for them a comfortable' home, where she hoped to especially care for these and other unfortunate little ones. Before she could consummate her plans that much dreaded monster, yellow fever, came upon her like a raging tyrant whose grasp she could not break, and to whom she fell a victim October 10, 1867, with the following words that passed her dying lips: "I belong to God, our Father."

A tender plant, a mighty and sainted worker, like a flourishing flower, cut down in the days of a useful and glorious work, yet a conqueror, because she still lives to inspire many to follow her example.

CHAPTER XXI.

MRS. ELLA V. CHASE WILLIAMS.

A very excellent lady, who stands high among the females engaged in the the work of education, was born in the city of Washington, HD.C. Her father, William H. Chase, who was a blacksmith by trade, moved among the leading citizens of the District of Columbia dring his day, and died in 1863 leaving a wife and six children.

Her mother (whose maiden name was Miss Lucinda Seaton) was an immediate descendant of a very respectable family, of Alexandria, Va. She was a woman of strong will, energy and perseverance, as is evidenced by the career of her daughter, Mrs. E. V.C. Williams of whom we are now writing, who was educated at the famous Howard University. In 1879 she began her much loved work as a teacher, for which she is so well fitted, and into which she puts so much energy. From the beginning of her chosen work in 1879 up to December 1, 1882,

she taught in the public schools of Washington, D. C., and was considered one of the best teachers then employed in the city. She resigned and was married to Rev. E. W. Williams, Presbyterian minister, who was also educated at Howard University. This was quite and occasion, and was witnessed by a large number of people at the Fifteenth Street Presbyterian Church, Rev. F. J. Grimkee, D. D., officiating.

In 1883 a parochial school, in connection with the church held in charge by her husband, was organized, which has steadily grown until now it exists under the name of Ferguson Academy. It is located at Abbeville, S. C., and is a co-educational institution for boarding and day pupils, and is presided over by Rev. E. W. Williams as president, and Mrs. Williams as principal.

This very modest Christian woman is also editor of the "Woman's Department" of the Atlantic Beacon, of which her husband is editor in general. This paper is sent forth in the interest of education and the general welfare and, elevation of the race. She is also president of the Woman's Synodical Missionary Society, within the bounds of the Atlantic Synod. She has made public speeches in the interest of education, missions and temperance. In 1885 she represented the Presbyterian women of the South at the Woman's Missionary Meeting, in connection with the General Assembly of the Presbyterian Church of America, which meeting was held in Cincinnati, Ohio. She was also a representative to the same body at its meeting in Minneapolis, Minn., in 1886, and also represented them at the Centennial Assembly, which met in Philadelphia, Pa., in 1888. Her stay of nine years at. Abbeville, S. C., her present location, has been entirely devoted to the work of education. The school which she so much loves and which has been under her fostering care from its incipiency is yet growing and has become a f ourishing little enterprise to her, and is doing a noble part of the work along this line. Long may this faithful servant of Christ live to do even greater work in His cause to lift up an humble people!

SCOTIA SEMINARY, CONCORD, N. C.

CHAPTER XXII.

SCOTIA SEMINARY
(CONCORD, N. C.).

This school is under the control of the Board for Freedmen of Northern Presbyterian Church. It is the outgrowth of a parochial school established by Rev. Luke Dorland and his wife, in 1865 or 1866, who deserve great credit for the zeal and perseverance with which they clung to their work through trying times. In 1870 the school was incorporated by the State as a seminary under its present name, having that year *twelve* boarding pupils in a little plank house 16 x 24 feet. In 1876 it sent out its first graduating class of nine members. During the same year the first brick building was erected. At present the accommodations consist of "Scotia" and "Faith Hall," both four-story brick buildings, containing chapel, class-rooms, dormitories for teachers and about 275 students (these buildings are heated with steam and are lighted by electricity), *Music Hall* for the department of music, and the *church building* used by the students and the congregation.

The property is valued at $60,000. Scotia is exclusively for girls and aims to combine, in the most effective way, *industry* with the culture of the *mind* and *heart*. It does not admit students of the lowest grades. Its work is in the two departments: (1) *Grammar,* (2) *Normal* and *Scientific.* from the beginning something like 2,500 persons have been enrolled, and about 300 have graduated from one or both courses of study. The number enrolled during the last year was 261, of whom 253 were boarders from ten different States. Rev. Dr. Dorland and wife remained in charge until the fall of 1886, when, on account of advancing years, they were relieved, having made their indelible impress upon the Church and the colored people.

Rev. Dr. D. J. Satterfield and wife took up the work where their predecessors had left off. The present faculty is composed of the president and principal (Dr. D. J. Satterfield and wife), with eleven lady teachers and two assistants.

While seeking to develop a high type of womanhood in its students Scotia has two special lines of work:

(1). The training of teachers for our own schools. For this some technical instruction is given, but the main point of concentration is the *preparatory* and *grammar departments*, where the drill is made as thorough as possible. (2). Still more stress is laid upon the training of home-makers. The entire industrial system has this end in view—to prepare the student to be an ideal housekeeper; while the students also associate with the teachers,, who are of high culture and refinement and piety, with the view to add to their culture of heart, without which the best housekeeper can never make an *ideal home*.

It is in this way the friends of Scotia account for the fact that their graduates have not become conspicuous social leaders or in public life. As queens of the home, many of them have done well. Many of the graduates of Scotia are the faithful wives of noted presidents and professors in many of our best colleges and universities.

CHAPTER XXIII.

SUSAN S. McKINNEY, M. D.

ore has been done along all the lines of popular education for the higher and broader development of woman during the last twenty-five years than possible during any quarter of a century in the history of American civilization. Especially is this true with regard to professional and industrial education.

The idea of woman as a regular graduated practicing physician is growing more and more popular each year, and to-day the doors of quite a number of medical colleges are open to her which were closed thirty years ago against her. *And why should she not enter,* as well as her brother, and prepare *herself* for usefulness in life? The law of God has never excluded her, nor has the law of man the right to deny to her admission into this important field of labor. Indeed, she deserves recognition and should enjoy every right in the profession that is accorded to her brother.

Such a physician of character and ability as Susan S. McKinney, M. D., of Brooklyn, N. Y., will add dignity and refinement to the practice of medicine.

Graduating, as she did, at the HEAD of her medical class in 1870, by the united choice of both professors and students, she has, from the beginning of her practice, taken a high stand in the profession and has enjoyed a large and lucrative practice in *medicine and surgery among both white and colored* citizens of Brooklyn, N. Y. She enjoys the distinction of being the sister of that highly respected and honored man, Rev. Henry Hyland Garnet, D. D., who bore a national reputation. She also enjoys the distinctive honor of being the *first genuine colored woman in the United States to enter the medical profession.* She has been called upon to read papers of importance before both the State, and County Homeopathic Medical Societies, of which she is a member. She also belongs to the College Alumni Association and is attached to the Memorial Hospital Dispensary Staff.

The *Brooklyn Times* of June 27, 1891, contained the following concerning this distinguished professional lady, who undoubtedly deserves every word that has been said in praise of her merits:

When she commenced practicing here, twenty years ago, under her maiden name of Smith, she found it up-hill work to get established, sex, color and school being all against her; for in those days homeopathy was not so favorably regarded as now. Being quite young in years, and even more youthful in appearance, was another disadvantage. When about a year in practice she married the Rev. William G. McKinney, formerly located at Flemington, N. J., but now retired. Dr. McKinney is a bright little woman with sparkling black eyes and frank, pleasant expression. She has fairly outdone her white sisters in proving that a married woman can successfully follow more than one profession without neglecting her family, for she has not only acquired a reputation as a practitioner but is also a musician of acknowledged standing, being organist and director in the Bridge Street M. E. Church, where she has charge of a choir of thirty-five voices. She was a pupil of Zundel and Henry Eyre Brown, and has recently been elected Musical Director of the Brooklyn Literary Union, with her daughter, Miss Anna McKinney, who is studying music in the Pratt Institute, as assistant. Her boy is a clerk under C. P. Huntington, and both children are bright, handsome and healthy-looking and show careful nurture.

Of course, such, a busy woman has no time for social life, but is devoted to her family and her profession. Being the family doctor in many homes, she has a number of gentlemen patients, for the boys and girls of some families have grown up from childhood under her medical care. Many male doctors send their special female cases to her, one eminent physician having placed his mother in her care for treatment. In short, she meets with naught but courtesy and consideration from her fellow-practitioners of both sexes and schools. Two years ago she took a post-graduate course at the Long Island College Hospital, where she was the only woman student at the time. "Courage, 'grit' and physical strength are needed," she says, by the successful physician. "She must be willing to study hard with a determination to succeed."

Dr. McKinney is an important element in the society of Brooklyn, as well as a strong supporter of the best interests of her fellow-citizens in all that pertains to their well-being and happiness. She is broad, liberal and decided, yet kind, unassuming and gentle.

CHAPTER XXIV.

MRS. CHARLOTTE SCOTT.

When the rumor of war had wrought this country into anxious excitement; when the men of the North had been called upon to take up arms on the one side, and when the men of the South were being trained to keep time with drum and fife on the other side, the slaveholder, no doubt, had some fears as to the results of the proposed bloody conflict.

But there was another class of beings who also predicted the results; the slave saw fully as far into the future of this war as did his master. By the eye of faith he knew the days of a wonderful change would soon come.

As strange as it may seem, thousands of bond-men and bond-women assembled together at the dead hour of night, when patrol and master were victims to sleep, and prayed with full confidence for this war to result in the breaking of their shackles. Their belief that this long-prayed-for day would come was as strong as if God had, in an audible voice, promised it to them.

They declared that it would so end, and although many died without the sight, yet it did come, to the glory of the God in whom they trusted.

During this long and fearful struggle, that drenched this Southland with some of the best blood of the nation, there lived an old slave woman who fully believed in the providence of God. She was born in Campbell County, Va., and was the slave of a Mrs. W. P. Rucker, who at the close of the war, possibly, lived at Marietta, Ohio.

Charlotte Scott at this time was about sixty years old. Her father was named Thomas Scott. When the news of Lincoln's proclamation was flashed over the country, Charlotte Scott, with four million of her brethren, *rejoiced.* When the news of the death of the immortal hero was heralded throughout the country, she, with the rest of her brethren, *was sad.*

It was through this proclamation that she had been declared free, and now, unlike the nine that were cleansed, she desired to return and "give thanks," for

She knew he had *died in the cause of justice.* When her former owner informed her of this sad fate of her *immortal deliverer and friend,* she exclaimed, "The colored people have lost their *best friend* on earth; Mr. Lincoln was our best friend, and I will give five dollars of my wages towards erecting a monument to his memory." She was first to propose a monument and first to contribute to the carrying out of her proposal to erect the famous Lincoln Monument which now stands in Lincoln Park, Washington, D. C., and was unveiled by General U. S. Grant, April 14, 1876. It cost $20,000.

Is there any honor in her actions and love for the dead Chieftain? Is there any glory in the efforts for this monument? Has any sacrifice been made for which the world would give praise? If so, let them all fall first and heaviest upon the head of Charlotte Scott. She showed a gratitude characteristic only of a true heart and a well-trained conscience.

When this monument shall have crumbled and fallen; when the hands that placed it there shall have been forgotten in the grave, and when the spot upon which it now stands shall be used for other purposes not now known to mortals, the deed of this woman, the emanation of a thankful heart in kind remembrance and sacrifice, shall not be forgotten by the God in whom the bonded slaves trusted for deliverance.

CHAPTER XXV.

THE HYERS SISTERS

I t was probably April 22, 1867, when the Metropolitan Theatre of Sacramento, California, was filled with an anxious crowd of eight hundred or more human beings to witness the public beginning of two young Afro-American singers whose joint reputation since that time has stood without possibly a parallel in American history. These two young sisters, so often called the "Hyers Sisters," Anna Madah and Emma Louise Hyers, exhibited an aptness to imitate operatic performers when quite young. This peculiar and yet very natural quality led their parents to give them a chance. Opportunity at home was afforded with which the girls made such remarkable progress that professional teachers were soon a necessity.

Mr. James M. Trotter makes the following statement concerning them and their teachers:

After one year's instruction it was found that the girls had advanced so rapidly as to have quite "caught up" with their teachers (their parents), and it was therefore found necessary to place them under the instruction of others more advanced in music. Professor Hugo Sank, a German of fine musical ability, became then their next tutor, giving them lessons in vocalization and on the pianoforte. With this gentleman they made much progress. Another change, however, being decided upon, our apt and ambitious pupils were next placed under the direction of Madame Josephine D'Ormy, a lady of fine talents, an operatic celebrity, and distinguished as a skillful teacher. From this lady the sisters received thorough instruction in the Italian language, and were taught some of the rudiments of the German language. It is, in fact, to the rare accomplishments and painstaking efforts of Madame D'Ormy that the Misses Hyers owe mostly their success of to-day. For she it was who taught them that purity of enunciation and sweetness of intonation that are now so noticeable in their singing of Italian, and other music; while under her guidance, also, they acquired that graceful, winning stage appearance for which they have so often been praised. Although, as was natural, quite proud of the rich natural gifts possessed by their children, and extremely delighted with the large degree of their acquirements in the art of music, their sensible parents were in no, haste to rush them before the public, and it was therefore nearly two years after leaving the immediate tutelage of Madame D'Ormy when these young ladies made their debut. They also went to San Francisco and other places in California, where they gained great renown. After these concerts they retired to severe study preparatory to making a tour of the States. Finally deciding to proceed East, they sang to highly appreciative and enthusiastic audiences in several Western towns and cities. At Salt Lake City they were received with the very highest marks of favor. On the 12th of August 1871, they gave a grand concert in Salt Lake Theatre, offering some five operatic selections.

The *Daily Herald,* of St. Joseph, Mo., had the following to say concerning them:

Whoever of our readers failed to visit the Academy of Music last evening missed a rare musical treat. The concert of the Hyers Sisters was absolutely the best; furnished those in attendance with the choicest music which has been in St. Joseph since we have resided here.

The Hyers Sisters are two colored ladies, or girls, aged respectively sixteen and seventeen years, but their singing is as mature and perfect as any we have ever listened to. We have read the most favorable reports of these sisters in the California papers, but confess that we were not prepared for such an exhibition of vocal powers as they gave us last night.

Miss Anna Hyers, the eldest, is a musical phenomenon. When we tell musicians that she sings E flat above the staff as loud and as clear as an organ they will understand us when we say she is a prodigy. Jenny Lind was the recipient of world-wide fame and the most lavishly bestowed encomiums from the most musical critics in Vienna twenty years ago. Parepa Rosa, it is claimed, reached that vocal altitude last summer. But the sopranos who did it flit across the planet like angels. Several competent musicians listened to Anna Hyers last evening and unanimously pronounced her perfectly wonderful. With the greatest ease in the world, as naturally and gracefully as she breathes, she runs the scale from the low notes in the middle register to the highest notes ever reached by mortal singers. Her trills are as sweet and bird-like as those with which the "Swedish Nightingale" once entranced the world.

After a real triumph in New York City and Brooklyn the *Brooklyn Daily Union* had the following to say:

Not only was every inch of standing room in the Young Men's Christian Association Hall occupied, but the ante room and the stairway were completely jammed. In spite, however, of the uncomfortable crowding everyone was pleased to be present and all were delighted with the concert. The young ladies are gifted with remarkable voices and sing together with perfect harmony, displaying the full compass and beauty of their voices, which are sweet and clear.

A Boston paper said of them:

We were invited, with some fifty other persons, this forenoon to hear the singing of two colored young ladies, named Anna and Emma Hyers, of San Francisco, at the Meionaon. They are aged respectively sixteen and fourteen years, and, after a casual inspection, may be called musical prodigies. They are, without doubt, destined to occupy a high position in the musical world.

Mr. Trotter said:

In Boston they made many personal friends, receiving from many of its most cultured people very flattering attentions; and here too were pointed out to them, in a candid and friendly spirit, such defects in their voices or manner of singing as only those skilled in the highest technique of the musical art could detect. All such suggestions were readily received by the young ladies, who, acting upon the same, made much advancement in the technical requirements of the lyrical art.

They lingered in Boston, being loath to leave its congenial art circles, and to leave behind its many facilities for improvement in their profession. Finally deciding to start again on their travels, they visited many of the towns and cities of Rhode Island and Connecticut. Their singing everywhere gave the utmost satisfaction, and cultivated New England confirmed, in words of highest praise, the verdict of the West and New York.

CHAPTER XXVI

MADAM LILLIAN R. BUNDY.

This lady, eminent in her profession, was born and educated in New England, where she received a very thorough English and classical education, graduating with honors from the Warny, R. I., Academy, where she had spent much time in study under the honorable Professor Isaac B. Cady. At the age of seven years she began the study of music under the most proficient masters of that day—Prof. H. P. Pierce and Prof. Ebon Tonyee of the Boston Conservatory, under whom she finished as teacher of the piano, church organ and vocal music. At the age of fifteen she made her debut at a grand Organ Recital, given at St. Peter's Episcopal Church, of which her parents were the only colored members. It was at this very aristocratic church that she received the high praises of the entire audience and competent judges as being master of the immense organ, which she manipulated with perfect ease and grace. She has, since this great triumph, filled positions of honor among the wealthy masses of New England cities; was the first colored teacher and singer in old Mixion Academy of Language at Providence, R. I., serving for a period of four years and teaching many pupils of both races.

Soon after coining to New York her services were engaged as organist at the renowned Shiloh Presbyterian Church, of which Rev. Henry Hyland Garnet, D. D., was pastor for nine years. Although it is said that prejudice exists to an extent in that city, she can boast of some of the wealthiest white people among her scholars and patrons. Prof. G. Jardine, of great organ fame, quotes her as being the most brilliant colored organist of the city. With a most graceful and attractive appearance she has a bright future before her. Madam L. R. Bundy is one of whom the race may well be proud as a skilled and noted musician.

CHAPTER XXVII

HOME --LIFE OF LIBERIAN WOMEN.
"The hand that rocks the cradle
Is the hand that moves the world."

Nowhere is the truth of this familiar adage more clearly exemplified than in the young negro republic—"The Lone Star "—Liberia.

As we look back through the vista of years to the time before Liberia's corner-stone was laid, at the very beginning of the country's existence, we find woman at work, exerting her influence and exhausting her talents and strength to make its foundation sure. Her influence, the lever power which raises nations, which moves the world, has ever been a potent factor in advancing the welfare of the country. She has ever been willing and ready to share its burdens, encounter its obstacles and struggles and endure its hardships. This assertion is evidenced by the fact that soon after the arrival of the first colonists or emigrants in the country, which was at Monrovia, in 1821, the. Native chiefs perceived that, in all probability, the coming to their shores, to live in their midst, of Christian women would interfere with their nefarious traffic in slavery, which had long prevailed in the neighborhood. Therefore, regardless of the treaty by which they had ceded the territory, they determined to destroy the settlement if they could. The temporary dwellings that had been slightly and hastily put up were consumed by the torch in the hand of these natives. In the wake of the flames came the African fever, but the pioneer Liberian women said that

" The bravest are the tenderest,
The loving are the daring."

And thus saying, they faced these, braved them undaunted, and continued to battle with and hold at bay the natives, rebuild their houses, and in June, 1822, with the assistance of their brothers and copartners in the struggle, laid the corner-stone of the *Republic of Liberia,* upon the site whereon "today stands the beautiful capital city, *Monrovia.*

When, in these dark days, these trying ordeals through which Liberian womanhood passed, they were importuned to quit these anxious scenes of warfare and flee to British settlements or return to America, they replied, in the language of the brave, heroic leader, Elijah Johnson, and said, "No, sirs; we have been for years hunting and searching for a home, and we have found it and shall stay here." They stayed, too, and labored faithfully until their change came—until they were invited to cease toiling and cross over the silent river of time and rest beneath the tall palms that dot the fair plains of eternity. But ere their departure they solemnly enjoined upon their daughters to prove themselves polished stones in the nation's temple, the foundations of which only the judgment day will reveal the hardships, the sorrows and anguish which their mothers experienced in assisting to lay—in short, to be nothing less than true, faithful women of purpose and determination.

The pioneer women of Liberia were missionaries, soldiers and counselors, and directors in matters of state as well. They were women of peace, too, just the angels that young Liberia mostly needed at that time; and while they exhausted every effort to preserve it, they failed. Hostilities and famines were their constant companions. The native chiefs, the very ones who had sold the land, would have no pleas for peace. With these brave heroines it was now battle or famine unto death, with the greatest doubts as to the results. These women of peace here became of war. They helped their stronger allies plan fortifications, mount cannon, distribute ammunition; they served as picket guards, and in other ways encouraged, assisted, stimulated and inspired those who struggled to strike, strike till there could be no relaxation of vigilance--- till the enemy were repulsed. The energetic pioneers, enfeebled by severe and protracted self-denials, would spend sleepless nights with fever and then work all day building breast-works, stockades and clearing the dense forest in front of their few pieces of artillery. Thus, passed *many dark and rainy days.*

"Some days must be dark and dreary"

Until early in November in that year more than eight hundred natives, with war-paint and whoop, made a concentrated attack on the settlers' most outlying stockade. And had these natives, numbering more than ten to one of their antagonists, not stopped to plunder, they could have swept the settlement by one determined rush into the sea. Danger so imminent was a tonic that not even the African fever could withstand.

Having performed duty oft and well, as preachers of righteousness, as missionaries of peace, they, as Liberia's pioneer women, are now called on to experience the greatest battle in the history of the country in which women were participants. When in this crisis the women rallied the men retreating from the stockades, brought a cannon to bear upon the plunderers, which was fired by Mrs. Newport, whose memory is yet fresh in the minds of and will ever be preserved in the casket of precious recollections by every true Liberian. The Newport Guards, a military company of Monrovia, has, ever since her hazardous but decisive fire of cannon, perpetuated her memory by bearing her name. This woman, with other noble heroines, heading a charge as the natives hesitated, panic-stricken, by sudden and unexpected discharge of cannon, drove them, crestfallen, to the cover of the forest, and Liberia was saved.

"The oak grows stronger
By the winds that toss its branches."

It will not be putting the remark too strongly to repeat with emphasis, that from the very foundation of Liberia woman, with her modest demeanor and decision of purpose, has made as great and glorious an impress upon the pages of Liberian history as have the most illustrious of their sterner companions; yes, she has wrought equal with others to achieve glory for, and to enhance grandeur and magnificence of the country.

Among the sainted women who were present and assisted in laying the foundations broadly and deeply on which the fabric of Liberia's liberties shall rest to the remotest generations; among the noble-hearted women who labored assiduously and arduously, in sunshine and in rain, to push forward the civilizing work among the heathen natives of Liberia and raise the bright and morning star of freedom. and religion over this portion of Africa; good women who possessed great souls and breathed a sentiment which said:

"Give to the winds
Thy fears!
Hope, and be undismayed;
God hears thy sighs and counts thy tears,
God shall lift up thy head";

women who, though dead, still live in the hearts of Liberians, are Mrs. Newport, the warrior; Mrs. Elijah Johnson, the far-sighted statesman; Mrs. Teage, the jurist; Mrs. Wilson, Mrs. Yates, Mrs. Richardson, Mrs. Moore, Mrs. Payne and Mrs. Elizabeth Roberts.

Much of the prosperity which Liberians enjoy to-day is largely due to the ceaseless efforts of the good women whose names are mentioned above. But there are still some few remaining who have not yet gone on to join their mothers in that rest, sweet rest; who have caught hold where the pioneer sisters left off and have gone on steadily to work, building and fostering the nation's institutions.

These women are now actively on the stage of responsible. life in Liberia, giving inspiration, influencing the building of breastworks and stockades, not, however, like those which their mothers erected, of stocks and staves, but of earnest prayer, consecrated to God: Mrs. President Cheeseman, Mrs. ex-President Johnson, Mrs. ex-President Payne, Mrs. General Sherman, Mrs. L. A. Johnson, Mrs. E. J. Barclay, Mrs. H. A. Williams, Mrs. Henry Cooper, Mrs. Caroline R. Moore, Mrs. Martha Ricks, Mrs. A. D. Williams, Mrs. C. T. O. King, Mrs. A. B. King, Mrs. W. D. Coleman, Mrs. Georgie Dennis, Mrs. Z. H. Roberts, Mrs. J. H. Deputy, Mrs. Watson, Mrs. I. N. Roberts, Mrs Bishop Ferguson, Mrs. G. W. Gibson, Mrs. F. B. Perry, Mrs. I. C. Dickinson, Mrs. Colonel Jones, Mrs. June Moore, Mrs. Solomon Hill, Mrs. Decoursey, Mrs. Hagans, Mrs. T. W. Howard, Mrs. A. Barclay, Mrs. Sarah Blyden, Mrs. Dr. Moore, Mrs. Travis, Mrs. C. A. Pittman, Mrs. J. E. Sharpe, Mrs. E. C. McGill, Mrs. J. S. Washington, Mrs. Clement Irons, Mrs. Worrell and Miss E. C. Payne.

To give, or to even attempt to give in this short chapter, a sketch of the life and labors of each lady whose name appears herein is a task quite impossible for the writer to perform now; suffice, however, to say that these ladies have moved a long way from the lowly huts of the pioneer women.

Among them is represented every known grace and re inement which the women of other countries enjoy. They live in a goodly land, occupy comfortable, yea, luxurious homes, where none dare molest—where none can make them afraid.

E. E. SMITH,   Recent United States Minister to Liberia.

MRS. A. E. JOHNSON

CHAPTER XXVIII

MRS. A. E. JOHNSON.

T his very excellent lady was born in Toronto, Canada, in 1858, and was educated in Montreal, where she was also converted and baptized, joining the Point St. Charles Baptist Church when quite young. She is the daughter of Levi and Ellen Hall, formerly of the State of Maryland. Upon the death of her father her mother returned to Baltimore, where she and her daughter both reside at this time. Mrs. Johnson was teaching a day school in the Water's M. E. Chapel, in Baltimore, when she and Rev. Harvey Johnson, D. D.; became acquainted; as a result of which they were married in 1877, and now are proud of one daughter (four years old) and two sons, respectively eight and ten years old.

Mrs. Johnson began her literary career by writing for race papers. It was in 1888 she saw the necessity for a paper such as would draw out the latent powers of our women by developing a taste and aptness, upon their part, to write on such topics as would interest the young people and kindle in them a thirst for reading; consequently she began the publication of *The Ivy,* a monthly of eight pages, which she sent forth as a herald of light to guide and elevate *our own young people.* The matter in these columns was original, pure, instructive and interesting. A large number of our good women wrote for this paper, the contents of which were extensively read and much praised by the public.

In speaking of this spicy little beacon-light *(The Ivy) the Baltimore Baptist* says:

The contents were original and the general tone very creditable to the editor. * * * So far as it has gone, the editor must be conscious of having done a good work and shown the way for some others to follow.

Her next attempt was to write a book that could be used in Sabbath-school libraries. This she did, and it was accepted and published by the American Baptist Publication Society in 1890. This society is one of the largest of its kind in this country. The title of the book is "Clarence and Corinne." In May 1891 she wrote a story, entitled, "Dr. Hayes' Wire Fence," which was purchased by the *Youth's Companion,* of Boston.

At this time the American Baptist Publication Society has the manuscript of her second book, which will possibly appear during this year, having already been accepted. She now has on hand a new project with which she, we are quite certain, will soon strike another fatal blow upon the head of some "Thomas" of olden times, who sits hard by, ever ready to doubt the ability, skill and power of thought possessed. by Afro-American women.

But, alas! the world shall yet see as it has not yet fully seen, and shall know as it has not yet known, the whole truth in this matter (at least it shall acknowledge much that is now denied), for indeed the women of this race are steadily climbing and "every round is *higher* and *higher."*

The following are some more of her writings and also some press notices. The *National Baptist* (Philadelphia) has reproduced her story, "Nettie Ray's Thanksgiving Day," and also short poems from her paper. The *Sower and Reaper* (Baltimore) has published "The Mignonette's Mission." She has also been editor of a "Children's Corner" in this paper.

The *National Baptist,* in speaking of her book ("Clarence and Corinne"), says:

It is a pathetic little story.

The *Baltimore Baptist* says of the book:

The interest of the reader is early excited and held steadily to the close.

The *Baptist Teacher* says:

One feature of this hook makes it of special interest. It is the first Sunday school book published from the pen of a colored writer.

The *Missionary Visitor* says:

This, we believe, is our first Sunday-school library book written by a colored author. Mrs. Johnson is the wife of a noted and successful Baltimore pastor, and in this hook shows talent worthy of her husband. * * * The tale is healthy in tone, holds the attention and is well adapted to the intermediate classes of Sunday-school readers.

The *Baptist Messenger* (Baltimore) says:

The fact of its being published by the American Baptist Publication Society speaks volumes of praise for the book.

It also says:

This is one of the silent yet powerful agents at work to break down unreasonable prejudice, which is a hindrance to both races.

There are other strong sayings of the *Home Protector* (Baltimore), *National Monitor,* the *Sower and Reaper,* the *American Baptist,* the *Indianapolis Daily Journal, all* of which show conclusively the value of the writings of this noble woman. Her article recently published in the New York Age in the defense of Afro American literature as *original productions* is sufficient to hush in *eternal silence* the *enemy* of the progress the race has made, who now bobs up and claims that our literature is not, original. Mrs. Johnson gives this false doctrine such original blow from the gigantic intellect of an Afro-American, and pursues her enemy with such vehement logic that she not only confuses, but, like a champion of the truth, she refutes and conquers him.

The writer has often admired this little silent preacher in print, and feels confident that, with such success as Mrs. Johnson has already achieved, we, as a race, may very reasonably expect to garner a fruitful harvest of golden grain from her pen in the future.

MARY V. COOK, A. B., A. M.

CHAPTER XXIX.

MARY V. COOK, A. B., A. M.

Those who pursue the path of duty which takes its beginning among rocks and thorns are rewarded by being able to mount into clearer light and penetrate fairer regions.

It was by perseverance and faithfulness to duty that Miss Mary V. Cook raised herself to a point of distinction and honor which may serve as an example to others who find the road rough and uninviting. Miss Cook, like her mother, is of a lovable disposition, always kind and true.

The city of her nativity is Bowling Green, Ky., and, like many other cities of the South, was not especially inspiring to the colored youth, for whom there was no nourishment upon which to subsist. There was everything to discourage and humiliate a child of such tender feelings who had already used every advantage the town gave for improvement. Being ambitious, she entered many contests and in every case came out victor. In the winter of 1881 she was made assistant teacher in the school presided over by Rev. C. C. Stumm, then pastor of State Street Baptist Church. Though the pay was meagre she worked as diligently as if getting a larger salary. She often had occasion to shed tears because of the hard work and the unexpected demands made upon her already very small income, and upon one occasion she said, "The sun will yet shine in at my door." How, she knew not, for her parents were unable to send her off to school, but she felt that the way would be opened. At last the dawning of better advantages appeared. Rev. Allen Allensworth, seeing in her the elements of true womanhood, used his influence in getting for her a scholarship in the State University, Louisville, Ky., of which Rev. William J. Simmons, D. D., was president. October 15, 1881, a letter from Dr. Simmons reached her stating that the American Baptist Woman's Home Mission Society of Boston would defray her expenses if she would matriculate within three weeks and give pledge to remain until she had completed the course. She hastened from the school room to inform her mother of the good news, and immediately wrote complying with the conditions, and was registered in that school November 28, 1881.

May 13, 1883, she graduated from the normal department as valedictorian. As the president presented to her the Albert Mack gold medal, he testified that she had so conducted herself during the entire course that there had not been occasion to discipline her in a single instance or even impart to her a word of warning. In writing of the graduates of the school he made the following statement concerning her:

As a student, she was prompt to obey and always ready to recite. She has a good intellect and well-developed oral faculties, and is very refined, sensitive, benevolent and sympathetic in her nature, and well adapted to the work of a Christian missionary.

She served the University during her scholastic years as student-teacher and was at different times dining-room matron and record-keeper of daily attendance. She was honored by the students with the presidency of both their societies, which position caused her to lose much of her timidity and developed her faculties for thinking and speaking. During the last year of her normal course she won the Dr. E. S. Porter gold medal in a contest in written spelling, and soon afterwards Miss Cook carried off the Dr. D. A. Gaddie silver medal for proficiency in oral spelling. The students were lavish in their commendations and congratulations. Shortly after this Mr. William H. Steward offered a silver medal for proficiency in penmanship and Miss Cook was again victor. May 17, 1883, the trustees elected her permanent teacher and principal of the normal department, in which she held the professorship of Latin and mathematics. Her department was the largest of the University, but she performed her work with credit to herself and school. By an act of the board of trustees she was allowed to continue her studies in the classical department, from which she graduated, taking the degree of A. B., May, 1887.

As a teacher she has proved a success and seems to exert a magic power over her pupils; though always pleasant, yet at the same time commanding and ruling without trouble; she is yet a hard student, ever keeping abreast with the issues of the day. She is especially good in Latin, biography and mental and moral philosophy. She loves her race dearly and has been connected with nearly every prominent cause for its elevation.

When the Baptist Women's Educational Convention of Kentucky was organized in 1883 she was found among them. In 1884 this body made her Second Vice-President and also placed her on the Executive Board. The latter position she holds to-day. In 1885 she was made Assistant Secretary. In 1886 she was chosen Secretary of the Executive Board. In 1887 she was chosen Corresponding Secretary of that body (the Convention), which position she held till 1890. In 1891 she was again made Assistant Secretary. She is universally esteemed by the women of the State and is ever ready to do their bidding. Miss Cook has very many times addressed the Convention upon important subjects, and at the jubilee meeting, January 18, 1889, she gave the history of the Convention, at which time the *American Baptist* said:

The history of the Convention by Professor Mary V. Cook, their Corresponding Secretary, as a concise and comprehensive paper. She left the well-beaten tracks of most of the lady speakers and dealt entirely with facts, and without sentiment traced the Convention from its incipiency until the present time. It was an interesting paper, brimful of information, and was well received. Miss Cook is never more in earnest than when saying a word for the women's work.

She has often spoken and read papers before the public with much credit, viz.: At Mobile, Ala., she read a paper before the American National Baptist Convention, August 27, 1887, subject, " Woman's Work in the Denomination." The same year she appeared before the National Press Convention at Louisville, Ky., and read a paper, "Is Juvenile Literature Demanded on the Part of Colored Children?" September 25, 1888 at Nashville, in the great meeting of the American Baptist Home Mission Society, she read a paper on "Female Education." September 1890, she was invited to prepare a paper on "Woman's Work for Woman," to be read before the Foreign Mission Convention, but sudden illness in her family called her home before the programme of this body was called. September 1891, before the National Convention at Dallas, Texas, she read a paper on "Women in Medicine." She has appeared before the State Teachers' Association three times, viz.: In 1887, at Danville, "Woman a Potent Factor in Public Reform"; 1890, Hopkinsville, "Professional Women and Their Achievements," and 1892, Henderson, The Colored Women in the School-room."

Miss Cook made her *debut* in journalism in 1886. Her contribution, "Nothing but Leaves," in the *American Baptist,* was one of her best productions. Having been converted in 1876, she showed in this article a noble Christian heart and a soul deeply affected by Divine grace. In 1887 she was editor of a column of the *South Carolina Tribune* and also a column in the *American Baptist.* She has recently written for the *Georgia Sentinel.* Her position as editor of the "Educational Department " of *Our Women and Children* gave her wide scope in editorialwork,in which she took much pleasure. In the " Negro Baptist Pulpit," by Dr: E. M. Brawley, Miss Cook has an article on " Woman's Work," and is the only female writer in the book. Dr. J. M. Pendleton highly commended the article in his criticisms on the book and recommended it to the Northern Societies in their missionary work. Miss Cook is a terse, vigorous writer, who loves her race as she loves herself, as her articles will show.

September 5, 1889, she visited the New England States by invitation of the Board of the American Baptist Woman's Home Mission Society, Boston, as a representative of the colored women South and the State University in which she was teacher. The president and trustees granted her a leave of absence, and they (the president and trustees), in connection with the faculty, students, board of managers of the Baptist Women's Educational Convention of Kentucky, the Union District Sunday-school Convention and the State Street Baptist Church, Bowling Green, Ky., of which she is a member, sent to the New England Societies testimonials bearing upon her worth as a Christian and cultured woman. These appeared in the *American Baptist,* Louisville, September 6, 1889. She was away four months and spoke in all the important cities and towns of Maine, Massachusetts, Rhode Island and Connecticut. She was everywhere well received and every comfort and pleasure they could give were hers. Newspaper encomiums were profuse as to her ability. One clipping we give from the *Journal,* Augusta, Maine, September 24th·

In accordance with a notice on Saturday a large audience on Sabbath evening in the First Baptist lecture-room greeted Miss Mary V. Cook, Principal of the State University, of Louisville, Ky. Possessing a clear, musical voice, and with modest, refined manners, the speaker was well calculated to hold the close attention of her listeners for the hour occupied by her address. She spoke of her gratitude in being permitted to visit Maine and to look into the faces of the many friends of her people. She spoke of the colored people generally and of their schools. She told how rapidly the race is increasing and said the only remedy for the fear that power in the hands of an ignorant people would prove disastrous to the country was a Christian education that would include the head, heart and hands. She pleaded for this and for an educated ministry, and for better homes that better citizens might be given to the country. She was glad to note the Christianity here that recognized its brother though he be clothed in black. She spoke of her agreeable surprise in finding, as she entered the previous meeting of Christian Endeavor, that a colored brother led that meeting, and the eagerness that was depicted on each face as he spoke to them. She prayed that God would speed the time when men all over this broad land should he known not by the color of their faces, but by their intellect and moral standing. After the meeting she received the warm grasp of many a hand, and as she goes forth again to her work, she may be assured she leaves behind her an added circle of friends to remember her in prayer and kindly interest.

For four years the children of that State had paid her salary as teacher in the State University; so she found as well as made many warm friends not only for herself and work, but for the race. A private letter to a friend in Maine, in which Miss Cook spoke of the oppression of her race, was published in the *Home Mission Echo*, Augusta, Maine, August 1892. When she returned to her work the teachers and students received her with an ovation which she nor they will ever forget.

May 1890, she was requested by the same women of Boston to come to the Baptist Anniversaries, which met in Chicago, and represent their work. She did, much to their satisfaction. The best accommodation in that city were hers, at their expense.

In 1890 she resigned her position at the State University, against the protest of the trustees, but she thought of taking a course in medicine after needed rest was taken. But, alas! that boon was not to be hers, for in September, while attending the National meeting in Louisville, she was stricken with the sad intelligence that her mother had been paralyzed. Being compelled to give up her plans for studying medicine, she accepted a position with Rev. Robert Mitchell as teacher of Latin and science in the Simmons Memorial College, Bowling Green, Ky. Her burdens seemed to increase, for shortly after the affliction befell her mother, her father sickened and died, leaving to her the care of mother and grandmother. Under all she keeps cheerful and faithfully discharges her duty. The Lord has blessed her in many ways. As general solicitor for Eckstein Norton University, Cane Spring, Ky., she has been able to visit many Southern States and has learned a great deal about the race by observation and immediate contact. Miss Cook has been offered many positions as teacher within the last year, viz.: In Mississippi, New Iberia, La., Indian Territory, Florida, and four in her own state.

147

April 15, 1892 she, with three other ladies, was called to Frankfort, the State capitol, to address the legislative committee against the enactment of the Separate Coach Bill. That event will be a bright page in the history of the colored people of Kentucky.

She has been asked to prepare a paper for the National Educational Convention, which meets at Savannah, Ga., September 1892.

Miss Cook is an all-round scholarly woman. Her judgment may be depended upon. She is favorably known by almost all the leading men and women of the race in the country, and is more widely known, possibly, in the New England States than any other colored woman. She has done and is still doing much for her race, and it is hoped that what she has done is simply an introduction of what she is yet to do. She lives comfortably in her own home. Let all who read be encouraged to go forward, and success is theirs.

CHAPTER XXX,

MISS LILLIAN A. LEWIS.

The well-known and highly respected "Bert Islew" of the Boston Advocate is a remarkable young woman, of whom the race may be exceedingly proud. Pleasing as a writer, stylish as a lady, able as a thinker, fascinating as a speaker and wise as an editor, apt as a scholar, true and reliable as a stenographer and rapid as a typewriter, Miss Lewis, though young, is, nevertheless, destined to become a potent factor in the advance lines of the march of the race towards that higher and more refined plane of civilization to which she is striving, as a leader to carry her followers.

She has filled many important positions as an aspiring young woman; in all her efforts to labor for the race, she has been admirably successful. Her temperance lectures have been received with satisfaction, and so has her "Gossip" and her newspaper articles have all been read with much interest by the reading public.

Some of her writings are the following: "Man's Weal and Woman's Woe," "Dead Heads and Live Beats" "The Mantle of the Church Covereth a Multitude of Humbugs," "Idalene Van Therse." She has contributed to a large number of Afro-American journals. It is said that the Advocate was on the way to a collapse until the energy of this young woman was placed at the helm. Now the paper is again alive. So we may say she is the resurrection of the *Advocate* as well as a part of its life.

Miss Lewis is a very pleasant lady in disposition and in appearance, and is destined to become a power, invincible and active, in the affairs that make for the greatest good of the race.

Albertype: Forbes Co., Boston.   GEO. E. BARRETT.   C. W. PAYNE.   F. J. LOUDIN.   B. W. THOMAS.   Allen & Rowell, Photo., Boston.

PATTI MALONE.   MATTIE L. LAWRENCE.   MABEL R. LEWIS.   JENNIE JACKSON.

                                    ELLA SHEPPARD.   MAGGIE L. PORTER.   LAURA WELLS.

=1871=   **THE JUBILEE SINGERS,**   =1881-2=

Fisk University, Nashville, Tenn.

CHAPTER XXXI.

LADIES OF THE FISK JUBILEE SINGERS.

As this volume is exclusively devoted to the *Distinguished Women* of the race it is hardly necessary, in the beginning of this chapter, to offer any apology for our exclusion of the male members of the Fisk Jubilee Singers. Therefore, let it be understood that we have no intention whatever to detract in any way a single one of the many honors due these gentlemen for the valuable and indispensable part which they played in the accomplishment of that great work. As we must necessarily be brief, suffice it to say, "Honor to whom honor is due."

The following are the names of the ladies who are said to have been members of that famous club of singers: Misses Ella Shepherd, Maggie Porter, Jennie Jackson, Georgia Gordon, Maggie Carnes, Julia Jackson, Eliza Walker, Minnie Tate, Josephine Moore, Mabel Lewis, A. W. Robinson, Pattie J. Malone.

We quote the following from the valuable little book, "The Story of the Jubilee Singers," by Mr. J. B. T. Marsh:

At different times twenty-four persons in all have belonged to the company. Twenty of these have been slaves and three of the other four were of slave parentage.

Whether the company was equally composed of twelve males and twelve females does not appear from the above quotation.

Mr. J.B. T. Marsh also makes the following statement with reference to their first three years' work, which furnishes another link to the chain of evidence that an humble *beginning* is by no means an assurance of failure in large and difficult undertakings of the Afro-American:

They were at times without money to buy needed clothing; yet in less than three years they returned, bringing back with them nearly one hundred thousand dollars. They had been turned away from hotels and driven out of railway waiting-rooms, because of their color; but they had been received with honor by the President of the United States: they had sung their slave songs before the Queen of Great Britain, and they had gathered as invited guests about the breakfast table of her Prime Minister. Their success was as remarkable as their mission was unique.

It is but just to state here that the ostracism which they received at "hotels" and "railway waiting-rooms" all, possibly, took place in our liberty-loving America, as we have never known of the denial of rights to *colored ladies* of America when traveling in foreign countries.

A letter just received from Rev. E. M. Craveth, D. D., President of Fisk University, contains the following, in answer to questions by the author:.

The University raised, through the Jubilee Singers in the seven years work, one hundred and fifty thousand dollars net in money, and secured books, paintings and apparatus to the value of seven or eight thousand dollars more. The Jubilee Singers sang in England, Scotland, Ireland, Holland, Switzerland and Germany. Mr. Lowden, who was a member of the company while under charge of the University, took a company, on his own responsibility, to Australia, India, Japan and around the world.

Some idea of what these young women *willingly* and bravely encountered, that their less favored brothers and sisters might in after years enjoy the advantages of an education, may be gathered from the following words of Mr. Marsh:

At Zanesville, also, their concert did not meet expenses; but a friend paid their hotel bill, which amounted to twenty-seven dollars. What figure it would have reached had not the six girls been put into a single room over a shed, where the bed-clothing was so offensive that they were constrained to roll the most of it in a bundle and lay it on the porch while they slept wrapped in their water-proofs, is not known.

The gross receipts of the last seven days of their tour through Connecticut amounted to more than $3,900.

The total receipts of one month's work in England amounted to nearly $20,000. These two items alone are arguments, strong and forcible, in favor of what great things the race may accomplish by concert of effort.

On their return from New York to Nashville, having secured a first-class passage, they were ejected from the waiting-room for ladies in Louisville by some local prejudice which it seems the superintendent of the railroad could not overcome. Thereupon, he placed at their disposal and for their own special comfort an extra coach. This he has willingly done every time since when they have traveled that road.

However many and severe the difficulties they had to meet, one thing is certain— that the results of their work have been far more elevating and inspiring; far more beneficial to themselves as matters of actual experience and travel; far more beneficial to their race as adjuncts to their education and helpers in the destruction of prejudice, than the indignities heaped upon them and the thrusts made at them can ever tear down or destroy.

While we have spoken. mostly of their financial success, we have been none the legs mindful of their rounded and fully well-developed success in every direction. Had we the available space many newspaper clippings would here appear which would do great honor to any company.

It will also be seen that we have said nothing of the personal history of these twelve young women, simply for want of space. The Supplement to the Jubilee Singers contains much valuable information as to their success under the new (colored) manager (F. J. Lowdin, its author, also), who deserves unmeasured credit for his bold and arduous undertaking, which was most wonderfully successful. Now, when it is remembered that the songs they sang originated, not in some musical conservatory of the North, or of the West, but are the promptings of religious zeal in the untrained minds of the slave in the cotton fields, or in midnight secret prayer-meetings on the sugar farms of the South; or they were the productions of untrained minds of the ex-slave in the heat of camp-meetings or in their lonely and loathsome huts in the "Sunny South " And then when it is remembered that they who sang them were not graduates of our best musical conservatories, but were the humble ex-slaves and the children of former slaves, whose gifts were the real and mysterious endowments of the all-wise and ever good God, then the glory of their accomplishments heightens and expands as it could not otherwise do.

In speaking of them, after they had spent some time in Germany, the *Berliner Musik-Zeitung,* a *very critical journal,* in passing its final sentence upon them, said:

Not only have we had a rare musical treat, but our musical ideas have also received enlargement, and we feel that something may be learned of these negro singers, if only we will consent to break through the fetters of custom and long use.

Long after this great building, "Jubilee Hall," which is dedicated to their memory, shall have crumbled to dust and shall no longer mark the spot upon which it now rests; long after its present occupants and the Jubilee Singers, who gave it birth, along with this humble author, shall all have returned to their mother, dust, and be no more among the living creatures of earth, still the deeds of this most wonderful company of self-sacrificing singers and ex-slaves will ever live as imperishable monuments to their memory. And then may they, with all the just made perfect, sing *jubilee songs,* even more gloriously triumphant than the songs of earth.

CHAPTER XXXII.

HISTORY OF FISK UNIVERSITY FOR TWENTY—FIVE YEARS.

Fisk University, the fame of which is world-wide, owes its origin and foundation to the generous and Christian efforts of the American Missionary Association under whose fostering care it still remains.

At the close of the war this noble Association felt itself especially called and providentially prepared to diffuse knowledge among the lately emancipated negroes of the South who had already showed such a surprising thirst for it. For this purpose various small schools were established in different sections of the South. In September 1865, the Association commissioned Rev. E. P. Smith as District Secretary at Cincinnati, and Rev. E. M. Cravath as Field Agent, with instructions to undertake the opening of Christian schools for the freedmen of Kentucky, Tennessee and portions of Georgia and Alabama. The two men reached Nashville October 3rd and found General Clinton B. Fisk in command of Tennessee and Kentucky, as Commissioner of the Freedmen's Bureau, with Professor John Ogden on his staff as Superintendent of Education.

Messrs. Smith and Cravath decided that Nashville was the natural and strategic center for the extensive educational movement which they had been sent to inaugurate in Tennessee and adjoining States. In searching for the location their attention was called to the United States Hospital, west of the Chattanooga depot, which was about to be sold as no longer needed for the use of the army. After due consultation the ground on which the building stood was purchased for $16,000. General Fisk secured the transfer of the hospital buildings from the Department of War to the Freedmen's Bureau and placed them at the disposal of the societies for school purposes.

January 6, 1866 the Fisk School was opened with appropriate public exercises and was placed under the joint charge of Professor John Ogden, of the Western Freedmen's Aid Commission, and Rev. E. M. Cravath, of the American Missionary Association.

Three years later the former society transferred its interest to the American Missionary Association. The school was named in honor of General Clinton B. Fisk, who had both personally and officially aided in every practicable way in its establishment.

As there were then no public schools in Nashville for colored children the number in attendance upon Fisk University the first year was over twelve hundred. Fisk University was incorporated under the laws of Tennessee, August 22, 1867 with a board of nine trustees, and opened for advanced pupils, the city of Nashville having started school for colored children.

The first normal class of twelve was organized in November of the same year. Early in the year 1868 $7,000 was received from the government, and repairs were made in the buildings so as to accommodate boarding students.

In 1869 the government buildings, then in use for the school, having been transferred to the Association, permanent foundations were placed under them. A dormitory building was also erected and a Gothic chapel. In 1870, Professor Ogden, who was especially interested in normal work, resigned, and Professor Spence took charge as principal, with the idea of developing college preparatory and college work. The new idea made better accommodations imperative, as the old government buildings were fast going to decay.

A resolute band of singers, afterwards known throughout the civilized world as the "Jubilee Singers," under the guidance of Professor George L. White, started out October 6, 1871, on their marvelous career, with little money and no experience. Space does not permit me to relate the struggles of this little band. But after many months of hardships the clouds began to lighten, and as a result of their labors, after seven years singing in the United States, Great Britain, Holland, Switzerland and Germany, they realized a net income to the University of $150,000, besides many valuable gifts of apparatus, paintings, etc. With this money Jubilee Hall was built. January 1, 1876, the University was transferred to this building, which is situated On the former site of Fort Gilliam, one of the most commanding and beautiful locations about Nashville.

Soon after the erection of this hall Rev. E.M. Cravath, who was elected as president of the school in 1875, came personally to manage the work. His labors, seconded by those of the college faculty, five in number, resulted in the rapid development of the higher educational courses. In 1875 the first college class was graduated, and also the first normal class, and regularly from that time students have graduated from the college and normal departments.

Livingstone Missionary Hall is the other large building connected with Fisk University. The plan for the erection of this hall took shape in 1876 with the Jubilee Singers, who were then in England, and the first contribution to the fund, outside of the Jubilee Company, was given by Mrs. Agnes Livingstone Bruce, of Edinburgh, daughter of the great African explorer.

The honor of completing the work and securing the erection of the building is due to Mrs. Stone, of Malden, Massachusetts, who gave $60,000 through her agent, Rev. W. H. Wilcox, D. D. This beautiful building was dedicated October 30, 1882.

The building for the gymnasium and mechanical department had its origin in a gift of $4,000 by Colonel Howard, for years a distinguished citizen of Nashville.

I am pleased to note that the Theological Seminary, so long talked of, hoped for and prayed for, has at last been erected, at a cost of $25,000. This building contains three large lecture-rooms, a library and reading-room, and thirty-seven dormitory rooms. Two professors, newly elected, are at present conducting the work. Others will be added as the growth of the Seminary demands.

The legacy of $28,000 left by General Fisk is to be used in erecting a memorial chapel during the present year.

Thus from the old government buildings has arisen Fisk University, one of the leading universities in the country for educating the colored youth of America. Fisk sustains to the colored youth of this country the same relation as the leading white colleges to the white youth of this country. Even in the Dark continent some of her number are sowing the seeds of truth and Christianity, which shall spring up after many days.

Fisk University seeks to instill within her pupils a desire for higher education, thereby enabling them to cope with the scholars and the thinkers of the age. In this she has not been disappointed, for over one hundred and ninety-one graduates are making honorable records and winning great favors as educators, ministers, physicians, lawyers and businessmen. The estimated value of the property of Fisk University is $300,000, with an additional amount of $21,000 endowment.

Probably more than 7,000 young people have registered, from time to time, as students.

LENA T. JACKSON, A. M.

MRS. JULIA RINGWOOD COSTON

CHAPTER XXXIII.

MRS. JULIA RINGWOOD COSTON.

"Let us ever glory in something and strive to retain our admiration for all that would ennoble, and our interest in all that would enrich and beautify our life."

It will be a source of much gratification and genuine pleasure to the many readers and admirers of *Ringwood's Journal* to be formally introduced to the editress of this Excellent magazine.

Beautifully situated in the town of Warrenton, Va., is the "Ringwood Farm," so called because of its resemblance to an ancient homestead of the same name in Colchester, England, in fulfillment of a promise made to his young wife by its owner that their home should be called "Ringwood" if the first-born were a girl. Upon this farm and after it Mrs. Coston was named.

She was brought to Washington, D. C., when an infant, and having been reared at the nation's capital, it is naturally regarded as her home. Her education was commenced in the public schools, which she attended until reaching the highest grade, when her mother's health failed and she was compelled to leave school. Accepting the position as governess in the family of a general of the United States army, she found time and received both assistance and encouragement in the prosecution of her studies. In the spring of 1886 she became the wife of Rev. W. H. Coston, B. D., then a student at Yale University, the Right Rev. J. M. Brown officiating. Two little ones have been born to them, the oldest a lovely little girl of five years, the youngest a boy of three years, named, respectively, Julia R. and W. H. Coston. So far along the journey of life this esteemed couple have proved that marriage is not a failure. They are mutually and justly proud of each other. Mr. Coston has found in his wife a helpmate" in whom his heart doth safely trust"; that pearl of pearls, a good woman, "whose price is far above rubies"; faithful, affectionate, earnest, Christian wife, who fills her position in his household and congregation with the dignity and grace which appertain thereto. From the fact that Mr. Coston is the author of "A Freeman and Yet a Slave" it will be seen that ambition has led him to venture forth upon the treacherous sea of literature; happily, however, without making shipwreck. By reason of the consonance of their literary tastes Mrs. Coston has received much sympathy, encouragement and help from her husband, whose practical experience has enabled him to suggest plans and methods for the realization of that cherished desire of her heart which will forever distinguish her among Afro-American women.

As a girl, Mrs. Coston felt deeply the ostracism of all the Anglo-Saxon journals of our common country as displayed toward anything of interest or credit concerning the colored people; she longed to see a colored face upon the pages of a magazine, and to enjoy the privilege of reading about its owner. This intense desire culminated in the conception and ultimate execution of *Ringwood's Journal,* the success and growing popularity of which amply prove her wisdom in launching bravely out upon an untried sea. That the readers of *Ringwood* may duly appreciate and understand Mrs. Coston's purpose and motives the following quotation from the initial editorial of this journal is subjoined: *Ringwood's Journal of Fashion,* published by Mrs. J. R. Coston, makes its advent to satisfy the common desire among us for an illustrated journal of our own ladies. The injury of the absence of the cultivating influence which attaches to a purely published, illustrated journal devoted to the loving interests of our homes, and to the weal of our daughters, was felt by me when a girl, and is recognized by me now when a woman. Knowing that this injury of absence could only be overcome by the *presence* of such a journal, without measuring the intellectual ability required, we have published *Ringwood's Journal.*

The quality of her fidelity to her age and her earnest ambition in behalf of her race are still further portrayed in the kind and commendatory words of one of her dearest friends:

There is nothing masculine or egotistic in the character of Mrs. Coston. She is a lovable woman, whose actuating desire is to serve the highest interests of the women of to-day, that their lives may be made more helpful by giving them modest publicity, and thus present them as worthy models for the emulation of our growing womanhood.

Woman, "last at the cross and first at the sepulchre," is always to be found in the van of progress. The noble enterprise to which Mrs. Coston is devoting hand, brain and heart deserves to be the pride and joy of all her sister women. Her success will depend mainly upon their sympathetic co-operation. Let them then rally loyally to her support. The Afro-American race must learn to respect and esteem the efforts of its own representatives if it would compel the regard of others. But whether Mrs. Coston succeeds or fails, the very endeavor to elevate the race by creating and maintaining a refined ladies' journal will be an enduring stone in the "Temple of Human Culture." She may not have a monument of bronze or marble erected to perpetuate a grateful memory, but she will live, not only in the hearts of her two precious little ones, who will rise up to call their devoted mother blessed, but likewise in the pure and exalted lives of the grand women of the dawning future.

"PILOT BUOY"

MRS. JOSEPHINE ST. PIERCE RUFFIN

CHAPTER XXXIV.

MRS. JOSEPHINE ST. PIERCE RUFFIN

Was born in Boston at a time when her fair-haired English mother and swarthy Negro-Indian father could not walk together unmolested even in the streets of the liberal (?) minded old Bay State. Her primary education was begun in the common schools, but after that she ran against a snag in the shape of a State law which prohibited the commingling of *white* and *colored* children in the higher schools. Josephine, unconscious of any law or reason to prevent this, had boldly and proudly entered the Franklin Grammar School, but at the end of six happy, triumphant months was brought face to face with that hydra-headed evil, race prejudice, the monster which has bruised the heart and broken the ambition of so many aspiring colored youth. Then began a contest; the law and the school committee on one side, and the then widowed mother and eight-year-old child on the other; it is needless to say which side won in this unequal fight (albeit the sympathy and moral support of the full corps of teachers of the school and that of the chairman of the school board was given to the legally weak side), for did not the law stand on the statute book and had not a saintly, philanthropic, but short-sighted soul, by the name of Smith, given a building to be forever set apart for the benefit of colored children solely?

Strange to say, at this time none of the cities and towns adjacent to Boston made any discrimination on account of color in the schools; so the next four years of the girl's life were spent in the schools of Charlestown and Salem, Mass.; then after two more years under private teachers in New York, she returned to her home just in time to celebrate the triumphant termination of the untiring efforts of the loyal men and women of Boston (white and colored) to blot out from the book the obnoxious law of a State whose founders were supposed to be nothing if not just. And so it came about that the child who had helped to bury the old law was on hand at the birth of the new order, and led the delegation of waiting girls who entered "old Bowdoin on the hill," when her doors swung open to all and the glorious reign of the now truly free common schools of Massachusetts began.

Before she was sixteen Josephine St. Pierce was married to George L. Ruffin, who, at the time, was a recent graduate of the Chapman Hall School. The high-spirited young couple, with a keen appreciation of the pains and penalties of being "colored" in slavery-cursed America, decided that they would not begin their married life in the miscalled "land of the free," so they went straight from the altar to New York, and from thence sailed away to England. After five months of foreign travel and observation Mr. and Mrs. Ruffin returned to America, satisfied that, with all her advantages, America was the *one* place for young people with more ambition than money; then, too, at that day every person was needed to take his place and go down into "the valley of the shadow of death" that through a bloody war the nation might rise to freedom, and these young people determined to dedicate themselves to the service of their people and the strict performance of every duty, the young wife and mother even giving her consent to the urgent request of the husband to let him go to the front with the afterwards famous Fifty-fifth Massachusetts Regiment, but when he presented himself as a volunteer he was rejected because of chronic nearsightedness. They afterwards became active members of that home guard who, through the medium of the Sanitary Commission, worked incessantly at home and at church, making, mending and praying for the soldiers at the front.

With the return of peace and prosperity came the opportunity to devote themselves to the making of their own and their children's lives an example and a stimulus to others; it was then (at the close of the Civil War) that Mr. Ruffin entered the Howard Law School, and at the same time such education of their children was begun as would enable them (the children) to compete for and hold an honorable place in the moral, intellectual and industrial life of their native city. The father lived just long enough to see his children all started on their different careers, and died one year after he had been made Judge of the Charlestown Court. Five years after the death of the husband and father the eldest born followed. During the life of her husband Mrs. Ruffin's interests were so identified with his that the history of one is the history of the other. In the useful and progressive career of Judge Ruffin the counsel and support of his wife were great factors, and through him the two were in turn councilman, legislator, lawyer and judge.

Since the death of her husband Mrs. Ruffin has been more than ever active in the charities and philanthropies which fill so large a place in the life of the true Boston woman. For fifteen years she has been one of the Board of Directors of the Moral Education Association of Massachusetts, and at one time its treasurer. She is also a member of the Board of the Massachusetts School Suffrage Association, one of the earliest and first of the members of the Associated Charities of Boston and was recently made a member of the N. E. Women's Press Association. For one year Mrs. Ruffin was editor-in-chief of the *Boston Courant,* but lately felt compelled to resign the active management of this paper, the following being among the newspaper notices of her retirement. The *Woman's Journal* says of her:

Mrs. Josephine St. P. Ruffin, who for some time was editor-in-chief of the *Boston Courant,* is taking a long vacation, rendered necessary by prostration from overwork. Mrs. Ruffin has unusual editorial ability and she made the *Courant* a leader among Afro-American papers and a credit to weekly journalism. It is announced that "it is not expected that Mrs. Ruffin will again resume the active management of the *Courant,* although it is her intention to be a contributor to its columns; the starting of a new and very comprehensive charitable work, together with her growing business of the care of the estates of widows and maiden ladies, promising to consume all her time this coming season."

The *Boston Courant;* September 3, 1892, also speaks as follows:

RETIRES FROM ACTIVE SERVICE.

It is due the many inquirers as to whether Mrs. Ruffin is the editor of the *Courant* to state that early in June, owing to prostration from overwork in many directions, Mrs. Josephine St. P. Ruffin was compelled to take a long vacation from all work. Since that time the paper has been in the very efficient hands of Mr. Robert T. Teamoh of the *Boston Globe.*

It is not expected that Mrs. Ruffin will again resume the active management of the *Courant,* although it is her intention to be a contributor to its columns; the starting of a new and very comprehensive charitable work, together with her growing business of the care of the estates of widows and maiden ladies, promising to consume all her time this coming season.

In personal appearance Mrs. Ruffin bears the reputation of being one of the handsomest women of Boston, her regular, commanding features, abundant black hair (now plentifully sprinkled with gray) and olive complexion making a noticeable and pleasing appearance.

CHAPTER XXXV.

THE GREAT PART TAKEN BY THE WOMEN OF THE WEST IN THE DEVELOPMENT OF THE A. M. E. CHURCH.

In reviewing the annals of our past history, we can discover no agency that has contributed more to the moral and religious development of the colored women of the United States than that of African Methodism. To her it was an open door by which to enter the arena of public action. Long had she waited for moral and intellectual recognition from the world. Too long had the vail of obscurity, like the gall of death, shut out the knowledge of her existence from the sisterhood of earth. Her patience and sacrifice in trials and her fortitude and heroism in adversity had never been recorded by the pen of a writer that others might read and admire her virtue, her patriotism and her piety. Her soul had never been stimulated by the genial influences of fraternity and hope of honor to grasp after higher attainments and that moral elevation which enables her to look above the common things of life to a nobler and more exalted existence.

Though her capabilities for intellectual expansion and mental development were as ample as were those of the more favored daughters of earth, yet was every bud of hope which expanded in her soul blighted by the withering blast of scorn, and when fancy spread its wings for an exalted flight the chilling winds of adversity brought her to the earth, where it drooped in sadness and pined in solitude. But she was not altogether discouraged with outward circumstances with which she was surrounded. She prayed and trusted and waited until the "day spring from on high visited her" and through the rifted cloud she could discover a brighter era. In religion she had always found a solace for a wounded heart and the ordinances of the Church had been precious to her soul; but even in these sacred rights she had been made unwelcome, and though willing and ready to perform the most arduous duties, with contempt she was pushed to the background. But when African Methodism appeared, bringing an array of obligations and duties in which she could bear an active and untrammeled part, she hailed it with that joy and readiness which only the spirit of God can impart.

Many intelligent Methodist women seemed to take it as a God-sent blessing. They flocked to its standard and enlisted heartily into the work. In the early days of the Church when its ministers were illiterate and humble, and her struggles with poverty and proscription were long and severe, and it required perseverance, and patience, and fortitude, and foresight, and labor, the women were ready, with their time, their talent, their influence and their money, to dedicate all to the upbuilding of the Church. No class of persons did more to solicit and bring in the people than they. They raised money to build churches and to support the ministers. They assisted in the prayer-meetings and class-meetings and Sabbath-schools and taught there to love the ordinances of the Church and to respect the ministry. Where there were no churches built, they opened their doors for public worship and gladly received the care-worn and weary traveling preachers into their families and provided bountifully for their necessities. They were not only zealous in labors, but also were talented in speech. Some were gifted in prayer; so much so that persons were often convicted by hearing them pray and were led to God and soundly converted and became useful members of the Church. Others carried great power with their religious experience when related in class-meetings or love-feasts. Many who had been hardened sinners dated their conviction and conversion from the time of hearing the Methodist women talk in their closed-door meetings.

There were notable preachers among their number also. In drawing off the Church from the white and establishing the A. M. E. Church in the West there was no one who took a more conspicuous part than Mrs. Jerrinna Lee; she was a preacher of great power and demonstration. The word of God from her mouth was like a sharp sword which pierced the sinner to the heart and like a healing balm to the heart of the believer; she was attractive in manners and pleasing in person and won the esteem of all who saw her. In the years of 1828, 1829 and 1830 she traveled and preached through the States of Pennsylvania, Ohio and Indiana. Great numbers of both white and colored people flocked to hear her. She sang well and prayed fervently, and when after her sermon had closed and the doors of the church were open to receive members numbers would come forward and joyfully cast their lot with the despised Methodist.

The holding of camp-meetings was one great method of making African Methodism known to the world. In these the women bore the heaviest burden, they would make great provision to feed the multitudes that would gather there and hundreds would enjoy the hospitality of those good and pious women, while their souls were being fed with the bread of eternal life from the sacred altar. They thought no sacrifice too great or labor too hard if it only tended to build up and expand the Church they so much loved. The freedom which they enjoyed in their worship and the satisfaction arising from equal rights in church privileges made the work more precious and secured to them greater hopes for future success. In raising funds with which to build churches no difficulties deterred them from their efforts and no dangers affrighted them from their purpose.

Through heat and cold and storms and fatigue and hardships they gathered a little here and there, while they made what they could with their own hands, which many times was only the widow's mite; but when these small sums were put together they were sufficient to raise a monument in the name of God to dedicate to His worship. Like Lydia of old they had long prayed for the time to come when they would be thought worthy to take an active part in the Master's cause; this was God's opportunity and well did they serve it. It is a significant fact that whenever there is especial work to do in any good cause God raises up and endows persons with peculiar abilities adapted especially for each department. Thus, it was with Methodism; her notable women were not only filled with the Holy Ghost, but were possessed with the energy and zeal of the Apostolic ages, and their love for God and His cause made them as strong as giants. There were honorable women, not a few, who deserve to be remembered by the Church; they are dead, but their works yet speak.

There were Mrs. Barret, of Columbus, Ohio; Mrs. Reyno; Mrs. Woodson of Chillicothe; Mrs. Leach, of Jackson, and Mrs. Broady of Cincinnati; also Mrs. Baltimore of Missouri; Mrs. Elsworth of Illinois, and many others who helped to build up the strongholds of African Methodism, whose names are recorded on high, and when the books are opened and their deeds of love for the Master made known, they will hear the welcome sentence, "Come ye blessed of my Father, enter into the joys of my Lord," and they, amid the swelling song of the redeemed and harps of angels, will enter in to come out no more.

MRS. SARAH J. W. EARLY.

MRS. ZELIA R. BALL PAGE.

CHAPTER XXXVI.

MRS. ZELIA R. BALL PAGE.

It was in the old aristocratic city of Alexandria, Va., that Zelia R. Page, *nee* Ball, first saw the light of day. She was not a slave. She was reared by her mother, a woman of remarkable ingenuity and foresight, who, during the dark days of slavery, helped many a poor bond-man on his way to Canada. At one time, while living with a wealthy Southern family in Washington City, she kept concealed for one week in the attic six slaves, waiting for the password to march. This mother, seeing and knowing the degradation and misery of slavery, was determined that her daughter should know as little of it as possible. She, having faith in the girl's future, was deeply interested in her education. Having many friends in New England, and knowing of the educational facilities that colored youth had in that section of the country, she made up her mind to take this child to New England, but the question was how to pass through Baltimore and Havre de Grace alone with her child. Being intimately acquainted with the family of the celebrated Dr. Peter Parker, who had recently returned to Washington City from China, and knowing that they intended to visit the East, she consulted them about the matter. Dr. Parker told her the only way she could travel with his family was to go as far as New York as their slaves, she and her child. She readily consented; and thus, one Saturday morning in the month of June the mother with her child arrived in Providence, R. I. She found after reaching Providence that the educational facilities were not as good for the colored youth as those in Boston, so she sent Zelia to Boston to school.

This girl possessed great dramatic and artistic powers. During her stay in the New England school she would always be called upon to declaim in the presence of visitors. She declaimed before the great educators, Bigelow and Green. They said to her, "Go on; you have talent; improve it." But, alas! like many others, she had no one to depend upon but a poor mother for her support.

Her mother sent her to Wilberforce in 1870. She was graduated in 1875. She returned to Providence. In 1878, June 27th, she married Inman E. Page, the first colored graduate of Brown University, and now President of Lincoln Institute at Jefferson City, Mo. Her life has not been one of continual sunshine and yet it has not been at all times the opposite. Having a strict moral principle, she could never wink at anything that was wrong or seemingly wrong. Perhaps if she had been so constituted as to be able to close her eyes to what she supposed to be wrong-doing she might have prevented a good many hard statements that have been made about her. She is a diligent student, constantly seeking to add to her store of knowledge some new truths from the different departments of learning. She has written several excellent papers that have been read before the public and published by request. Before she was twelve years old she had read the works of Scott, Milton, Dante and other noted authors. She has been to Lincoln Institute fourteen years and during the greater part of that time she has served either as matron or as teacher of natural science.

She has been the means of doing much good in Jefferson City. She organized a Union Training School for the poor children, September 25, 1891, which meets every Saturday afternoon. The value of the instruction which she gives to these children will be seen in future years. She has often said, "Oh! if I were only rich. I do not want money for myself, but I would like to be rich in order to do some good in this world. I would build an institution of learning simply for the poor colored young men and women of my race and have them to learn everything that would enable them to vie with the Anglo-Saxon race."

She is a devoted Christian, and always seeking to do what good she can and to help others. Mrs. Page will long be remembered by the students of Lincoln Institute, and especially the poor students, for her deeds of kindness to them.

JOAN IMOGEN HOWARD, A. M.

CHAPTER XXXVII.

JOAN IMOGEN HOWARD, A. M.

Then this very excellent lady, of whom the race is proud, Joan Imogen Howard, was born in the city of Boston, Mass. Her father, Edwin F. Howard, is an old and well-known citizen of that city, and her mother, Joan L. Howard, now deceased, was a native of New York. She has one sister, Miss Adeline T. Howard, the principal of the Wormley School Washington, D. C., and one brother, E. C. Howard, M. D., a prominent physician in the city of Philadelphia. Having a mother cultured, refined and intellectual, her earliest training was received from one well qualified to guide and direct an unfolding mind. At the age of fourteen, having completed the course prescribed in the Wells Grammar School, Blossom Street, Boston, she graduated with her class and was one of the ten honor pupils who received silver medals. Naturally this souvenir of her girlhood is greatly prized.

Her parents encouraged her desire to pursue a *higher* course of instruction, and consequently, after a successful entrance examination, she became a student of the Girls' High and Normal School, as it was then called. She was the first colored young lady to enter and after a three years' course to graduate from this, which was at that time the highest institution of learning in her native city.

A situation as an assistant teacher in Colored Grammar School No. 4, now Grammar School No. 81, was immediately offered. Here she has labored ever since, endeavoring to harmoniously develop the pupils of both sexes who have been committed to her care, so that their physical, intellectual and moral powers might be so trained as to produce human beings of a high order. Many of her pupils have become men and women of worth and hold positions of honor and trust.

For several years an evening school, which was largely attended and of which she was principal, was carried on in the same building. As time advances more is required of all individuals in every branch of labor. Teaching is no exception, and in recognition of this she took a course in "Methods of Instruction" at the Saturday sessions of the Normal College of New York City. She holds a diploma from this institution (1877), and thus has the privilege of signing "Master of Arts" to her name. This year (1892) still another step has been taken, for after a three year course at the University of the City of New York she has completed the junior course in the Department of Pedagogy and received the degree of "Master of Pedagogy."

The position on the Board of Women Managers of the State of New York for the Columbian Exposition was entirely unsought by her. Her experience has been a very pleasant one thus far, as she has received the most courteous treatment from the other ladies with whom she is associated in this vast undertaking. Her special position on the Board is as one of five of the Committee on Education.

MRS. HARRIETTE ESTELLE HARRIS PRESLEY

CHAPTER XXXVIII.

MRS. HARRIETTE ESTELLE HARRIS PRESLEY.

But He has not been unmindful of the good deeds of His faithful servants, and has so ordained that their memory shall be perpetuated as living examples of faithfulness for the benefit of posterity.

So we well remember the deeds and are impressed with the character of this devoted young woman, Hattie E. Presley, who was born in Buckingham county, Va., in 1862 , of humble parents

When quite young she was taken by an aunt to Richmond, Va., and adopted. She was well cared for and reared with most beautiful manners and a lovable disposition—not only " pretty " in person, but in manners. She was a pupil in the public schools of Richmond for many years, standing well in classes and in the favor of teachers and school-mates. When quite young she became a Christian and united by baptism with the First Baptist Church, of which Rev. J. H. Holmes, the model Christian, was pastor. Some time after becoming a Christian she entered the Richmond Institute (now Richmond Theological Seminary) and was for awhile in the classes taught by the writer, who was then a "student-teacher." She was a consistent Christian, and was always engaged in some good work, either among the poor and wretched, or in the Sabbath-school or in the church. She seemed to have an ever sympathetic heart, ready to bestow a blessing wherever it was possible for her to do so. In her classes she was always obedient, meek, kind and gentle. While thus a student in the Richmond Institute she and Rev. J. H. Presley, who was also a student, became fond friends, and this friendship grew into blooming love for each other. Rev. Presley was preparing to go to Africa as a missionary. Hattie began also to prepare to go with him, they having so agreed. In June 1883, they were united in the bonds of matrimony, and sailed for Africa on December 1st of same year, accompanied by Rev. W. W. Colley and wife, Revs. McKinney and J. J. Cole. The gathering at the First Baptist Church on a Sunday evening in November 1883, was a memorable occasion, for it was here that hundreds, if not thousands, of Christian people met to bid "farewell" to the missionaries; and, in the case of this dear woman, it was a " farewell " until these Christians shall meet her in heaven. When they had been in Africa only a short while Rev. Presley, her husband, was taken quite ill, and remained so for some considerable time. She was ever faithful to him in this great trial, and even when all was as dark as night, when all hopes for his recovery were fast fleeing, she still was true, and when high temperature and the infected poison of fever deprived him of consciousness, and hopes yet fleeing, she was also true to him, and, like a clock, she was ever on the watch for a chance, an opportunity, to supply some necessity. During this severe trial of her faith and strength the little infant that had been born to them was laid in the cold grave, and yet she stood by an afflicted companion far in a heathen land. Finally, while he is still sick, her nerves take on a reaction from the great strain to which they had been subjected, and now her own strength fails, and she, in the midst of a terrible crisis, dies like a hero in the heat of battle.

Thus, one of the fondest of our missionaries died at her post, giving up her life that she might be of service in leading some poor heathen to forsake his idol and turn unto the Lord and live. The writer delights to think of her as he knew her, a pure and faithful Christian woman. We cannot lay hands upon any creditable statements as to her real work as a missionary apart from that already referred to, but knowing her as we did, we are confident that it was all well done, kindly and freely done, with willing hands and heart.

In her death, the mission has lost a vigorous and energetic worker. How her place will be filled we know not, nor by whom, but some good seeds have been sown that may yet make our hearts glad with the sight of a fruitful harvest.

"My word shall not return unto me void, but it shall accomplish that which I please"
(Isa. 55:11), are very consoling words in this case as we think of our mission and its loss, but we may be sure that she is

"Gone to the rest of the ever blessed

To the New Jerusalem;

Where the children of light do walk in white, And the Saviour leadeth them."

MRS. SUSIE ISABELLA LANKFORD SHORTER.

CHAPTER XXXIX.

MRS. SUSIE ISABELLA LANKFORD SHORTER.

Soon after the death of her mother the family moved to Baltimore, Md., where her father was pastor of Bethel A. M. E. Church. A little incident occurred which no doubt helped shape her future course. One evening near sunset a minister called to see her father; he had every look of a traveler—dusty, weary, hungry, almost forlorn. However, he was soon made presentable, and in the meantime Susie had spread a refreshing meal. He enjoyed it very much, he said when he had finished, and pronounced the *biscuit* excellent (he had managed to consume eleven, though they were *not* very large). The young housekeeper was delighted that her father's guest, a stranger to her, had been made so welcome.

The minister was a Professor of Theology, and resided with his family near Xenia, O. Chief among his friends there was a bachelor professor, to whom, as soon as they had welcomed each other, he related the little incident in Bethel Parsonage, and recommended at once the little girl who could make such good biscuit as a suitable companion for a wife. Soon after this the second marriage of her father took place, and what with a new wife and fashionable hired girl it was plainly seen that Susie was not needed; so she was allowed to return to Wilberforce, where, in spite of herself, she must come in contact daily with this bachelor professor, and he taught her all about the verb "love" and "to be" loved. They were married in 1878 by this *same* professor and minister who had enjoyed her hospitality so long ago, Dr. T. H. Jackson, assisted by Dr. B. F. Lee. It was many years afterward e'er Susie knew anything of this revelation, when the Doctor mentioned it in her presence, in general conversation with Professor Priolean and wife, at their residence. Early in life she was inclined to write. She wrote a poem on the death of her mother, at the age of fourteen years, which was highly complimented. For many years she wrote occasional papers for the *Christian Recorder,* and is at present the contributor to the "News Column " of the same. She is possessed of a missionary spirit, and aids willingly any enterprise that has for its object the bettering of humanity.

For many years Mrs. Shorter was President of the Ladies' College Aid Society of Wilberforce University, and did much, in a quiet, unostentatious way, to help worthy students through school. She is the author of a work entitled "Heroines of African Methodism. "She is a real "doer," and not merely a hearer and talker. She is a very modest creature, and therefore ranch of the writing that has dropped from her pcn has never reached public print.

She now edits a corner in *Ringwood's Afro-American Journal of Fashion* for the *especial* benefit of our girls.

MRS. LUCY WILMOT SMITH

CHAPTER XL.

MISS LUCY WILMOT SMITH

One reads with a glow of enthusiasm the life and career of such women as Miss Smith. Great was her work for the race, and her noblest efforts were put forth in raising the standard of womanhood. She was the daughter of Margaret Smith and was born in Lexington, Ky.

Like the difficulties that come to may colored girls, she found it no easy task to satisfy her soul with the culture for which it longed. Her unusual brightness attracted much attention. Friends of the family took an interest in her and directed her reading by placing in her hands books which should prove the most beneficial. The result was at maturity she was considered among the best informed of the race.

Seeing how hard her mother had to labor for the support of her children, Miss Smith felt that she must lend a helping hand. Though young she took a position under the Lexington School Board, where she labored faithfully and satisfactorily. In 1881 she was elected teacher in State University, taking charge of the model school as principal. She was a model teacher as well as an exemplary Christian woman and left a lasting impression upon those under her care. She lifted the men up to the apprehension that a noble character and a cultivated intellect are more enduring graces than mere beauty of form—that to be manly was their first duty. She taught the young women to despise mediocrity, to trust their own brain and to aspire towards all that is noble and grand. Her indomitable will, perseverance and originality gave her success in all her undertakings.

For some time she served as private secretary to Dr. William J. Simmons, by whom she was led into prominence. She was painstaking and accurate and sacrificed much of her pleasure and time that his work might not lag. All that she did was with that cheerfulness of spirit that not only sweetened her own life, but also made life easier for others. Dr. Simmons often spoke of her worth and helpfulness. Though burdened as teacher and private secretary, she took up the studies of the normal department and graduated in 1887. Out of her means she supported a sister in the University; after this sister's graduation, she assumed the education in the same school, of a sister's daughter and that of one of her own brothers at the same time. She never forgot her mother's comforts and provided for them. One loves to think of her as he knew her, and to know her was but to admire her.

In 1884, Miss Smith left the State University to try the West. She there filled a position in Wyandotte, Kansas. Here her efficiency was recognized and honored, for she became President of the Sewing Circle of the Wyandotte Baptist Church, also of a society connected with the Methodist Church, and Secretary of the Women's Christian Temperance Union: Upon the urgent request of president and trustees she returned to her old position at State University, September, 1885, where she served as financial clerk and city missionary for the Young Men and Women's Christian Association; she also served this body as president. She became a Christian, December 1872, under the influence of Rev. James Monroe, and lived a consistent member of the Baptist Church. It was a point of her life to give one-tenth of her means to the Lord, and her large-heartedness never allowed her to turn her back on any worthy cause.

When the call was made in 1883, by Dr. Simmons, for the Baptist women of the State to come together and organize for the benefit of the educational work, Miss Smith was among its foremost workers and was secretary of the organization. Her interest in that work never weakened from the first, and she was willing to serve wherever placed. She was a member of the Board of Managers for years and was Secretary of Children's Bands, an auxiliary of that body. She wrote a pamphlet of thirteen pages, setting forth the work, constitution, order of business and work children could do to earn their own money, which proved beneficial and was quite instructive to the little ones. She was of a national disposition, and every such meeting she could reach was greeted by her smiles. The first National Baptist Convention, which met in St. Louis in 1886, listened to a paper from her on "The Future Colored Girl," which is published in the "Journal" of that meeting. She was also elected at that time as Historian of that body, and served it several years as one of the Executive Committee. In 1888 she again appeared before this body with a paper which showed carefulness of thought and logical arrangement.

Her newspaper work began in 1884, when she controlled the "Children's Column" in *The American Baptist,* of Louisville, Ky. In 1887 she accepted a position on the staff of *The Baptist Journal* of which Rev. H Coles, of St. Louis, was editor.

She furnished sketches of newspaper writers, among the women of the race , for the *New York Journalist,* in the interest of artists, authors and publishers. Her work was very much praised and also reproduced in the Boston Advocate, the Indianapolis Freeman and other papers. She was a forcible writer, using good English, and always produced something readable. She edited the department of "Woman and Woman's Work" in Our Women and Children, a magazine of Louisville, Ky. In this work she took much pride. She was greatly interested in the elevation of woman and was always outspoken on woman suffrage, as a clipping from one of her articles will show:

It is said by many that women do not want the ballot. We are not sure that the15,000,000 women of voting age would say this, and if they did, majorities do not always establish the right of a thing. Our position is that women should have the ballot, not as a matter of expediency, but as a matter of pure justice.

It was her intention, had life been spared her, to establish a female seminary that a more thorough education might be given the girls of head, heart and hands. She had also begun a book on "Women and Their Achievements," which her friend, Miss M. V. Cook, would gladly finish and publish if the manuscript could be gotten. Miss Smith was a warm enthusiast on temperance and was always ready to talk or write on that subject.

She felt that the mortality of women is due to their timidity in expressing themselves freely to male physicians, and with this fact in mind, she determined to alleviate their suffering by making herself proficient in medicine, especially to that part which pertained to female ills-and their remedies. Like all else she did she threw her whole soul into it, having a private teacher from among the best and most skilled physicians of Louisville. What woman, who reads this sketch, will take up the work she so nobly began and make the most of it for the good of the race and humanity at large?

As a writer the following is said of her:

She frequently writes for the press and wields a trenchant pen; is ambitious to excel and will yet make her mark.

(The American Baptist).

Mrs. N. F. Mossell says:

Miss Smith writes compactly, is acute, clean and crisp in her acquirements, and has good descriptive powers. Of strong convictions, she is not slow in proving their soundness by a logical course of reasoning. Her style is transparent, lucid, and in many respects few of her race can surpass her.

But, alas! "Death loves a shining mark—a signal blow."

In the fall of 1888 overwork began to tell on her features, then a dreaded cough set in. Her friends became alarmed from the first and begged her to give up work and take rest. She only smiled at such requests and said, "It will be all right." Everything was done for her, yet deeper and deeper fastened the disease 'upon her. Physicians were consulted and assured anxious friends that all would be useless unless she gave up work. Yet she worked right along without a complaint, without a frown, without a murmur, but with a smile she would greet all. Summer came, she went off for vacation, but too late then to do much good. September 1889, when school opened, she was found at her post of duty, feeble and emaciated, but with the same iron will and bright mind. She knew what the result would be and requested Dr. Simmons to preach her funeral; selected hymns and passages of scripture for the occasion, though to others she never hinted death, but talked of her future work for her sex, etc. Her mother came to be with her and, if possible, have her go home, Lexington, Ky., but she stoutly refused. October 15, 1889, she consented to go home, and was accompanied by the matron, Mrs. Jane McKamey and Rev. C. H. Parrish. Before leaving she said to the matron, "I waited to see Miss Cook," who was then in the New England States, "but I must go now." She arose every morning, dressed and received her friends till the morning of her death, December 1, 1889, at 5 A. M., when she rested from her labors.

MISS ADA C. HAND

CHAPTER XLI.

MISS ADA C. HAND.

The subject of this sketch was born in Westmoreland county, Va., December 25, 1862. When she was but little more than a month old her parents braved the perils of that unsettled period, and moved to Washington, D. C., so that for all practical purposes she is a child of our capital city. Her mother was free, but her father was a slave. This latter fact, however, had little effect upon the child's career, for both were practically free when she was born, and during all her life with them she was able to enjoy the full benefit of what time and ability they were capable of bestowing upon her. Her father was said to have been a man of uncommon natural ability, but of course had been denied all advantages which schooling would have afforded. Her mother was one of those amiable characters which seem filled with love for all and bred to innate nobleness and purity of life. She had learned to read and write a little, and what she knew was carefully imparted to Ada. She not only confined her teaching to what could be gained from books, but the fundamental principles of house-wifery were carefully taught, and although to the negro the term and use of the kindergarten were absolutely unknown, this mother intuitively grasped the idea in teaching Ada to plan, sew, cut and fit for a large doll of her own and to make all of the stitches common to ordinary needle-work, thus indelibly impressing upon the child's mind the practical bearing and relation which these things would have upon the necessities of real life.

When Ada was nine years old her mother died, leaving three children, an older sister and a younger brother. The sister soon married. Many persons were anxious to adopt Ada, because of her known usefulness and capability in household lines. The father, however, kept her and her brother together, Ada being housekeeper and "maid of all work". This condition of affairs obtained for three brief years, when the father was, in the wisdom of God, called to his final rest.

Ada and her brother then went to live with their sister, whose husband was particularly cruel and overbearing. Not desiring either of the children to secure the advantages of education, he ordered that Ada should be put to service as a nurse. Her independent spirit revolted at the indignity, and justly so, as she supported entirely her brother and herself and only needed his roof as a protection. Her present knowledge of books enabled her to secure several adult pupils at night, who paid her fifty cents per month each, thus giving her the scanty means of securing for herself and brother the degree of comfort which they enjoyed.

The failure to crush Ada's spirit was spent upon the brother, who was taken out of school and subjected to a street education, which Ada's good sense deemed hurtful. Finding herself unable to thwart the strong will of this brother-in-law, who seemed unrelenting in his course towards her brother, she planned to steal him away and place him in the charge of an aunt who resided at least sixty miles off in the country. Accordingly she started with him, took the steamer down the Potomac River, traveling all night, and reached the place to which she was destined about three o'clock in the morning. No inkling had been given to the aunt of the coming of the children, nor had Ada any idea of the time the boat would land her at the place she desired to reach; but the watchful care of that Father who never sleeps was around and about these precious treasures, and they were fortunate in finding their aunt's husband waiting at the landing to meet friends whom he expected by the boat. He conducted them safely to his home, where they remained for two months, Ada studying from the books which had composed a necessary part of her traveling outfit.

Having reached the high school course of our city schools, there were of course no schools sufficiently advanced to which she could go in the country. Her determination to have an education induced her to return to Washington, leaving her brother to the care of her aunt. She enjoyed the hospitality of a friend for one night after her arrival and was the next day invited to live with a cousin. This she did, but the struggle to get an education was not here appreciated, and Ada still had to strive against the burdens heaped upon her, which, at times, seemed greater than she could bear. Having arrived just in time for the examination in the high school, she was admitted, and, notwithstanding the loss of two months of actual training, led her class. This being her first year in the high school, and with such a record, nothing could now daunt her. Many a day she sat and drank in the instruction imparted without having had a mouthful of food, as the little money she was able to earn was not sufficient to provide shoes, clothing, light and fuel. These were necessities which her fingers and brain had to earn after her household tasks were completed for the latter were required as a bonus for a shelter.

192

Five years of care and deprivation had now passed, and with the class of 1879, of the high school for colored children of the District of Columbia, Ada was graduated and subsequently passed very creditably the examination for admission to the Miner Normal School, of which Miss M. B. Briggs was principal.

With the close of the school year 1879—'80 Miss Ada C. Hand was graduated with honors from the normal school, having passed successfully the entire curriculum of the public school course of the District of Columbia, and stood among the first for admission to the grammar, high and normal school. At the opening of the school year 1880 '81 she was placed in charge of a first grade (primary) school, where she distinguished herself through the native ability and aptitude shown for her chosen profession. So marked was her strength in the school-room in every point of her work that she was made training teacher in the normal school the second year she taught, which position she has held consecutively for ten years, shooting clear above all others in methods and plans of work.

She has attained considerable prestige as an artist, particularly at portraits; paints, draws and sketches any object she desires for use in connection with the object or language lessons in her school-room. In 1878 she received a medal for the best original design. She has made a complete set of charts to facilitate the work of teachers in presenting in the most attractive and pleasing way the text-books required by the first year course of our school.

Miss Hand has for ten years taught one hundred pupils a day—a school of fifty (first grade) from 9 to 12A. M., and another of fifty pupils (second grade) from I to 4P. M. — besides keeping accurately the complicated record book required for each school. She is held responsible for the methods given pupil-teachers of the normal school in four subjects during the year.

Her manners in the school-room are decidedly pleasing and attractive, and her school is a model of excellence in every particular at all times. There is a great demand for admission to her school, and many parents gladly take their children from remote sections of our city to have them enjoy the benefits of Miss Hand's experience.

She spares neither time nor money in making her school first-class in every particular. This year she has purchased, at her own expense, a symphonion which will play an unlimited number of pieces, for the purpose of meeting the want she felt of a piano to conduct her classes in writing and calisthenics.

She is very unassuming and her unpretentious manners have endeared her to many hearts in our city. She has a few friends whom she has tried and to these she is true, but she has no fondness for society or notoriety.

Having been properly directed in her earlier years as to the value of work, the child of ten years was a fair index of the woman of today, for the tidy, lady-like appearance which she always made when her own hands washed and ironed the spotless garments she wore as a child still follows her, and it can now be said to her credit that, although she has not earned less than $80 per month for the past six years, she still makes every article of clothing she wears, such as dresses, cloaks, underclothing, etc., which most young women regard as such an irksome task.

Miss Hand is a member of the Presbyterian Church and has had charge of the infant department for the past eight years.

CHAPTER XLII.

CAROLINE V. ANDERSON, A. M. M. D

C aroline V. Anderson, A. M., M. D., the daughter of Hon. William Still, of " underground railroad" fame, was born in 1849. Reared in the " Quaker City " at a time that "tried men's souls," she early gave evidence of an aspiring mind and intellectual powers not of the ordinary. As a graduate from Oberlin College in 1868, at the age of eighteen, she had, in a measure, realized the rich promise of her early girlhood.

She entered actively thence into the work for which by nature and accomplishments she was especially fitted. The work of teaching engaged her attention for a few years. Her instructions in the classroom were always clear, comprehensive, progressive, embellished by all the lights and graces which admirable common sense, observation and extensive reading could give. Her geniality was inspiring although it did not prevent her from being firm to her convictions, when convictions had to be maintained against assaults.

In 1875 and '76 she held the position of teacher of music and instructor in drawing and elocution at Howard University, Washington, D. C. The movement in the direction of greater freedom to women, opening up avenues before closed and widening those already opened, found an earnest advocate in Dr. Anderson. In 1876 she entered the Medical Department of Howard, completing her course at the Women's Medical College in Philadelphia. Independent as she was resolute, the young physician by her unaided efforts built up a practice which was of several fold importance to her, to her sex and to her race; important to her not only from its pecuniary stand-point, but also in her deservedly receiving the respect and high esteem of her brother and sister 'practitioners of both races; for her sex and race it is a vindication; in several of the hospitals of the city she has served as resident, visiting and consulting physician. As the wife of Rev. Matthew Anderson, pastor of the Berean Presbyterian Church, she finds a special channel for various other energies in that work that is doing the most to humanize and elevate mankind. She is ardent in all Christian Work, public-spirited and affectionate, and as a teacher, physician, mother and wife her life has been rich in incident, and with a modesty equal to her talents she invariably ascribes the attainment of her distinctions to persevering attention rather than to unusual mental capacity.

CHAPTER. XLIII.

ST. AUGUSTINE SCHOOL, RALEIGH, N. C.

St. Augustine School, Raleigh, N. C., was founded in 1867 by the Rev. J. Brinton Smith, D. D., and has thus already completed its first quarter century. It is under the care f the Protestant Episcopal Church; which has always taken great interest in the support of higher schools for the Christian training of young men and women. It embraces Preparatory, Normal, Collegiate and Theological departments. At the present time instruction is also given in carpentry, in tinsmithing, in shoemaking, in bricklaying for the young men, and in sewing, cooking and the care of the household for the girls. It is hoped that industrial instruction may be extended in other directions very soon.

The girls and young men are together in the recitation-room, at their meals and in occasional social reunions, but otherwise the girl's department is managed separately and in a different building. Each girl is provided with her own dressing-room, furnished with a bureau-closet, each provided with a separate lock and key. Trunks are all kept in a trunk-room. Beds stand in the dormitory just outside of each girl's dressing-room. The grounds of the school are situated on an eminence just outside the city of Raleigh and particularly well situated with regard to health and beauty. Especial care is taken of the health of the students. In order to discourage extravagant dressing and cultivate taste for neat and tasteful dress the girls wear uniform dress of dark blue. While every effort is made by those in charge of the school to make the students happy and contented, there is yet an earnest belief in such strictness of discipline, compliance with regular duty, vigorous work with mind and body as shall train the character and fit the students for the important work that is before them in actual life.

Several hundred students have already been trained as teachers and a number of young men have been prepared for the ministry of the Protestant Episcopal Church. The grounds of the school, embracing some forty-two acres, are devoted to a campus, surrounding the various school buildings, and to a garden in which supplies of fresh vegetables are raised for the school table. The whole property is situated on the outskirts of Raleigh, near enough for convenience and far enough out to be away from the distractions of city life.

While every effort is made to inculcate a respect for manual labor, yet nothing is allowed to interfere with progress in the various studies of the school. The faculty is an able one of ten teachers. Three of them are college graduates, four are graduates of the school, one of another normal school, and the author of this book is lecturer on physiology and the laws of health.

The invested funds of the school at present amount to something over $30,000, the income of which, along with the aid received from the Church, is used in carrying on the school. Total value of funds and school grounds, with buildings, is $65,000. The school charges $7 a month for board and tuition. All of the students are able to reduce this to about $5 per month or somewhat more, in needy cases, by manual work on the school grounds.

Progress is now a watchword of the school, but it is a progress that is conservative of the past as well as hopeful of the future. No progress is of any avail which does not lay its foundations in the molding of Christian character in teaching young men and young women to help themselves rather than depend on others, to be gentle men and women in word and manner, to hate sham and respect truth. The present principal is the Rev. A. B. Hunter.

MISS EDNORAH NAHAR.

CHAPTER XLIV.

MISS EDNORAH NAHAR.

The race has produced few young women possessing more push and real energy than the courageous little personage whose name marks the beginning of this chapter. Born in the city of Boston, Mass., she quite naturally attended the most excellent public schools of that great city, where she necessarily laid a broad foundation upon which she has built a more recent and most tasty structure. She is of foreign and American parentage and has always given evidence of that thrift which is now an important characteristic of her.

After spending sufficient time in the public schools, she entered Fort Edward Collegiate Institute, New York, where she was further prepared for life's duties, into which she has so earnestly entered. She began public service on the 16th of November 1886, by reading for a concert of young talent. It is needless to say more of her first effort than that it was a success. Since that time up to September 1892, she has given nearly eight hundred concerts in thirty-one States of the Union and has also appeared with much acceptance in Halifax and St. John, New Brunswick. She has appeared before the public in Boston, Mass., more than sixty times with great satisfaction and credit; at the *Boston Theatre twice,* before about five *thousand persons.* She has also appeared in Philadelphia and was there greeted by an audience of over five thousand on the 17th of November, 189o, at the Academy of Music. At Fanueil Hall she read for the Irish League after a speech made by Ben Butler. In the National Pageant, given by Cora Scott Pand, she took part in four speaking tableaux in the Boston Theatre, at Newport, R. I., and Union Square Theatre, N. Y. She spent one season at Bouccicault's Dramatic School in New York, and was pronounced by him a genius as an actress, as well as by ex-Secretary Noble, Hon. Fred Douglass and many other Afro-American and Caucasian men who may be regarded as fittingly competent to judge.

She manifests an interest in the cause of humanity and has given many hours of her valuable time and much talent in this direction. The very high esteem in which she is held in her native city and the large crowds that have so repeatedly thronged to hear her at home, on more than sixty different occasions, in less than six years of her early public life, are strong and weighty evidence of her sterling worth and ability in her chosen profession.

With the exception of twenty-one concerts, managed by J. C. Price, for Livingston College, Miss Nahar has been her own manager, and has successfully managed a few church concerts in Boston, but lately has entered the managerial field as a full-fledged manager. In Chicago, where she now resides, in January 1893, she signed a contract with J. B. Pond, the Black Patti's manager, for the Madam for four concerts, $600, two of which she gave to Bethel Church, Chicago, on February 6th and 7th, and two in New York, March 7th and 8th, to Zion Church—a brave venture for a little woman and so young a manager. Both were grand successes; each church was packed both nights, Bethel Church receiving as its one-half net profits more money than from any other concerts ever held in the church by *any* manager. On February 27th and 28th, before leaving for the New York concerts, just three weeks after the "Black Patti" concerts, Miss Nahar filled Bethel again almost to suffocation two nights with a children's cantata and a pantomime. She has at present many engagements to manage both concerts and dramas during the Word's Fair.

The height of her ambition is to build and put into active working order a home for friendless girls—not a refuge, but a home, with all that the word means—that hundreds who otherwise would be thrown out upon the world friendless and alone, and might drift into vice, may find a shelter where Christianity, self-respect and self-support will be taught. Chicago will probably be the place chosen to build. The present prospects are also in favor of her becoming an actress under one of the best managers in America.

It pleases those who have heard her to hear her again. Her appearance is most excellent; her manner of gesticulation is graceful;.she has the ability to get out of herself into her author's spirit, feelings and thoughts—a good imitator of the sublime. She is kind and interesting in the social circle and very much at home with those with whom she converses. We may predict for her a life of great usefulness. The following are some of the sayings of the press concerning her:

Miss Ednorah Nahar is a reader of talent. Her gestures are easy, graceful and to the point, while her stage presence would do credit to many a professional actress—Boston *Daily Advertiser.*

Her general style is good, her manner pleasing; added to this she is most fortunate in the possession of a voice which is a marvel of sweetness and purity of *tone.*

(Boston Evening Traveler).

Miss Nahar's rendition of the "Chariot Race," from "Ben Hur," was a revelation, and too much cannot be said in praise of it. With a clear, resonant voice, full of fire and dramatic action, she electrified her hearers and held them spell-bound to the end. She has a fine voice, and an earnest and expressive face— *The Boston Pilot.*

Miss Nahar in her description of the "Chariot Race," from "Ben Hur," showed a notable dramatic *skill. (Boston Evening Transcript).*

Miss Nahar has won for herself the title of "Boston's favorite elocutionist."— Boston *Advocate.*

Her art is no art, but nature itself. She is both elocutionist and actress. (Newport (R. I.) *Daily News).*

Miss Ednorah Nahar, iri her dramatic readings of the "Sioux Chief's Daughter," made a strong hit, and her two *encore* pieces showed a versatility rarely seen. (*Halifax* (N. B.) *Morning Herald).*

As a dramatic reader Miss Nahar has few equals. Of her readings we can say nothing but words of praise. *(St. John* (N. B.) *Globe).*

Miss Nahar as an elocutionist is superb. Her voice is well modulated, her enunciation is very clear and distinct, and she possesses perfect control over her vocal organs. Her recitation of the "Organ Builder" and the "Pilot's Story" were pathetic, while the curse scene of "Leah, the Forsaken " was a piece of stage work hard to be beaten.

Miss Nahar's humorous pieces took the house by storm. "Aunt Jemima's Courtship" and "The Lords of Creation" were charming, while the rich Irish brogue she brought out in her rendition of "Low Back Car" was perfection *itself.* *(Danville Daily Register)* (Dem.)

Miss Nahar is an elocutionist of rare ability and power. Her diction is clear and her gestures full of grace. Her selections are the best.

It is not saying too much of her to say she reminds one very much in her stage movements and easy manners of Modjeska. (Greensboro *North Slate*).

Miss Nahar's appearance here was a success in every particular. She made herself a favorite in her first piece, " The Pilot's Story," and the enthusiasm kept up during the entire readings. Her manner is decidedly easy and graceful on the stage. In the curse scene from "Leah " she not only sustained her reputation as a clear reader, but also gave evidence of considerable histrionic power— *Washington Correspondent of New York Age.*

Miss Ednorah Nahar received a great amount of applause, and her rendition of the curse scene from "Leah, the Forsaken," was as *fine a* hit of acting as we have *seen. (Charlotte Chronicle).*

Miss Nahar, of Boston, was particularly greeted to the echo in her almost perfect rendition of dramatic selections—Norfolk *Evening Telegram.*

"Aux Italiens," by Miss Nahar, was interpreted with a newer and subtler meaning than ever before; it was pathetic, tender, loving, fire-full, fervid and dramatic, each following in place with a sequence that only comes with genius.— *The Philadelphia Weekly Sentinel.*

Miss Nahar is prepossessing in appearance, graceful in movement and confident in bearing. She possesses decided dramatic powers, has a fine voice, strong, pure, flexible and quite voluminous—Cleveland (O.) *Gazette.*

In "Aux Italiens" Miss Nahar displayed original conception as well as extraordinary powers of execution; she has command of her voice, and her renditions are more like interpretations than recitations. St. *Louis Advance.*

Miss Ednorah Nahar as an elocutionist is superb— *The Daily Record* (Columbia, S. C.).

The honors of the evening were properly awarded Miss Nahar, who is a great favorite in St. John; her "Chariot Race," from "Ben Hur," was a masterpiece of stirring power, while in "Cleopatra" in Egyptian costume she brought out fully the tremendous passion of that poem--*Daily Telegraph* (St. John, N.B.)

In the "Chariot Race" and "Cleopatra" an elegant Egyptian costume afforded every opportunity for displaying to the best her wonderful abilities— *The Daily Sun* (St. John, N. B.).

Her voice one always remembers with pleasure. It is said the charm of Booth's voice remains with one who has heard him; this is not too much to say of Miss *Nahar. (Cincinnati Enterprise)*.

Miss Nahar is a talented lady whose "Sioux Chicf's Daughter," given in Indian costume, was finely rendered, while the "Chariot Race," from Wallace's "Ben Hur," was a revelation. (New *York Mail and Express.*

Her gestures are easy and graceful and she possesses rare gifts and powers as an elocutionist—Durham *(N. C.) Daily Sun.*

At the Hyperion Theatre about one thousand people attended the concert given by the Dixwell Avenue Church. Besides the Yale Banjo and Apollo Club, Miss Nahar, of Boston, a highly gifted elocutionist, was received with great applause —The *Palladium* (New Haven, Conn.).

Miss Nahar is, a reader of wonderful talent, very graceful and expressive; her selections are particularly *refined—Philadelphia Advance.*

MRS. LUCY ANN HENRY COLE.

CHAPTER XLV

MRS. LUCY ANN HENRY COLE.

This devout young lady is the daughter of Mary Elizabeth and Philip Henry, who resided at Rose Hill, three miles north of Richmond, Va., where the subject of these lines was born on the 31st day of March 1865. Her father was drowned when she was nine years old, leaving the entire responsibility of a large family upon her mother. Like most Afro-Americans, in those days, scarcity of means for support was an every-day reminder at this widow's house. However, there was *one bright character* in that gloomy home—Lucy Ann was always cheerful and ever with a book in hand seeking to know the contents thereof.

She exhibited such an aptness to learn and teach that she received the name of "teacher" among the children with whom she used to play. When she entered the Richmond public schools at ten years of age (the family having moved into the city) the little "teacher" had learned to read and write. The mother being compelled to work for "daily bread," and "Annie," being the next dependence for a nurse, could not enter school as early as most children do, and now entering at ten years, she could not expect to remain very long. Sure enough, when she had been to school only six short years, mother's health failed and the faithful child bade her school adieu to become the only sick-nurse to an afflicted mother.

However, by faithful study, she had finished the grammar grade. Although the mother's health was, after a long illness, partially restored, yet Lucy Ann could not return to school; being the oldest of several children, she was bound, by a sense of duty, to remain at home and lighten the burdens that fell heavily upon a disabled parent. She was never idle, though sometimes in poor health herself. On becoming a Christian, she united with the Ebenezer Baptist Church, of Richmond, and ever afterwards lived a devoted, faithful Christian life.

There is *one memorable fact* that we here note: From the very hour she was converted she declared that Africa was the field of labor to which her attention, in some mysterious way, had been turned. At various times she would ask her mother if she (mother) thought Africa would ever be reached by this anxious seeker for truth. Her mother, scarcely believing that she (daughter) ever could get to that faraway land, would carelessly reply, "The Lord will open the way." However dark and discouraging the way then seemed to Lucy Ann, she still cherished a fond hope in her breast that the Lord would *open the way.* In all this she had not failed in her devotion to her domestic duties, while, at the same time she taught a subscription school as a means of help in supporting herself. This school lasted two years, during which time she was also assistant missionary to Miss Helen R. Jackson. Possibly we are now reaching the point in this history when God, in "His own way," is ready to satisfy the desires and answer the prayers of this saint-like child of His. A tea-table is spread at the house of one of her brethren in Christ; she is invited, as were several other respectable citizens, among whom was Rev. J. J. Cole, a missionary to that land

"Where Afric's sunny fountains
Roll down their golden sand."

That land so far away, where----
" The heathen in his blindness Bows clown to wood and stone."
Here she met, for the first time, him whose wife she was evidently sure to become. This was not a fixed plan of any man or woman. Certainly, none of the parties on either side dreamed of any such results as did come. However, Miss Lucy Ann Henry and Rev. J. J. Cole met for the first time; they beheld each other; they liked each other, and finally they loved each other. Rev. Cole in a few days (or possibly the next day) found his way to the Henry residence, and again and again he made his way there. Her mother saw that God was about to "open the way." She became anxious about things, and one day when she thought that Rev. Cole was coming to get her consent to the marriage of Lucy Ann she left home, saying, "I will never consent."

During this opposition of the mother this brave and Christian girl said to a friend, "I will not marry until I get my mother's word, however anxious I am to go to that great land to labor." In the meantime God came to the mother and changed her about so that she freely consented, and all was well.

Lucy Ann felt the need of some further training for the great work now before her, so she entered the Hartshorn Memorial College at Richmond, Va., where she spent a short while and then turned her face towards the "Dark Land," and gave herself in marriage to Rev. J. J. Cole, on the 21st day of December 1886, at the Ebenezer Baptist Church, Revs. Richard Wells and J. A. Taylor officiating.

Who can solve this mystery? Who can fail to see the hand of God in this marriage of the happy couple that sailed on the 3d day of January 1887, for Africa, where they have successfully labored for so many years? Truly the Lord is great. His word is everlasting. Surely—

> "God moves in a mysterious way
> His wonders to perform;
> He plants His footsteps in the sea
>
> And rides upon the storm.
> "Deep in unfathomable mines
> Of never-failing skill,
> He treasures up His bright designs
> And works His sovereign will."

In her first letter after reaching Africa Mrs. Cole says:

DEAR MOTHER, HOME AND FRIENDS:- I feel that I must grasp the first opportunity to write You concerning our voyage across the sea and our safe arrival in Africa. After thirty-five days at sea, of which I shall write later, we arrived at Grand Cape Mt., W. C. Africa, February 7, 1887. The bark "Cardena," in which we sailed, cast anchor February 7th, about three miles off land. We were then carried in a boat, which was rowed by four men, to Cape Mt. Landing. The boat came within forty or fifty feet of land.

One by one we were carried ashore in the strong arms of the naked heathen. Rev. H. McKinney was first to greet us, after which the natives came one by one to bid us welcome. *   * After spending some time at the Episcopal mission, they left for their own special field some way off across the lake (Bendoo Mission).

Looking downwards we could see the bottom of the lake all covered with rocks. Mr. and Mrs. Topp began to sing "Let us build on a rock," and as we were nearing our last landing we all bravely sang " Hold the fort, for I am coming." Nearer and nearer we came to the shore, the last verse rang out loud and strong:

> " Fierce and long the battle rages,
> But our help is near;
> Onward comes our Great Commander,
>
> Cheer, my comrades, cheer.

And as the chorus died away and was lost upon the breezes we stepped upon the field " whereunto we are called."

As the day wore on evening came, and with it came family worship. In the little sitting-room we met in company with about fourteen natives, most of whom were naked; some had on their cloth. They sat on chairs, sofas, and the floor. As the organ poured forth the beautiful melody, "There is a fountain filled with blood," we sang it as we never sang before. * * * Some day you may see me when you looketh not for me. * * * Come over and help us dispel the darkness.

Yours in Africa,   LUCY A. COLE.

Rev. D. N. Vassar, D. D., who has very recently returned from a visit to the Vey Mission as Commissioner. of the Baptist Foreign Mission Convention of the United States, published the following account of Mrs. Cole and her work:

Mrs. Cole is a Christian lady of great integrity; she is indeed a helpmate to her husband. She is a hard worker and is going from morning until late at night. A look at the mission house would convince anyone that a woman's gentle hand played a daily part in the arrangement of everything around. The floors are kept perfectly clean. The bedding is thoroughly aired every day.

Little tidies and what-nots are so skillfully arranged that one almost forgets that he is in a heathen land. Indeed, everything is inviting, and when her husband returns after a walk or boat-ride through the hot tropical sun from his labors among the heathen he finds his wife waiting and everything in readiness to make him happy and to give the rest so necessary in that climate. Often, too, she accompanies him and leads the singing before and after preaching. Mrs. Cole has her school of sixteen children to teach. They love her as if they were her own children. None of them want to leave her, and when the parents of the children come for them to take them home, they cry and beg to stay with "daddy and mamee," as they call Rev. Cole and Mrs. Cole. When these children are brought to the mission, they come without any clothes. Not even a rag or string around the waist. Of course, it would be out of the question for them to be naked. What is to be done? There is no appropriation for this school, and the little money sent by the few friends cannot go far. The question is answered in the reality of the case, that these children are all neatly dressed and well fed. How is it done? The parents of the children do not give a single penny's worth to dress them, nor as much as a grain of rice to feed them. Indeed, it is a general thing that these children must be ransomed from slavery or a price paid to the parents to get them in school.

How is it done? It is done by self-denial and industry by Rev. and Mrs. Cole. All the clothing is made by Mrs. Cole with the needle and thread. She has no sewing machine.

It is wonderful how fast she can make the needle fly, even when her mind is not on her sewing. Would you look on the picture? Look! far over the lake you see yonder cloud as black as midnight; it is the sign of a hurricane. When it comes it will he furious. The waters of the lake dash like a heavy sea. A little boat five miles away is battling with the waves; you do not know who are in the boat, but if your eye was as well practiced as another's eye who is watching, you would see that they are Rev. Cole and three or four native Africans. They are pulling at the oars with all their might, lest the storm overtake them. But here at your side on the mission piazza stands Mrs. Cole. Look in her face and you will see deep care and anxiety seated there. Look in her hands. She holds a little dress half finished for one of her school-girls. The needle and fingers have never stopped. How fast they fly!!Stitch after stitch until the thread is used up, and then, for a moment the eyes are moved from the boat to re-thread the needle or to change to another seam, and the work goes on. Now the boat is at the landing; all jump out and pull the boat to the shore. Mrs. Cole heaves a gentle sigh as if a silent prayer is answered, and continues her *work. (African Missions, March 1892).*

CHAPTER XLVI.

MRS. CHARLOTTE FORTEN GRIMKEE.

The subject of this sketch was born in Philadelphia, of which city her grandfather, James Forten, was an old and well-known resident. As the facilities for educating colored children were at that time very poor in the city of her birth, she was taught privately for some time by an aunt, and then sent to Salem, Mass., where she attended the grammar school and afterwards admitted into the normal school, in which she was the only colored pupil.

She was treated with great courtesy and kindness by teachers and pupils and was appointed by her class to write the poem for one of the graduation exercises. Just before graduating she was, greatly to her surprise, she, offered a position as assistant teacher in one of the public schools in which there happened to be not a single colored pupil. After her graduation she took the position with many misgivings, for she knew that Salem, although far in advance of Philadelphia at the time as to liberality, yet was not entirely free from prejudice against color, and she feared also that some of the pupils might be insulting or rebellious, especially as the school contained some very unruly members—large boys who worked in the country during the summer months and came to school in winter determined to get as much "fun" out of it as possible. Some of these were larger than herself, hence there was some room for fear in case of conflict. But very soon she had the satisfaction of seeing these riotous spirits, like raging billows, calm down, and never did she hear a disrespectful word or the slightest allusion made to her color. Her relation to the pupils was a very pleasant one, and after teaching there for some time it was with much regret that she was obliged to resign the position on account of extreme ill health brought on by the severity of the New England climate, and return to Philadelphia. When she had, after a long period of invalidism, regained her health, she returned to Salem, where she had a position in the school which she had first attended. The principal, one of the finest teachers and noblest women she had ever known, was her dearest friend. The position in this school, in which there were only girls, was an extremely pleasant one, but after teaching there some months, she was again attacked by severe illness and obliged on her partial recovery to return to Philadelphia on account of the milder climate.

During her residence in Salem she had written articles for the *Anti-Slavery Standard* and other papers, at the same time indulging very earnest youthful hopes that she might become an authoress. During the war she was sent, with a friend, by the Freedmen's Aid Society in Philadelphia, to teach the freedmen at Port Royal, on the coast of South Carolina.

They were located on St. Helena Island. She spent several years there and found the work most interesting. While there she held correspondence with Mr. White and his sister, with whom she had spent many happy hours during her school-days. It was at a suggestion by Mr. White that she published some articles on their life among the freedmen in the *Atlantic Monthly*, for which she was liberally remunerated.

On her return North she went to Boston, where she was engaged for several years in the work of the New England Freedmen's Aid Society. Here she enjoyed her correspondence with the Freedmen's teachers, although suffering much from ill health. She was, however, able to do some literary work, translating some novels for Messrs. Scribner & Co, and also, short stories for *Scribner's Magazine*. She also wrote articles for the *Boston Commonwealth* and other papers.

Upon the breaking up of the Freedmen's Aid Society she went to Charleston, S. C., and taught school for one year, after which she returned to the North and remained in ill health for a long time. Upon improving in health she again attempted to teach in Washington, D. C., but after a short while she was thoroughly convinced that teaching was too great a taxation upon her strength. She resigned and took a clerkship in the Treasury Department. While thus engaged she again wrote articles and verses for the papers, the *Christian Register*, of Boston, especially.

In 1878 she was married to Rev. Francis J. Grimkee, pastor of the Fifteenth Street Presbyterian Church, of Washington, D. C. After a service of nearly eight years here Rev. Grimkee resigned on account of poor health, and accepted a call to the Presbyterian church in Jacksonville, Fla. He remained there (she with him) for about three years, and being much improved in health he accepted an urgent recall to his former charge in Washington, D. C., where he still resides. Her life in the District has not been an eventful one, much of her time being spent in church work, and therefore she has not done as much literary work as she had hoped to do. She sometimes tries to find some consolation in the thought that possibly this is why her long-cherished dreams of becoming an authoress have never been fully realized. Few Afro-American women have been more useful than Mrs. Grimkee.

She was faithful to the race when faithful friends were few and much needed. She came to the front in those dark days when it tried every nerve to the uttermost for one to be an aggressive defender of the rights of an oppressed people. Mr. G. W. Williams, the historian, says of her:

She comes of one of the best colored families of the State. * * * She proved to be a student of more than usual application. * * * She wrote both prose and poetry and did admirably in each.

CHAPTER XLVII.
MISS LULU C. FLEMING.

Miss L. C. Fleming was born in Hibernia, Clay County, Florida in 1862 at the time the great hostile armies North and South were gathering for the mighty conflict over slavery. Her mother was half Congo and her father half Caucasian, under the yoke of bondage, but not without deeply throbbing hearts for freedom.

When little Lulu was only about six weeks old her father resolved to go to the war. Thus, taking his wife and children and as many young slaves as were willing to join the army and fight for liberty, he bravely attempted to carry into execution his bold resolve. Concerting with the captain of a Union gun-boat, who had deserted from the Rebel army, the father not only found his own dear little band seeking refuge in the ship, but many others who were under bondage were of a similar spirit, and in a short time the gun-boat was well loaded with fugitives. But the bright hopes of the father only lasted for a very brief space of time. The captain now deserted the Union side and landed all the fugitives in Jacksonville, prisoners - Lulu's father in irons - and narrowly did he escape being hanged (some did not escape). Thus, again he with wife and little ones were reduced to slavery, although Lulu was too young to know what her father suffered in the days of slavery, for very soon after he was released from his imprisonment, he was found in the Union army fighting against slavery, and for two years he was in the service, and was only released by death without ever seeing his wife and children again.

The life of Lulu up to fifteen was marked only by the trials common to poor slave children generally, except being fortunate in having a mother, although a slave without education, who was deeply concerned for the welfare of her children, and doubtless her influence had good effect upon Lulu.

Touching her conversion, she must bear witness in her own happy words as copied from a private letter to a friend, and here introduced. After speaking of the "kind Heavenly Father's care" over her mother and children, she adds:

At the age of fifteen He drew me unto himself, and after passing through the shadow of doubts, I entered into the blessed light of His love, wherein to walk is fullness of joy, December 1877. I was a missionary like Andrew of old from the very day I found the Lord. Six years ago, while engaged as public school teacher in St. Augustine, Florida, I met in my Sabbath-school Dr. Kellsey, of Brooklyn, N. Y., who became deeply interested with the manner in which I expounded the Word of God to my class, which consisted of the pastor of that church, the licensed ministers and the adults generally of the school.

This gentleman, who was then in the rear of the room, came up and introduced himself to me, asking if I were a Floridian, and then he asked where I was educated. I told him. He thought I should have a higher course, as my heart was so much interested in missions. I told him my mother had educated me to the extent of her means, and that I was now on life's ocean for myself. He said, "I will see if I can't help you if you care to attend college." Accordingly he interested a company of young ladies in his church in me, and by them I was educated, graduating from Shaw University, Raleigh, N. C., May 27, 1885, with the honor of class valedictorian.

While teaching in Florida, before going to college, sympathizing deeply with the two most needy and lowly classes in the community where her field of labor belonged, instead of devoting her leisure time to such amusements and recreation as are generally hailed with delight by the average young and thoughtless teachers, Lulu was found with a devotion which was as rare as it was Christ-like, doing with all her might what her hands found to do, in aid of the aged and infirm and the poor little orphan children. On this line, for a time, she concluded that her mission work was to be consummated.

In 1883, she claims, while in school, Africa was laid on her soul, but she then yielded only to the extent of trying to have others become interested and go. After finishing her collegiate studies, with renewed zeal she returned to her former field in Florida.

Here again the narrative would not be complete if her own graphic language was omitted:

But the Lord had need of me in Africa, and the happiness that I used to enjoy in the work at home was marred from time to time with the shadow of the darkness of the "Dark Continent," and it was not until June 27, 1886, when I answered a personal request, coming from the Woman's Baptist Foreign Missionary Society, asking me to go as their *first* representative to that far off dark land, that I felt happy and free from the sin of omission of duty. I was truly happy then, and since I have set sail for the benighted country I am happier (she was on her voyage when these words quoted were penned) ; when I reach the doleful shores I shall be happiest. What comfort comes to us from doing the perfect will of God concerning us!

In due time the voyage came to an end; the desired haven was reached. Other than some very rough weather on a part of the voyage nothing occurred on the journey to mar her prospects, being providentially preserved from sickness all the way from the land of her nativity to her destined mission field in the Congo Valley. The unbounded sight of heathenism everywhere now to meet her gaze, turn whichever way she might, without the face of a familiar human being or friend to cheer her as she entered into her mission work, her faith in God was thus to be tested, and thus it was tested to the fullest extent. But on this ground there is no tale of disappointments or wavering, or of homesickness to relate, for this young missionary had sat down and thoroughly counted the cost before starting on this dreadful mission. In such an attitude as this to commence service for Christ and humanity it is about as hard to comprehend how this delicate young disciple could brave the peril before her as it is to comprehend how by having " faith as a grain of mustard seed" a mountain could be removed. Truly her life seemed to be hid with Christ in God, and she was simply happy in the faith that she was doing her duty, and that she had nothing to fear with the firm promises of her Heavenly Father to rest upon. All her letters from the mission field that came under the writer's notice were carefully examined and re-examined, not only to see the progress she was making from time to time, but to see if there were not spells when she would find herself overwhelmed in a state of dreadful horror. But, strange as it may appear, there was no evidence that she was ever given to such moods. Her letters were exceedingly instructive and interesting, and would occasionally find their way into public print, where, both in this country and England, they attracted considerable attention. But the space allotted for this sketch will barely admit of more than one-fifth of one of her private letters, dated "Palabala Station, Congo Independent State, S. W. Africa, June 6, 1890," which must suffice to indicate her attitude in the midst of her labors after having been in the field for more than three years.

Having a knowledge of photography and being equipped with instruments, which she had carried with her from Philadelphia, in writing home to friends she would occasionally send some original photographs for them to view. In the following extract containing reference to "pictures" it will readily occur to the reader what was signified in the allusion:

You must excuse the poor pictures; really, they are not worth keeping a letter for. However, such as they are, I gladly send you. I have made the study of the language and my mission work my first duty. Photography practice comes far apart, so I am proportionately far from perfection. Take the meaning they bring you and hope to get better ones next time.

When we parted in 1887, I hoped we should meet again this year. Well we never know to-day what to-morrow will bring forth. Having been so well all along I began in time last year to entreat my Board to allow me to stay out five years. No lady has ever stayed out so long, but I am sure it can be done; I have only begun my real work. Until Miss Gordon came, I had to be mother for our mission girls and teach our station school. This work she has taken and I have been able to do work among the town folks. My town school is not in a town, but by the public road-side, where the children from four towns have access to it. This takes up my mornings. In the afternoon, until lately, I teach an hour and give the rest of the time to preaching the Word.

The past two months I have had a native helper, who takes the afternoon class. This gives me my afternoons to preach in three towns, taking one an afternoon. I hope to get off on another jungle tour through this dry season; yet it seems too bad to have to close my school again, as it has already been twice closed for health reasons.

My native helper I will need with me. I am praying that the God of all missions will show me my duty in the matter. Out here we often wish it possible to divide ourselves and let half go on one mission and a half on another. Truly the harvest is great, and the laborers are few. There are coming more into the vineyard, praise the Lord, and in our day we may see many great changes. You know of your Church in the South beginning a mission out here? This makes three new societies to enter the field since I have been here.

The signs of the times say that the "coming of the Kingdom draweth nigh " in Congo Land. We have a mission house two miles away, where I work mornings in the capacity of preacher, teacher and doctor. All is very poorly done, but is done for the love of Christ and in His name. I hope to be allowed two years home in which to study medicine, so as to be better able to help this suffering people. They do trust so fully in my skill—poor creatures—and I know so little to do for them.

Thus, after laboring hopefully and incessantly for about four years she returned for much-needed rest and recuperation and to obtain medical knowledge. After all, however, she has found no great amount of time or opportunity for leisure or rest. Being a very interesting speaker, with a well-stored mind on missions, in particular, and Africa, likewise, she has been much in demand, solicitations coming from different denominations (from white and colored, North and South. It may not be out of place here to state that on one occasion she had the honor to be heard in Spurgeon's great chapel, in London, and to be very cordially greeted by that wonderful man. Let the young women of the race take courage and with the faith, earnestness of purpose, trust in God, with a willingness to do with all their might whatever their hands find to do, as characterized in the brief and simple sketch of the life of Lulu C. Fleming.

Press on, working in this faith and trusting in Christ the Lord; no obstacles or mountains in the way will be too difficult to be removed. And it is to be greatly desired that among the many FAITHFUL and TRUE women whose portraits may be found sketched in this volume may issue a never-failing source of inspiration which shall prove of lasting benefit to millions of our struggling young women who are aiming for a higher and nobler womanhood.

WILLIAM STILL.

MRS KATHERINE D. TILLMAN, A.M.

CHAPTER XLVIII.
KATE D. CHAPMAN TILLMAN.

This lady of much ability was born in Mound City, Illinois, February 19, 1870. Her mother was a faithful and gifted school- teacher and writer, from whom her daughter received much inspiration in early life.

This daughter of poor parents, Charles and Laura Chapman, has gained quite a reputation with the pen. She has written in both prose and poetry for the leading race papers. Her first published poem appeared in the *Christian Recorder* in 1888, entitled "Memory." Her first story appeared in *Our Women and Children.* Since then she has continued to write. Her education was obtained in the public schools and in the State University of Louisville, Kentucky; also, in the high school at Yankton, South Dakota, and in Wilberforce University, in Ohio.

Some very praiseworthy statements concerning her have appeared in *The Statesman, Appeal* and *Torchlight,* all of which did honor to this worthy young woman. The first poem that came from her pen, when only thirteen years old, was occasioned by a severe illness, and was entitled " The Dying Child." A sketch of her life has appeared in a leading New York journal, and, also, in the very excellent book by Mr. I. G. Penn, "Afro-American Press and its Editors." She is now preparing a volume of short stories for girls. Ill health has caused a laxity in her progress as a writer, but there is yet hope that she may become one of our greater lights, being yet young in years. The following is one of her poems on the condition of the race:

A QUESTION OF TO-DAY.

"And shall our people, long oppressed
By fierce, inhuman foe,
Not seek to have their wrongs redressed ?
No! by their manhood, no!
"You men do call us women weak.

By Him who ruleth all,
For what was ours we'd dare to speak,
Menaced by cannon ball.

Human we are, of blood as good,
As rich the crimson stream,
God-planned, ere creation stood,
However, it may seem.

"Oh! sit not tamely by and see
Thy brother bleeding sore;
For is there not much work for thee, While
they for help implore?

"From Wahalak came the news,
Our men are lying dead.
Did it not hatred rank infuse
When word like this was read ?

"And now White Caps, with hearts as black
As hell—of Ku-Klux fame,
Still ply the lash on freedom's back;
And must he bear the same?"

Thus, said a woman, old and gray,
To me, while at her door,
Speaking of what so heavy lay
And made her heart so sore.

"What woman! dost thou speak of war,
The weaker 'gainst the strong?
That, surely, would our future mar,
Nor stop the tide of wrong

"We must be patient, longer wait; We'll
get our cherished rights."
"Yes, when within the pearly gate, And
done with earthly sights,"

Replied the woman, with a sneer

Upon her countenance.
You men do hold your lives too dear To
risk with spear or lance."

"Naomi, at Fort Pillow fell
Three hundred blacks one day;
The cannon's roar their only knell,
In one deep grave they lay.

"Our men have bravely fought, and will,
When'er the time shall come;
But now we hear His 'Peace, be still!"
And stay within our home.

"Let but our people once unite.'
Stand firmly as a race,
Prejudice , error, strong to fight,
Each here in his place

"And not a favored few demand
Bribes of gold, position,
While many freemen in our land
Bewail their hard condition."

"Liberty, truly, ours will be,
And error pass away;
And then no longer shall we see
Injustice hold her sway.

"As Americans we shall stand, Respected by all men;
An honored race in this fair land,
So praised by word and pen.

"And those to come will never know
The pain we suffered here;
In peace shall vow, in peace shall plow,
With naught to stay or fear."

Said Naomi: "You may be right,
God grant it as you say.
I've often heard the darkest night
Gives way to brightest day."

CHAPTER XLIX.
MRS. A. J. COOPER.

If we should be asked to-day to name the greatest female educator the race has produced in North Carolina, we would be most, certain to mention that one that marks the beginning of this chapter. She is not only the greatest that we know of as a North Carolinian of color, but she is possibly the peer of any the State has produced, of whom we have any account, as a female educator in either race. Our more favored neighbors can well boast of many good and eminent women, such as Lydia H. Sigourney, Alice Carey and Phoebe Carey, etc., but they all came through only a *part of the great storm that negro women of eminence have to contend with.* It is simply remarkable, when one contrasts the two roads leading to eminence, to behold the difference.

In the pathway along which negro women have to travel may be found almost every conceivable difficulty to be overcome alone by the traveler; from *poverty; through humiliation (even upon public thoroughfares)*, to almost a *sacrifice* of friends and life. A long, up-hill and lonesome journey, and therefore the more remarkable, especially in the South, when compared with the easy pathway of our more favored sisters. When an Afro-American woman does arrive at any eminence it is well known that she has *fought a fierce and bloody battle* almost *every step of her way.* Despite all the opposition and conflicts within and without the ranks of the race, some of our women are *eminent,* among whom is Mrs. A. J. Cooper, who was born in Raleigh, N. C., August 10, 1858.

At a very early age she entered St. Augustine Normal School, being among the first boarding pupils at that institution. When she was possibly about eleven years old she was given a class as student-teacher, which was the beginning of her career as teacher, in which profession she has continued to this day. She was married in 1877 to Rev. G. A. C. Cooper, of Nassau, New Providence, West Indies, who was, at the time of marriage (1877), a teacher in St. Augustine School and pastor of the St. Augustine Church at Raleigh, N. C. In 1879 her husband died and left her a widow only twenty-one years old.

After filling with much credit in this school many positions, such as pupil-teacher, teacher, matron, and lady in charge of female department, etc., she left in 1881 for Oberlin College, where she entered the sophomore class, upon examination. While thus engaged in study in the classical department she taught classes in the preparatory department, and the students in the classes taught by this Afro-American lady were *white students.* She was also the private teacher of a class of white students outside of school hours. She graduated in 1884 and spent one year at Wilberforce University (1884—'85) as professor of modern languages and science. Then she returned to St. Augustine Normal School at Raleigh, N. C., and taught two years. In 1887 she was elected to a position in the High School of Washington, D. C., where she has been engaged in teaching ever since. She has just published a book entitled "A Voice From the South," which we have not as yet had opportunity to examine. That Mrs. Cooper is a lady of rare ability is acknowledged by all scholars who know her.

As great and as learned, as refined and popular as she is, she is still not exempted from humiliation on public railways in some parts of the South. Just a few days ago (the last days of 1892) she chanced to visit her old home and peep in upon her friends in Raleigh, N. C., and when leaving even this city of her birth she was *insulted* in a waiting-room at the depot, and ejected from the room. For what? Simply because she was a *colored woman.*

Insulted and ejected (with a first-class ticket in her hand) by a white man who is by far her *inferior* in every respect. [NOTE: I mention this treatment here as simply an opportunity to place it upon record, and let it go down in history to posterity.] Indeed, it is true that great negro women work hard and go through much that is far from being pleasant after as well as before achieving greatness.

However the storms, and whatever the difficulties, the women of this race have bright prospects of a better future in such pioneers and representatives as Mrs. A. J. Cooper.

CHAPTER L.

MRS. LUCRETIA NEWMAN COLEMAN.

A woman of good talent and refined manners, up with age in which she lives and an advocate of sound doctrines in all matters of morality and religion, a writer of thought and ability, are characteristics of the lady whose name heads this section of Women of Distinction.

Born in Dresden, Ontario, the immediate descendant of William and Nancy Newman, her father having died while she was quite young and her mother soon following him into the grave, necessarily left much responsibility upon this lady of whom we pen these lines.

Educated very largely in the common and high schools she graduated from the scientific department of Lawrence University and immediately began the work of teaching what she had learned to others. It was about 1883 when she was assistant secretary in the financial affairs of the A. M. E. Church, having already been a store clerk and teacher in music and in the common English branches.

The American Baptist, which was at this time so ably edited by our lamented friend and brother, William J. Simmonds, D. D., contained the following, in September, 1884:

As a writer her fame is fast spreading, not only in one or two States, but throughout the United States. Should she continue with the same success in the future as she has had in the past, she will be equal to Harriet Ward Beecher Stowe, if not her superior. Her poem, "Lucilla of Montana," and her novel, "Poor Ben," have been very highly spoken of by competent critics and newspapers.

She has contributed some very fine articles to the *A. M. E. Review,* and in all matters to which she has applied herself she has. well succeeded.

CHAPTER LI.

MISS A. L. TILGHMAN.

This lady was born in Washington, D. C., and is a graduate from the normal department of Howard University; has taught more than ten years in the public schools of that city. As a teacher and disciplinarian she bore a high reputation. Upon one occasion she desired to exchange her school of a higher grade for one of a lower, because of the latter being nearer her home. She did so, but in this exchange she entered a school that had been noted for bad order and being extremely unruly. When she had been there a few weeks the superintendent called one day and said with regard to the excellent condition of the school, "Miss Tilghman, how am I to account for this change?"

As a child she exhibited great talent for music and possessed a wonderfully sweet and sympathetic voice that touched every ear that heard it. Once when Bishop Payne had heard her sing, at a memorial meeting, a song called "Departed Days," he arose and said, "That child's parents had better spend a hundred dollars on her voice now than leave her a fortune when they die."

For several years Miss Tilghman was leading soprano of the Fifteenth Street Presbyterian Church choir, and was one of Washington's favorite *prima donnas*, appearing in concerts with Madam Selika, Madam Nellie Brown Mitchell, Miss Adelaide G. Smith, and other prominent singers, although at that time she was very young. In December, 1880 she was engaged to sing in New York, and the *National Era*, a paper published at that time, in speaking of her singing, said this:

Miss Tilghman's appearance in New York City was the bursting forth of a musical star of the first magnitude, whose brilliancy completely captured the praise and admiration of the critics, and forced from the many talented vocalists of the great metropolis a concession of her richly earned title, "The Queen of Song."

In June 1881, Miss Tilghman was communicated with and engaged as *prima donna* of the Sangerfaest, held in the Grand Opera House in Louisville, Ky., where she sang four consecutive nights amid great applause, and won for herself and her race laurels as a singer that can never fade. It was there that Miss Tilghman first saw the cantata of Queen Esther rendered, and she came back to Washington, gathered together the best musical talent and presented it upon the stage at Lincoln Hall, taking the character of Queen Esther, accompanied by nearly one hundred voices, full orchestra, and beautiful stage costumes. The entire cantata was magnificently rendered, and it is said that never before had the colored people of Washington produced anything upon the stage to equal it, either in stage costumes and settings or in the perfect rendition of each part.

The presentation of the cantata entailed an immense amount of *hard work* upon Miss Tilghman and, coupled with the regular duties of the school-room, proved *too* much for her physically, and within two months she was stricken with a severe illness that prostrated her for *five* months. The following summer she was urged upon to go away as soprano leader of a company of singers, and it was during that engagement, and while scarcely more than half recovered from months of illness, she was again stricken down, and this time with a fearful accident, from which she has not fully recovered, and possibly never will. It was during the engagement with this company, while singing in Saratoga, that the terrible accident befell her which disabled her for teaching and possibly changed the whole current of her future life. Many are familiar with the story of that sad accident, and many more may learn of it for the first time.

While passing down Broadway, Saratoga, a brick fell thirty feet from the scaffolding of the Collamar building, striking Miss Tilghman on the head, felling her to the ground and *fracturing her skull.* From this fracture sixteen pieces of bone were removed. There are some lives into which it seems that all kinds of afflictions are thrust and still they are borne with such patience as is to many simply remarkable. And even with this our afflictions seem as nothing when compared with what Christ suffered for us. Why not be patient?

Miss Tilghman attended the Boston Conservatory of Music expressly to study the Conservatory methods of teaching piano, and that she learned the system well and is a most efficient teacher is shown by the following letter:

What was said some months ago by Dr. C.N. Dorsette of Miss Tilghman's work in Montgomery is true in every sense, and she is truly building monuments of music in the homes of the colored people. A few years ago there were no colored pianists in Montgomery, and in no house where colored people lived did one hear in passing the artistic rendition of music as is now heard in almost every two or three squares. Nowhere had such a thing as a musical recital ever been heard of until Miss Tilghman went to Montgomery and parents sat and listened to their own children perform in public on the piano, and their hearts swelled with pride as they looked and listened. This young lady is doing a grand and noble work in that city. She has not been without her trials and afflictions in life, but no woman has ever fought through them more nobly and womanly than she. No woman has ever taken a truer stand for the right. She has won the highest esteem and respect of all who have met her and witnessed her work, and in years to come the young ladies who have been under her instruction and watched her womanly learning will rise up and "call her blessed." (The *Southern Christian Recorder,* 1888).

In 1886, while teaching music in Montgomery, Ala., Miss Tilghman first began the publication of the Musical Messenger, the first and only musical journal ever published by any one of the Negro Race. That the Messenger was well edited and was a credit to the race is fully attested by the following complimentary comments:

Miss A. L. Tilghman is the editress of the Musical Messenger, the only paper of the kind ever published by our people. Miss Tilghman is a young lady of much talent —*New York Freeman*

The *Musical Messenger* is the finest journal of the kind ever issued in the South. It is full of good matter, written by some of the best people in the country. —Herald (Montgomery).

Miss A. L. Tilghman, the well-known Washington *prima donna,* is the editor and proprietor of the *Musical Messenger,--- (Washington Critic).*

We welcome to our exchange list the Musical Messenger, by Miss A. L. Tilghman. Another woman joins the profession. May it be hers to enjoy much prosperity.— *Virginia Lancet.*

Miss Tilghman publishes the *Musical Messenger*, the first paper devoted to music ever published by the race.—*People's Advocate.*

Miss Tilghman, editing 'the *Musical Messenger,* and formerly a teacher in the public schools of Washington, possesses musical talent of no mean order.—*New Orleans Pelican.*

The *Musical Messenger* is the name of a monthly journal published by Miss A. I,. Tilghman. She is a graduate of Howard University, and was a successful teacher at Washington for several years.—*A. M. E. Church.*

The colored race have several newspapers of first-class merit ; but, musical as they are, none of them, until now, have started a musical journal. The new venture is the *Musical Messenger,* a monthly of considerable promise.— *American Machinist* (N. Y.).

We are in receipt of the Musical Messenger, a monthly published in Washington, D. C., by Miss A. L. Tilghman, and devoted to "the highest moral, social and intellectual interest of the people." That. the race stands sadly in need of such a journal should be freely admitted. It is our earnest hope that the editor's hands may be strengthened and her soul fortified in this very creditable venture. --*(Tribune,* Philadelphia, Pa.).

Miss Tilghman was correspondent for *Our Women and Children,* published by the lamented William J. Simmonds, who was a faithful and energetic worker for the race. As a writer, as well as a singer, Miss Tilghman stands in the front rank of our young Afro-American women. She has composed several very fine poems.

In closing this sketch we feel that it is fitting to give our readers the poem which she composed in honor of Queen Victoria's seventieth birthday and which was published in the *Musical Messenger:*

236

DEDICATED TO HER GRACIOUS MAJESTY, QUEEN VICTORIA, OF ENGLAND.

Reign on! most glorious
Queen! And let thy scepter sway,
Till Ireland's people are redeemed,
Their darkness turned to day.

Reign on! till right shall rule,
And wrong shall buried be,
Reign on! most generous, noble soul!
The world needs such as thee.

Reign on! ne'er let thy power
Be ever rent in twain
Thy life so noble, good and pure
Be tarnished with one stain.

Reign on! for God doth guide
Thy sovereigns at His will,
And He who stills the raging tide
Will bid thy foes he still

Reign on! unequaled Queen,
Till man to man is free,
Till not one shackle shall he seen,
And nowhere slaves shall he.

Reign on! reign ever on
Not in this world alone,
But may thy pure and holy life
Be echoed at God's throne.

Reign on! till Heaven is gained,
And thou with the redeemed
Shall there receive the victor's crown,
Most noble, glorious Queen!

CHAPTER LII.

MISS N. ANTONIA GORDON.

The subject of our present sketch was born to James and Sarah Gordon, August 25, 1866, at Augusta, Ga. She stands third oldest in a family of nine children and was always the personification of gentleness and kindness to, her brothers and sisters. As a daughter she loved and obeyed in a way which most children never attain. As a younger sister, she fondly served and looked up to her brothers, making them her ideals of youthful manliness; while as an elder sister she never sought her rights. Often the younger members of the family imposed slaps or other childish freaks on her without her even reporting them to their parents. The mother soon noticed in this child a peculiar domestic turn. Whatever the mother attempted to do her oldest daughter would be on hand offering help. At the age of six years she completed a *patchwork quilt* which excited much attention in the neighborhood, and the mother was pressed to place it upon exhibition at the State Fair.

At an early age this child was in school, and soon proved herself to be above the average aptness. Her book was put before everything in her mind, even her food. As she grew larger this love for books deepened. At her domestic duties she would have her book open on a table or chair so her hands and head could both be called into action at once. Her parents' pastor, Rev. A. W. De' Lamotta, saw in this child something out of which there could be made a great woman, and advised her parents to send her to a school for women and girls, then just opening in the basement of the Friendship Baptist Church of Atlanta, Ga. In the fall of 1882 this child took leave of home and dear ones for the above school, which afterwards became *Spelman Seminary*. Misses Packard and Giles, the founders of this now famous institution, soon discovered this child's rare qualities, and, as was their habit, they inquired of her whether or not she was saved. On receiving an answer in the negative, these two soul-winners set out to win this precious soul for Christ. And, in the midst of her term with them, their hearts were made glad by her salvation. With her birth into the kingdom came her call to Africa; this desire burnt upon the table of her heart from the very day she was converted.

The years that followed in her career at Spelman were full indeed, and might of themselves fill a volume with very interesting facts. But as our space is so limited suffice it to say that she stood foremost as a soul-winner and a scholar. As a student-teacher she often had the joy of seeing scores of her pupils saved under her teaching. As a teacher she is winsome, firm and gentle. Wherever she has taught she could teach again, so greatly loved is she. At Spelman she was and is still their pride. Here she graduated with the honor of Class Poet in 1888, when a position was offered her in the Mitchell Street Graded School of Atlanta, Ga.

Her plans for beginning work in Africa were fast formulating, but being pressed she consented and served at said school till Christmas, 1889. By this time the ladies of the Woman's Foreign Missionary Society of the West had selected her to be their second representative in the great Congo Valley. Then came the task of giving up a devoted grandmother, who declared she could not live through a separation from her, as well as Misses Packard and Giles, who had endeared themselves to her beyond mention, and a host of others who formed a circle of as true and fond friends as ever lived. This trial daunted not the frail, beautiful girl's faith, but she attended the tearful farewell services arranged at Spelman and took a joyful leave of this host of dear ones for Africa on the 10th of March 1889.

After a long journey from Atlanta to Boston she looked out for the first time in her life upon the sea and thought what other than a divine call to Africa could induce her to face the *perils of the sea.* On the 16th day of the same month she embarked by the Cunard Line from Boston. While waiting for an African bound ship in London this " Daughter of the King" had it revealed to her that it was even as the grandmother had said—her parting was too much and had proved God's means to gather her to Himself. She mentioned this to Miss Royal, her traveling companion, with a sweet peace and resignation that she herself could not understand. This was no longer a vision when, on her arrival in the Congo, she found a letter there awaiting her telling her what she had for weeks known. Still this peace was hers, and she set herself about learning the language and the work with cheerfulness.

Her father had been for years a deacon in the Baptist Church. She loved him above all earthly objects. He delighted in his child's devotion and sent her from him with a fatherly, devoted "God bless you, my child, and use you to save the heathen, God bless you!" In less than eighteen months after she had begun this work of "saving the heathen" this dear father was gathered with those found worthy to wear the crown. This news was enough, to cause our heroine to say, "This is harder than I can bear," and give up in heart, but the brave heart said, "Though He slay me, yet will I trust in Him." In speaking of her sainted father, she would say, "I miss his *prayers so much!*" She kept joyfully at the task of winning the heathen to Christ. And ere her heart had time to heal came the startling news that her mother in the Lord, Miss S. B. Packard, had also joyfully gone up to wear the crown. This news found her just taking up new work at Lukunga Station, where more than five hundred lambs of God had been gathered in and awaited her devoted service. In two short years three of her dearest were heavenly! This urged her on to greater devotion, and today finds her in charge of a large press-work on the Station, a teacher in the first Congo Seminary, she being one of the founders, and having the oversight of three district schools taught by native teachers. Of the family of girls she took charge of at Palabala we see naught but what gladdens our hearts, as all have been saved through Christ. Africa has never had given her a purer life, a heart more devoted to her welfare and the salvation of her millions than is this devoted missionary. May her life be long spared to lift up this benighted nation by the press and by personal contact with the word of God! The following is the last poem that she wrote for the press, and explains itself:

MISS PACKARD'S BIRTHDAY.

This is the holy Sabbath,
The third day of the year,
The birthday of Miss Packard,
Whose memory is dear.

Our *Alma Mater,* Spelman,
Will celebrate this day,
And we will join in spirits
Though we're so far away.
Our hearts will always praise Him
That she was ever born to save
The girls of our dear Southland
By ignorance enslaved.

Of all her noble life-work
I need not tell to you;

Of all her noble life-work
I need not tell to you:
Seven years we shared together
Her love and care so true.

Alas! our hearts are stricken,
To speak of it gives pain;
We've lost our benefactress,
But O, to her what gain!

We do not mourn as others,
Our hope gives joy and peace, For we
have this assurance:
Her work shall never cease.

Rest on, our weary loved one, Secure
in Jesus' arms;
Earth's sin and toil and trials
Can never do thee harm

Your work shall live in thousands
You've taught the way of life; We'll
spread the glorious message Despite
opposing strife.

And she whom thou hast left us, We'll
keep with jealous care, Lest Heaven
takes her from us Your joy and bliss to
share.

Oh, God! do hear our pleadings, And
spare our dear Miss Giles, That she
may bring more lost ones To know
Thy love and smiles.

And daily bless our Spelman, Enrich
her by Thy love;
Grant that her girls and teachers All
meet in Heaven above.

L. C. FLEMING

MISS MARY A. BURWELL

CHAPTER LIII.

MISS MARY A. BURWELL.

I n condescending to choose human beings as his missionary messengers of love and mercy to the countless millions of earth God has not assigned them all to a circumscribed pulpit or church, either in heathen lands or in civilized countries, But has been pleased to send some of them to the poor in every land, even unto little children in our own "land of liberty." He has said, " Suffer little children to come unto me, and forbid them not." For the especial care of orphan children there is a peculiar fitness, not at all possessed by the majority, either as an acquired or as an inherited possession.

As an earnest laborer in this field among the poor, needy children of the race few of our young women have been more active, according to opportunity, than "Little Mary" Burwell, who was born in Mecklenburg County, Va., of (recently) slave parents living in humble circumstances.

Her mother, though in very poor health, was nevertheless kind and affectionate, and no doubt would have willingly done all possible in the discharge of her duty towards her only child. However, an uncle of this "only child " came on a visit and was so attracted by the lovable disposition of Mary, asked for her and, upon promise of educating her in the city schools of Raleigh, his request was granted, and he and little Mary were soon in the "City of Oaks," where she entered the Washington School at about eight years of age. After spending some time in the primary school she entered Shaw University, from which she graduated after remaining therein six years, taking a diploma from the Estey Seminary course. She was a member of several classes taught by the author, while upon the faculty of Shaw University, who was always impressed with her meek yet earnest disposition as a student. After graduating she taught for several years in the public schools.

She was then called as lady teacher to the orphanage at Oxford, N. C., which position she accepted and gave up her school out of a desire to do something to help that struggling asylum, notwithstanding she knew it to be heavily burdened with debt and without one dollar in its treasury. She said, "Any assistance I can render in the work it will be my pleasure to do so.

"Did she expect pay from this institution in the shape of a big salary? No; none was offered, as there was nothing to offer her as an inducement. In June 1890 she entered upon her new work without any promise of earthly reward. Then the asylum consisted of one wood building of three rooms, containing eight little children. It was indeed a poor home. Finding talent among these children, she began to train them for concerts with a hope of getting better quarters for them. In July, just about one month from the time she went there, she took them out to travel. They created much interest through the State. The General Assembly of North Carolina gave the institution $1,000, and up to November 1892, less than two and one-half years, she has raised an additional sum of more than $1,500 and has also solicited many annual contributors who will continue to give. So she has done much to help furnish and build additional rooms. Now, instead of one building with three rooms containing eight children, there are many new additional rooms, well furnished with comforts, enjoyed by forty children. Miss Burwell has given new life to things in general at the Colored Asylum at Oxford, N. C. She is yet young in years, and has visited most points of interest in the State with these children, holding concerts and soliciting aid for the school, having not a dollar with which to start (except previous savings of her own).

She has been able to receive only some very small compensation for her work, and yet she is as earnest and as determined as ever. Her future is evidently bright, and her chances to do good are many. She became a Christian when fourteen years old, and was baptized into membership with the First Baptist Church, Raleigh, N. C. She is an active, energetic, Christian worker, regarding no task too hard.

IDA GRAY, D. D. S.

CHAPTER LIV.
IDA GRAY, D. D. S.

(A PRACTICAL DENTIST).

As a library deprived of some one of its necessary books, or a machine without one of the component parts, or a chemical laboratory that is void of a most important reagent, is incomplete and, therefore, inadequate to fully fulfill the ends of its existence, so a nation without a full system of government, or a navy without a cannon, or a race of people who have not the diversified acquired facilities essential to achieve greatness, must strive in vain to become great. The Afro-American, like all other races, the conditions being the same, is affected similarly by his environments. He now enters every avenue into which his brethren have been going. In this spirit of push and pluck our present subject affords a living example.

Dr. Ida Gray, a practical as well as a scientific dentist, was born in Clarksville, Tenn., March 1867. Her parents subsequently moved to Cincinnati, Ohio, where this very excellent young lady has since lived and where she now has an office and is regarded as a first-class dentist. She serves a large number of the best colored and white citizens of her city. So far as we are able to find out Miss Gray is the only female Afro-American dentist at the time of this writing. Her example is indeed one of great importance to our young women, who may take notice and find a field that is not only useful and already ripe for the harvest, but in which they, as laborers, may reap a rich and an abundant crop.

Ringwood's Afro-American Journal of Fashion, July 1892, makes the following very pleasant statement concerning this professional lady:

The accompanying portrait is of Dr. Ida Gray, the only Afro-American lady dentist. Miss Gray resides in Cincinnati and was one of the very many who received their educational start in Gaines High School. On leaving this school she entered the dental department of the University of Michigan, from which she graduated in 1890. On returning to her home she opened a very cozy office on Ninth Street, and has, in these two years, built up a large practice, having as many white as colored patients.

Miss Gray is a very refined little lady, of whom the editor of the *Planet* says: " Her blushing, winning way makes you feel like finding an extra tooth anyway to allow her to pull."

As a result of strict attention to business and the thoroughness of her work she is kept constantly busy. Cincinnatians are proud of their Afro-American lady dentist, and she in every respect proves herself worthy of their confidence and admiration.

CHAPTER LV.

MARY CHURCH TERRELL, A. B., A. M.

A daughter of Robert R. Church, a very popular man of Tennessee, and a resident of Memphis, Mrs. Terrell, at an early age, was sent to Ohio to be educated. She graduated from the famous Oberlin College in 1884 with the degree of A. B., being the youngest member of her class. She has since that time been further honored by her Alma Mater with the degree of A. M. In 1891 the registrarship of the college was extended to her, which honor she declined for private reasons.

She has, at one time, occupied a place upon the faculty of Wilberforce University and has also been connected with the High School at Washington, D. C., as teacher in the department of modern languages. The period from 1888 to 1890, inclusive, was spent in study and travel in Europe. As a resident pupil in Paris, Berlin and Florence she became quite proficient in French, German and Italian; and also cultivated herself in the fine arts. Mrs. Terrell is a musician of creditable rank and an art critic of discriminating taste. The Bethel Literary and Historical Association, of Washington, D. C., recently honored Mrs. Terrell with the position of president, this being the first time this well-known and influential society has elected a woman to that position.

Mrs. Terrell was married to Mr. Robert H. Terrell, a bureau chief of the United States Treasury, in October 1891. She is evidently a worthy wife and a well-qualified helper to her race, having filled many positions of trust and honor with great credit to herself.

GEORGIE COLLEY

CHAPTER LVI.

GEORGIE COLLEY

Mrs. Georgie Colley was born at Portsmouth, Norfolk County, Va., October 25, 1858; is the older of two daughters, the only children of her mother. She was educated under missionary teachers from the North, all of whom were ladies. Chief among them was Miss Julia M. Bartlett, at one time a teacher in the Wayland Seminary , Washington, D.C.and afterward the principal of the Colored Orphan Asylum in the same city.

Mrs. Colley was very carefully reared and trained by a faithful Christian mother, who spared no pains nor means to rear this child to be an honor to the home and community, and to be a faithful worker for God when converted. She was converted at the age of eighteen, under the ministry of Rev. E. G. Corprew, who baptized her into the Zion Baptist Church, Portsmouth, Va., first Lord's day in December 1876.

Mrs. Colley grew up in the Sunday-school of Zion Baptist Church, and became a teacher in that school at the age of fourteen years; was elected teacher of the most advanced class of young women in the school; was also elected assistant superintendent of the same school, which position she held for one year.

Before the organization of the Virginia Baptist State Sunday-school Convention, while the work of Sunday-schools was reported to the State Convention of Churches, Mrs. Colley then, from twelve to fourteen years of age, competed for prizes in the conventions, winning the second prize in the convention at Lynchburg, Va., and the first prize in the convention at Danville, Va., for the greatest number of scriptural verses, repeated from memory, with the fewest mistakes, before "judges" appointed by the Baptist State Convention. The first prize was won at Danville, Va., when she repeated the 119th Psalm without making a single mistake, several of the judges on this occasion being of the white Baptist ministers. Rev. Henry Williams, Jr., now pastor of the Giffield Baptist Church, Petersburg, Va., presented the medal.

Mrs. Colley, before she was married, taught public schools, holding good certificates from the County Superintendents, teaching five years in Norfolk and Nansemond 'counties, Va.

APPOINTED MISSIONARY TO AFRICA.

"Miss Georgie" became Mrs. W. W. Colley, by marriage, November 1, 1883, in the Zion Baptist Church, Portsmouth, Va., Rev. C. H. Corey, D. D., President of the Richmond Theological Seminary, officiating, assisted by the pastor, Rev. J. M. Armistead. A large number of ministers were present and took part in this solemn service.

The Foreign Mission Convention of the United States had a few weeks before this closed its meeting in the First Baptist Church, Manchester, Va., where it was voted that Rev. W. W. Colley, the founder of the Colored Baptist Foreign Mission Convention inAmerica, and their mission work in Africa, might takeunto himself a wife and be ready to leave for Central Africa, in company with other missionaries, to open the Colored Baptist Mission in the "Vye" country. The subject of this sketch had been duly consulted on the question of becoming a wife and a missionary. Dr. S. H. Dismond and Mr. J. B. Cable were chosen as first and second "best men," and in thirty days from marriage she was on the Atlantic Ocean sailing as missionary to Central Africa, under the Baptist Foreign Mission Board of the above convention.

Their union has been blessed with four children, two of whom were born inAfrica. Mrs. Colley stood the climate of Africa better than any of the six missionaries who went out with her.

One writer has said that "A woman's best qualities do not reside in herintellect, but in her affections. She gives refreshment by her sympathies rather than by her knowledge." She enjoyed her work among the heathen and they were devoted to her.

Much might be said in this sketch that would make friends for African missions, but space will not permit. The work of the missionary's wife and theunmarried woman, as teacher, not only of the Bible, but everything that comes in the line of woman's work, makes woman's presence in all heathen lands, as a missionary, as indispensable as that of the minister of the Gospel.

CHAPTER LVII.

MISS ELLA D. SPENCER.

Ella Spencer was born in New York City, her parents being well-known and highly respected residents. From a child she possessed an eye for beauty in color and form, particularly in birds and flowers, and when as she grew older and entered old Grammar School No. 1, over which presided with gentle rule John Peterson, whose memory the children of a decade ago, though clothed in trailing skirts and lengthened trousers, revere with touching tenderness, her drawing teacher, Miss Newbery, noted with delight her aptness in that direction and devoted special attention to developing her very evident talent.

After leaving school Miss Newbery, who had become not only her guide in drawing but a warm personal friend as well, feeling proud of the splendid promise of her pupil, registered her name at Cooper Union Art School. The first year the class of applicants was so large that Miss Spencer was obliged to wait for the following year. Though the authorities of the school did not know the young lady was colored, with the exception of a little show of surprise her work was so commendable no particular attention was paid to her from a prejudiced standpoint. Indeed, she was popular from the beginning of the term. From the drawing class she passed to that of casts, photo-color and crayon, the entire course covering six years. She received her diploma from the hand of that grand philanthropist, Peter Cooper, himself. From the moment she emerged with her treasured testimonial she has occupied a proud place in the hearts of New Yorkers, where her work is well known and much sought after. It is a rare thing to enter a New York home without finding some specimen from Ella Spencer's brush and pencil, and now that her work stands for itself she quietly pursues the even tenor of an artist; works continuously, almost forgetting the social world around her, perfectly happy and contented with the result of her labor. And while she is well known as a crayon artist, she is kept busiest, especially holiday seasons, decorating a miscellaneous assortment of goods, Christmas and Easter cards, porcelain placques, fancy cushions, screens, plush and velvet draperies, sachets, fancy boxes, mirrors, etc. Among the portraits that established her reputation are a life-size crayon of Richard Allen, the founder of African Methodism, drawn for and exhibited at the centennial anniversary of the A. M. E. dispensation held in New York at Bethel Church, 1887; a life-size portrait of Bishop Dickerson, now in the possession of Mrs. W. B. Derrick. Her work is not confined to our people, for some time ago she made a fine likeness of Augustus Schell, the well-known financier, which was so well liked by his family that Mrs. Schell ordered it at a handsome price. Ever since she has been working among these people, one lady introducing her work to another, in such a way as to keep her employed all the time she cares to devote to the work.

Miss Spencer painted for the New Orleans exhibition a large water-color, entitled "A Summer Day in Pompeii." The rare delicacy of the work of this one picture has been claimed by many to be sufficient to sustain the name "Timid Footsteps." "The Alsatian" and a portrait of her cousin, all in watercolor, are well known and admired by all who see them. A short while ago Miss Daly, her last teacher, attested her high regard for Miss Spencer as an artist by appointing her as her (Miss Daly's) assistant at her studio. Unfortunately, her health, which has never been robust, failed her, and a trusted physician. told her she would have to relax her labor else serious consequences would allow About that time her mother purchased a commodious dwelling in Flushing, Long Island, a pretty rural town seven miles out of New York, and after a short rest she is fast regaining her health. Not yet in the prime of life, and judging by the work already accomplished, there is no reason that the race at large should not expect many brilliant things from her. She expects to have some work represented at the World's Fair.

CHAPTER LVIII.

MRS. LILLIAN MAY THOMAS.

Lillian May Thomas was born in the city of Chicago, Ill., in 1857, and was the oldest child of Rev. Byrd and Jane Jeanetta Parker. When but nine months of age her parents removed to the city of Oshkosh, Wisconsin. Her father was a man of great native ability and a historic character in the story of "Negro Methodism in America," being pastor to Quinn Chapel, Chicago, many years ago, followed by pastorates at St. Paul's, St. Louis and Bethel, Indianapolis. Here mother was a graduate of the well Quaker institution of learning Spiceland University, of Indiana, and long before the public school system of Indiana was created became the first pay-teacher of the colored youth in Indianapolis, afterwards teacher in St. Louis and other cities.

Lillian inherited to a marked degree her father's controlling traits of mind and at a very early age gave signs that she was the worthy offspring of a superior parentage. Her school-days were spent in her adopted city of Oshkosh, but she was not permitted to finish what from the beginning gave abundant promise to her preceptors of being a very brilliant course of study and application. Her favorite studies while at school were grammar and composition, although not behind the average student in all of the English branches. With completion of the junior course of the Oshkosh High School her days of schooling ended, in a palpable sense, by her marriage, which, in lieu of her youth and the probable distortion, from a practical stand-point, of a brilliant literary career, was regarded by her friends as a lamentable incident, but while she was no longer found in the school-room, in reality her studies had but just begun, since, from that time to the present, she has been a most unflagging delver after knowledge, and a veritable "book-worm" on learning's humid page.

She early became a creature of luminous ideas and a much solicited contributor to that great dissemination of public opinion, the weekly and daily press. Among the first papers to solicit and publish contributions from her pen was the *Northwestern,* of Oshkosh, and the *Evening Wisconsin,* at Milwaukee, at about which time, in the event of the United States Supreme Court declaring the Civil Rights Bill unconstitutional, her column and a half article on "The Rights of Colored People," or "A Plea for the Negro," which appeared in the *Northwestern* secured for her at a leap, as it were, no mean place in the galaxy of women writers of either race, and distinctive encomiums for her quaint diction and rare logical disseminations, an idea of which may be leaned from the following excerpt from the article mentioned above:

When a man quits his home and goes upon a public street, enters a public car or hotel, we say he becomes one of the public and has no exclusive right of occupancy. He has no right to say that a man tall or short, white or black, shall not receive the same civil treatment as himself. This we call a civil right; and we hold that to be in a car or in the same hotel does not make one man society for another any more than to occupy the same air makes all birds of one feather.

And public practice does not accord with this theory, as can he readily shown; for instance, what lady or gentleman would avoid any of the first-class hotels upon it becoming known that a Frank James, or even a Guiteau, had taken quarters there? And if the propriety of their sharing the same roof was questioned, they would quickly say, "It is a public house; we do not call it associating with them," and indignantly recoil at the mere mention of these characters as their associates. But under precisely the same circumstances when it comes to the black man it is called "social equality," and the question arises, Who shall he blamed? If we question the ticket-seller or hotel-keeper they profess to only conform to the wishes of the public (meaning white, of course), or, in other words, are governed by the spirit of the times, implying that to the American people the negro is obnoxious and to insure the prosperity of their business he must be excluded. But we ask, is this the sentiment of the people or of a few rebel-hearted men who would inflict their outrages under the plea of a public necessity? If not, why stand by and with the cry of "unconstitutional" permit this human wrong to go unmitigated? Or, if we accept the theory that the negro is obnoxious, how shall we explain his presence in all dining and sleeping cars, in the largest hotels in our country, and at all pretentious receptions and parties? We have known instances in this city where the presence of the negro was so essential to the dignified aspect of entertainments to be given that they were brought from other cities for the occasion, the odium imported. And yet we cannot see why these persons courting the approval, in the matter of railways and hotels, of the most fastidious public, and in the elegant social gatherings of their most esteemed friends, would mar the equilibrium of their guests by having the negro present.

"But," you say, "we have always considered them invaluable as servants, and are willing now as ever to concede to them the highest position as menials; it is only when they rise above what we consider their natural sphere that we protest—when they would become our equals." But we say to you, this is despotism and hardly consonant with true American principles. You have adopted as a fundamental doctrine that all men are created equal, with certain inaliable rights, namely, life, liberty and the pursuit of happiness. You pity England, with her Lords and Commons ; Russia, with its Czar and subject, and yet practically acknowledge that you have a people among you of American birth whom you consider by God created for your servants, your inferiors by nature rather than by condition. We would ask also, if not in the land we have enriched with our labor, where would you send us that we may enjoy the civil treatment we ask?

Would you say to England, France or Ireland, "Though in times of oppression in your countries we have afforded your oppressed an asylum on American soil, strange to say we have a people among us who, because of a color which to us is a badge of inferiority, we cannot suffer equal rights with ourselves, and we would ask you to take them from us, and give them what they ask"? And you might add, by way of proviso, "If you find them to be possessed of qualities which would promote our national welfare you may return them to us at such a time as our prejudice shall have abated toward them, but for the present we pray you take them ˆ ɔm our midst."

After a lapse of several years, being thrown on her own responsibility for maintenance, she came to Indianapolis about the year 1885, where she soon attracted the notice of the *literati* of the city and was accorded that consideration due her intellectual gifts. Being a lady of fine voice and attractive personality, through inclination coupled with the suggestions of friends, she took a series of instructions in the art of elocution under Madams Prunk and Lucia Julian Martin respectively. During a professional tour extending through six weeks her reception was a flattering one and would have turned a less balanced head. In September 1891, her old love for journalistic work asserting itself, she was offered and accepted a position on one of the race's greatjournals*The Freeman,* as correspondent editor, feature writer, etc. Her " friendly reminders" which appeared weekly in that splendid publication dedicated to the women of the Afro-American race, have been read wherever the negro is found and will be accorded a positive and lasting place among the refined literary creations of her day. s a writer Mrs. Thomas' strength lies in her acute and very rare power of discrimination and analysis. Possessing a keen sense, of what might be termed intellectual intuition of the eternal fitness of things, she is quick to detect the grain and discard the chaff.

Writing with her is not indulged in for reason urges by the mere literary *dilettante,* viz., pastime or mental diversions, but for a purpose, and that the lifting up of her fellow-man, the directing of human thought forward, as far as it lies within her power, and onward to those idealistic spheres where lofty souls find solace and assuagement, and where the coarse and uncanny seldom confront. In ideas and thought she is original, in treatment and application much so, and in order to present in their most invulnerable guise the children of her pen's creation she does not hesitate to waive those literary rules that intellectual inconsequential shudder to violate and mediocrity pays abject court to. Being a most womanly woman, she Is, however, the possessor of a dual intellectual composition, in that she reflects the grasp of the best masculine minds on the one hand, and all the sympathy of touch and deftness of treatment of gentle woman on the other. A remarkable growing woman, an honor to her race and her sex, and in consideration of 'her superior attributes of nature, Pollock's lines suggest themselves to our minds, which we quote with slight transposition:

> With nature's self,
> She seems an old acquaintance,
> Free to jest at will,
> With all her glorious majesty.
>
> * * * * * * * *
>
> Then turns, and with the grasshopper,
> That sings its evening song,
> Beneath her feet converses.

CHAPTER LIX.

MRS. DELLA IRVING HAYDEN.

At the close of the Civil War we find the subject of our sketch in the town of Tarboro, N. C., without a mother's care, her mother having in the early days of the. war moved to the Old Dominion. In her incipiency she knew the care of none but a grandmother, to whom she was devoted with all of the devotion a child could bestow.

From the old Webster spelling-book she made her start, and soon learned as far as *baker*—a great accomplishment in those days. After getting a foretaste of an education she, then a young miss, became very anxious for an education. Free schools were not yet in existence, so she entered school seven miles away in Nansemond county. This school was under the control of the Freedmen's Bureau and taught by a Mr. A. B. Colis of New Jersey. The next year her parents moved from Nansemond County to Franklin, Southampton County, Va., where she entered the public school.

In school. she was obedient, docile, kind and punctual, out of school she was the delight of her playmates and apparently the life of the school. Early in her life she was converted and joined the Baptist Church. As a Christian she was a shining light and an ardent worker in the cause of Christianity. Years and deeds having hastened her near the verge of womanhood, she became a faithful teacher and an earnest worker in the Sabbath-school, to which work she became very much attached. She was secretary for Sunday-school and church clerk for several years.

In 1872 she entered Hampton Normal and Agricultural Institute with very limited means, with none to look to but a widowed mother. But she was not too proud to do any work assigned her to assist her in paying school bills. Lapse of years having brought her to womanhood, we may now call her Miss Irving. During her school-days at Hampton she stood high in the esteem of both her school-mates and teachers. In her second term in school she made the acquaintance of Mrs. G. M. Jones, of Philadelphia, who gave some financial aid and has ever since been a warm and devoted friend.

In 1874, Miss Irving (as she was then), having a determined will of her own and hearing the continual appeal of her people to "come over in Macedonia and help us," could no longer resist the pitiful cry, and laid down the pursuit of her studies, and, with that burning zeal of a missionary, laid hold of the work that she had so long desired. By so doing she did much to dispel the gloom which overshadowed her people, and financially enabled herself to resume her studies in 1875. Her first school-house was a little log cabin in a section of her own county known as Indian Town. Her first term was marked with great success and she filled the first place in the hearts of the people among whom she labored. There she organized a Sunday-school, for which she acted as teacher, chorister and superintendent. So great was the love of the people for her that they said they didn't believe the county paid her enough for the valuable services she rendered them, and as a unit came together and made up the deficiency as nearly as they could, for they thought that currency could not compensate for the great good and the blessings that she had been the means of bestowing upon them.

Her second term was taught four miles from this place, where it was difficult to find a family near the school with sufficient room to board a teacher, most of the houses having only one room. She was sent to such a house to board. This was too much for the young teacher. The people looked upon her as a jewel and would do anything to please her, so she called the parents together and they willingly united and built another room to the house, the teacher furnishing the nails.

In 1875 she returned to Hampton Normal and Agricultural Institute and resumed her studies. In 1877 she graduated with honor and was the winner of a $20 prize offered to the best original essayist of the class. On her return home to resume the work among her people, to which she felt so closely espoused, she was elected principal of the town public school. Here she met with some competition for the position, but energy, push and competency always hold sway over all opposition, where fair play is granted. She outstripped her rivals and filled the position with credit three years.

She was looked upon as the spiritual, educational and political adviser of her neighborhood for the colored people. In the church and Sunday-school she had no peer, for both minister and Sunday-school superintendent sought her advice as to the best means of spiritualizing the church and enlivening the Sunday-school. She stands in the ranks among the best educators of her race. Through her influence and recommendations a great many young men and women have gained admission into some of the best institutions of learning in the United States. Many of them she assisted financially, while in school, from her scanty income, which was a sacrifice but a pleasure. Quite a number of them have graduated and are filling honorable positions.

As a politician she was so well informed and could discuss so intelligently the public issues of the day that in her town, in the campaign of 1884, she was styled the politicians' oracle. She, as did Paul, ceased not day nor night to warn her people of the danger that awaited them. While teaching she did not fail to practice economy, for she saved means to lift a heavy debt off her property which she mortgaged to secure means to finish her education.

In 1880 she married Mr. Lindsey Hayden, an accomplished gentleman, who was principal of the public school of Liberty (now Bedford City), Va. Unfortunately for her Mr. Hayden lived only a few months after marriage. During his short illness Mr. Hayden found in her every requisite of a true wife and ever his administering angel. After the death of her devoted husband she resigned the position as first assistant teacher in the school in which her husband had so recently been principal and returned to Franklin to live with her widowed mother. Notwithstanding all hearts went out in sympathy for her in her bereavement there was a sort of mingled joy at her return to her old field of labor, since it seemed a matter of impossibility to fill her place as a worker among her people. In the fall of 1881 she was elected again principal of the town school, which position she held for nine years.

As a temperance worker and lecturer in general the United States cannot boast of one more ardent. She served three years as president of the Woman's Christian Temperance Union and the Home Missionary Society, organized by Mrs. Marriage Allen, the wonderful messenger of England, four years as recording secretary of the county Sunday-school Union, one year as corresponding secretary organized a great many temperance societies, and hundreds have taken the pledge. She is at present president of the Virginia Teachers' Temperance Union. In 1890 she was elected lady principal of the Virginia Normal and Collegiate Institute, which position she now holds.

Says Gen. S. C. Armstrong, Principal of the Hampton Normal and Agricultural Institute:

Mrs. Della Irving Hayden was at Hampton school four years and made a most excellent record. We all here, teachers and friends, expected a great deal of her, and have not been disappointed. She married a noble young man, Mr. Lindsey Hayden, who soon died — a great loss. Since her bereavement Mrs. Hayden has devoted herself nobly to her people. We hope she may be spared many years. She is among the famous women of her race.

Says Miss Maggie I. Stevens:

Mrs. Della Irving Hayden well deserves the name woman. I was a pupil in school under her thirteen years ago. It was through her I gained admission into the Hampton Normal and Agricultural Institute. It is to her (through the help of God) I owe my success in literary attainment. She has no peer as a quick thinker and an earnest worker.

James H. Johnston, A. M., President of the Virginia Normal and Collegiate Institute, says:

Since Mrs. Hayden's election as lady-principal of this institution she has exhibited unusual tact and ability in the performance of her duty, thereby gaining the love and esteem of the students and commendation of the Board of Visitors. As a temperance worker she has been exceedingly active and has succeeded in getting hundreds of our students and teachers of the annual summer session to sign the pledge. * * * She does not fail to use her pen and power of speech, which she possesses in no ordinary degree, to advance the Master's kingdom. Dr. J. P. Bryant, County Superintendent of Southampton County, in speaking of her qualifications as a teacher, said:

Mrs. Della I. Hayden taught twelve years in the public schools of Southampton to the entire satisfaction of patrons and school officers—the most of the time under my supervision. She was principal of a large graded school in this place. Her executive capacity is of a high order, and she manages a school of a hundred or more pupils with as much dexterity and ease as most teachers with twenty or twenty-five pupils. Her ambition in her chosen profession is unbounded, and she never tires. Beginning with a third grade certificate she was enabled to attend the Hampton Normal and Agricultural Institute, teaching one year and returning to the school the other, until she graduated with distinction at that institute. She finally obtained a professional certificate, the highest grade, under the public school system, as a reward for her perseverance, energy and ability.

The foregoing statements will give our readers a faint view only of the wonderful and useful life that Mrs. D. I. Hayden has lived for years among her people.

WILLIS B. HOLLAND, Principal of Public School, Franklin, Va.

CHAPTER LX.

MRS. N. A. R. LESLIE.

Modest, zealous, aspiring and faithful to duty; economical and yet philanthropic; conservative and kind, are traits characteristic of this very devoted laborer in the cause of Afro-American education. She was born in Amelia county, Va., and is the fourth daughter of Nannie and Charles P. Coles. She has taught school most of her life, beginning with the English primary branches, has gone upward from a mere teacher of moderate grade to the position of a founder and principal of a great enterprise in our educational work. She labored for some time under appointment of the Freedman's Bureau at a time when it took nerve and will to teach among our people, for in those days opposition to negro education in the South was strong within our own ranks as well as without. Nevertheless she began this work in 1865 and continued in the same as long as the government supported and continued the schools in the South under its supervision. For quite a while she was jointly employed and paid by the first public school board in New Orleans and the American Missionary Association at a salary of $70 from the former and $25 from the latter per month, making a salary of $95 per month. She was married to Rev. R. A. Leslie in 1874.

After teaching for some time in the State of Mississippi, they moved to Indian Territory, the native home of her husband. They remained there awhile and then they returned to Mississippi, soon after which he died, April 1884. She then returned to Indian Territory (after spending some time at the Boston Conservatory of Music).She, now having developed herself along musical lines, has done much for her race in giving instructions in music.

The *Texas Pioneer,* June 15, 1886, said of her:

Mrs. N. A. Leslie of Paris, Texas, is an educated and accomplished lady and a successful teacher of *instrumental music.* Mrs. Leslie has a large collection of newspaper clippings that are very complimentary to her and speak wonders of her work for the race. Space forbids us at this late day to quote many of them. She is now located at Corpus Christi, Texas, where she is doing a noble work as an educator and a musician. She has saved her earnings and is in possession of considerable property and cash. Mrs. Leslie is indeed a great woman.

CHAPTER LXI.

MISS ALICE ELIZABETH McEWEN.

Miss McEwen first saw the dawn of day in Nashville, Tenn., July 29, 1870. Her parents were Anderson N. and Elizabeth H. McEwen. She was taught the first principles of English by her mother. She entered Rodger Williams University and doubtless would have finished her course here, but moving from Nashville, and her parents feeling that better care would be taken of her, she entered Spelman Seminary the fall of '85. It was also in this year that her first article for publication appeared. She was a regular correspondent for the *Montgomery Herald* from this time until its editor was forced to leave Montgomery.

Three years. little Alice (as she was called) was in school trying to fit herself for usefulness. In 1888 she graduated from Spelman Seminary, not as a member only of her class, but as the one standing head. Those who know her can readily testify to her ability as a scholar. Since her graduation she has held prominent positions. It has been said of her that "As a scholarly woman she has acquitted herself most creditably."

Her first article, entitled "The Progress of the Negro," excited much comment. From time to time she has given the world her ideas through some of our leading newspapers. Her subjects have been varied. Among her best productions are her graduating oration, "The Advantage of Adversity," published in almost all the leading newspapers of the South; "Women in Journalism," a paper read before the National Press Association in Washington, D. C., and "Signs of the Times," a paper published in the *Freeman* (Christmas, 1891), and afterwards published in the *Southern Watchman,* of Mobile, Ala.

Aside from a journalist Miss McEwen is a professional teacher. Though young she has made a bright record in this profession. She has taught in the leading schools of Montgomery, Talladega and Huntsville. She has given perfect satisfaction wherever she has labored. As a scholarly, Christian teacher she stands among the first of our country. She was elected secretary of Huntsville

State Normal School last September, which position she held until she resigned to accept work elsewhere. Miss McEwen is now principal. of a large school conducted by the Odd Fellows at Moss Point, Miss.

Aside from her work in the school-room Miss McEwen is pursuing her study in elocution, which course she will soon complete. She is also reading medicine preparatory to entering school to finish a course in this great profession. In the near future she will become an author. She is ascending slowly the ladder of fame. She is a reader of the best works and keeps abreast of the times. She has many accomplishments that mark her a cultured lady.

May heaven bless her! The future of few female writers is prospectively brighter than that of Miss Alice E. McEwen. Her aim as a writer is not for mere social attainments, but for the betterment of her people.

CHAPTER LXII.

MRS. CHRISTINE S. SMITH.

Eleven years ago a girl of fifteen summers stood at a washtub in the kitchen of one of her neighbors in Muncie, Indiana. This neighbor, a white lady, was in need of someone to do her washing, and she engaged to do it the subject of our sketch, who lived next door and who was attending the city high school. As the the girl stood in the tub with her bare young arms playing in and out of the foaming suds, the lady for whom she was working asked what she intended to make of herself. The brown-eyed girl, whose complexion was not less fair than that of the woman for whom she labored, quickly responded, "A school-teacher". Some years later this same lady told Miss Shoecraft that she never thought she would make a teacher. The gulf between the little washer-woman and a school-mar' in was too great to be bridged by this young colored girl —so thought her once employer. But she has changed her mind since she has seen how much Miss Shoecraft has accomplished by her indomitable will and strength of purpose. These essentials to success are so overshadowed by the womanly graces of our subject that even many of her friends fail at first to note these sterling qualities. Doubtless a short sketch of her life will be an incentive to girls who may find themselves surrounded by difficulties that rise as walls of adamant between them and long-cherished desires. Her highest aim in life was to get a thorough education, and then touch the sleeping heart of the masses and set it throbbing with a newer and a better life.

Miss Christine Shoecraft was born July 1, 1866 in Indianapolis, Indiana. Her parents were A. R. and Mary B. Shoecraft. Her mother died when she was but two and a half years old, and the care of the motherless little one rested upon her father and grandmother, who, when Christine was eight years of age, moved to Muncie, Indiana. It was in this city that she received her education, finishing from the high school when seventeen years of age. During her last three years in school many difficulties barred her pathway. But, nothing daunted, she went right on, assisting in the house-work, washing and ironing, and at the same time keeping abreast of her class. When it came time for her final examinations, instead of using the intervals between them for cramming, she washed and ironed. In this way was the money earned with which she bought her graduating dress.

The girlish heart thrilled with genuine joy when she received her diploma. She felt a long-cherished hope realized. She saw her efforts crowned with success. She had grappled with the stern difficulties that stood between her and the consummation of her desire, and she had conquered. At seventeen years of age she set her little bark adrift with no fear of the future. Had she not won in that dark, tried past as a girl, and would she not win in that as yet untried future as a woman? She trusted the Saviour. She learned to love and serve Him when she was thirteen years old. Now she went forth for battle filled with pure, noble motives, burning with pent-up zeal to do something in the world, and to do what she could in the awakening of the young minds of the race. Has she succeeded? Read her history in the school-room and in the A. M. E. Sunday-school Union and you will find an answer to your question. Miss Shoecraft was offered a lucrative position as assistant principal in the State Normal School of Alabama. She accepted it. Rev. W. H. Councill, its principal, in speaking of her work in connection with the school, says:

"Miss Shoecraft was a success in every particular. She gained and holds the hearts of her fellow-teachers, the students and friends of the institution. She is, indeed, not only a born and cultivated teacher, but a leader and a commander. She was faithful and competent in any position in which she consented to serve, whether in charge of the whole school, or a class, or laboring for the people in church or Sunday-school. A consistent Christian, she carried an earnestness and consecration into her work which would not admit of defeat. She kept constantly in view the greatest good of those whom she served. She is unquestionably the most popular teacher ever connected with the Huntsville Normal School. Under the greatest trials she was the most composed, and in the darkest hour her womanly virtues shone most brilliantly and placed upon her brow a halo which called forth the admiration of friend and foe.

"In her dealings with the community, as well as her conduct towards her pupils, she lost her self-interest in her efforts to serve others, and Fred. Douglass himself was never more devoted to the welfare of the race than she. "As Hamlet said of his father, we say of her:

"A combination and a form indeed,

Where every god did seem to set his seal,

To give the world assurance of a woman."

"She resigned her position in December 1887, and the following year married the distinguished Dr. C. S. Smith, Secretary of the A. M. E. Sunday-school Union, located at Nashville, Tenn. In this age of advancement all avenues are open to both colored men and women. But few of our women have entered the business arena and by their ability proved to the world what a colored woman can do in this line. Mrs. Smith has successfully done this. In becoming the wife of Dr. Smith she allied herself to and became interested in the largest publishing house in the world owned and controlled exclusively by colored people. During her connection with this institution she has held, at different times, every position in the clerical department—cashier, book-keeper, entry and order clerk. For a year she has been the assistant manager of the establishment. It is the first time in the history of the Union that such an honor has been conferred on a woman. At the annual meeting of the Board of Managers of the Sunday-school Union, in April 1892, her efficient management was highly commended.

In the school-room, in the counting-room, or as manager of the Union, Mrs. Smith has been conscientious in the performance of duty, and has shown marked executive ability in every position she has held. Notwithstanding the arduous labor in connection with her position in the Union she superintends her household affairs and devotes not a small portion of her leisure moments to her baby boy, C. S., Jr., and to the study of art. Today she is modest, unassuming, kind and tender-hearted; a friend to the needy, a pure and noble woman, quietly and nuostentatiously performing her duties as if they were not out of the regular line of woman's work.

MISS CLARA A. HOWARD

CHAPTER LXIII.

MISS CLARA A. HOWARD.

One of the first eleven daughters of "Spelman Seminary," of whom we may say, "They bore the heat and burden of the day." When Rev. Quarles had gotten his people's brick structure for worship completed, he began to pray for a school in Atlanta which would be solely for girls and women of color. One happy day, while he was on his knees praying thus, a rap called him to his feet, and at the door of his study he found two God-sent women, Misses Packard and Giles, whose hearts longed to do *just* the work for which he had been praying. They told him their desire. He told them his story, and added: "I have had His promise, 'And it shall come to pass that before they call, I will answer; and while they are yet speaking, I will hear'. I was just on my knees praying for such a school." He then told them that he would open his basement to such a school and do all in his power to help them. On the eleventh day of April 1881, Spelman Seminary was born in the above-mentioned basement. Few were present, but they mark the birthday of an institution to be the *Alma Mater of* this our subject.

This life began at Greenville, Ga., January 23, 1866. She is the only daughter of King and Mary Ann Howard. The first thing this child astonished her parents in was her advanced conduct as a babe; she appeared to notice everything about her. The day on which she was eight months old she stood on her feet and walked. This was too much for the fond parents to keep to themselves. Their daughter soon showed a disposition to be alone, and this gave them much concern, as they feared she would grow up to make a selfish woman. At the age of six she began her school life, becoming a member of the Haines Street public school.

She advanced rapidly as the years rolled on, and after four years here entered a private institution known as the Staw School of Atlanta. Two years fitted this aspiring pupil to enter the well-known Atlanta University. She was studying.

at this latter when the above ladies arranged with "Father Quarles" to use his church basement as a school-room.

The father of our subject being a deacon in that church at his death, the dear widowed mother had brought up her sons and daughter faithful to the Church, and they had been gathered in while young. "Father Quarles" baptized this Daughter of the King in 1881. Miss Howard left the University to take up her studies with ten humble pupils in the basement. She advanced as Spelman advanced, and graduated with the first class in the history of the school, May, 1887. Being a widow's daughter, Miss Howard had to work hard during her school-days, even working late at night. Her mother and brothers disliked seeing her under such pressure and used to urge her to retire with them. Her reply would always be, "Do not worry about me; I have an object in view, and will have to work to make it; I have to finish my education, and will have to work to do it." This great strain told on the strength of our subject. It was then arranged that she board in the institution. Here she remained a boarder even after her graduation, so attached was she to her "Spelman Home." Before a graduate Miss Howard taught at Wodley, Ga. Here she was very much loved by parents and pupils. As teacher in the model school at Spelman she distinguished herself as a disciplinarian, as well as an affectionate teacher. She was therefore highly recommended to the Board of Education of the city of Atlanta for a position in the Sommerville Graded School of that city. Here she taught with much acceptance until 1890, when she offered her resignation to take up work in Africa immediately. This was the "object in view" of which she used to so often speak. When first she told her mother what her "object" was the mother laughed her away, saying, "You are going to bed, that is where you are going. You do not know what you are talking about." The devoted daughter would have gone immediately after her graduation but for her health.

April 24th found farewells over and the last preparation made for the long journey. On this day she took a joyful leave of dear ones to begin her long-cherished work in Africa. She was assigned to Lukunga Station, where she found hundreds already gathered in school and church. She took the place as teacher ere she had time to begin the study of the language of this hungering people. English studies had been begun by some of the Lukunga pupils, so it made this immediate beginning possible. Along with Miss Gordon she founded the Lukunga Seminary, and the two have sole charge of the same. Eternity alone will determine the good this consecrated life is doing for this benighted land in lifting up its people by the school and by personal pleading for their salvation. Her peculiar tact in reaching the hearts of children and managing them without apparent effort has made it easy for her to reach older people, and thus gather from all precious souls which must shine forever and ever as the stars, For her we pray a long life in which to engage in this work so blessed in its character and so glorious in its reward.

L. C. FLEMING.

CHAPTER LXIV.

MRS. CARRIE E. SAWYER CARTWRIGHT.

The life we are now to review is indeed a conspicuous one. "Some are born great; some achieve greatness, and some have greatness thrust upon them. But to be truly great is to be truly good." This is a characteristic of Mrs. Cartwright, who was born in Pasquotank County, North Carolina. Her mother's name was Emeline Sawyer, her father's name Henry Fesson, each taking name after their former owners respectively. She was among the first young women attending Estey Seminary at Shaw University. Shortly after her school life began here she had the misfortune of losing her faithful, devoted mother, leaving a large family of undergrown children. This sainted mother requested Carrie to remain at home and become mother for her brothers and sisters. To most young women, thirsting for an education and seeing before them the opened way, having already begun to walk therein, this would have been a great trial. To Carrie it was a delight. No sacrifice seemed too dear for her to make for those little hearts hanging on hers. Plans for their best good engaged her mind the last thing at night and the first thing in the morning. The father was often conferred with and urged into vigilance respecting the welfare of those dear ones. When sick they claimed even her time for sleep, so close was her vigilance and untiring her efforts to render them comfortable.

In 1882, after almost ten years of the above service, this faithful woman entered once more Estey Seminary. Like all sensible girls she had been wooed and loved, but when she found out that the suitor objected to her spending three years more at school to complete her course she *unselfishly freed him* from his obligation, at the same time inviting him to seek in someone else a help meet. It was the good fortune of the writer to enter school in the class of '85 alongside her. The three years we spent together in the Seminary afforded ample opportunity for the writer to see into the life of this unselfish soul-winner. Her efforts among the unsaved in school were untiring. During revival efforts no soul among the saved was more burdened with the salvation of the unsaved than was this earnest one. Not only were these needy ones in school the objects of the most prayerful attention, but twice a week, in connection with the city mission work of the Young Women's Christian Association in Estey, this devoted woman took her Bible and sought the habitations of the poor, the sick and the souls in sin and darkness. The city Sunday-school knew the power of her influence for Christ. When her last examination had been successfully passed and she was to be no more among the earnest workers of the University she was still remembered in the city and school. She, in 1883, decided, with the writer, upon Africa as the field of her life's work. To this choice she remained faithful, and in 1886, when Rev. Cartwright, of Liberia, came to this country seeking volunteers, this waiting daughter of Zion said to the Z. A. M. E. Church, "Here am I; send me." As she only answered thus the venerated missionary deemed it best to woo her and take her back to share his work. Accordingly they were married and sailed for Africa a few hours after the ceremony— July 10, 1887. After a voyage of thirty days' duration she set foot on the field beside her devoted husband and began on that day the work of saving souls in Africa. As in this country the church, the day-school, the Sunday-school and individual souls alike claim her efforts and prayers. Last year her husband returned to this country, but the faithful wife stood alone at their post and cried "Behold the Lamb!"

Often when he spent the night with his gun in hand as a protection to life and property, she felt undisturbed, for her heart was bold and brave, never faltering, never fearing, never failing.

L. C. FLEMING.

HARTSHORN MEMORIAL COLLEGE.

CHAPTER LXV.

HARTSHORN MEMORIAL COLLEGE

Hartshorn Memorial College is one of the two institutions under Baptist control devoted to the separate education of colored young women. This institution is located in the City of Richmond, State of Virginia. The work of instruction began November 7, 1883. It is chartered by the State of Virginia with full collegiate and university powers, the charter bearing the date of March 13, 1884.

This institution was founded for the secondary and collegiate education of young women. This purpose is more fully expressed in the charter as follows:

Be it enacted by the General Assembly, That the following named persons, with their associates and successors, are hereby incorporated under the name and style of the Hartshorn Memorial College, for the purpose of founding and maintaining an institution of learning of collegiate grade for the education of young women, to give instruction in science, literature and art, in normal, industrial and professional branches, and especially in Biblical and Christian learning, with such departments, schools and courses of study as the trustees shall deem proper and needful, and to confer such literary and honorary degrees as are wont to be conferred by colleges and universities in the United States.

Hartshorn Memorial College received its name from Deacon Joseph Charles Hartshorn, of Providence, R. I., afterwards (at the time of his death) of Newton Centre, Mass. by whose benefaction the institution was planted. As suggested by the name the institution stands as a memorial for Mrs. Rachel Thurber Hartshorn, whose death occurred shortly before its founding. The spirit in which the school was founded is expressed in the following mural inscription:

FOR THE LOVE OF CHRIST, WHO GAVE HIMSELF FOR THE
REDEMPTION ALIKE OF EVERY RACE, AND
FOR THE LOVE OF COUNTRY, WHOSE WELFARE DEPENDS UPON THE
INTELLIGENCE, VIRTUE AND PIETY OF THE LOWLY
AS WELL AS THE. GREAT,
AND WITH TENDER SYMPATHY FOR A PEOPLE FOR WHOM TILL LATE
NO DOOR OF HOPE HAS BEEN OPENED AND
ASPIRATION HAS BEEN VAIN,
AND WITH DESIRE AND HOPE FOR THE ENLIGHTENMENT OF THE DARK
CONTINENT, THE FATHERLAND OF THE COLORED RACE,
IN MEMORY OF HIS SAINTED WIFE,
RACHEL HARTSHORN,

THAT HER FAITH AND CHARITY MIGHT BE REPRODUCED AND
PERPETUATED IN THE LIVES OF MANY, THIS
INSTITUTION WAS FOUNDED BY
JOSEPH C. HARTSHORN'
OF RHODE ISLAND.

Hartshorn Memorial College emphasizes the Christian elements in education. It does this for two reasons: First. It is believed that the Biblical and Christian element renders education better and more complete. It makes better and stronger thinkers, and nobler and more womanly women. This, and this only, can develop character which stands victorious over the world. Secondly. The work of lifting up and blessing the race must be done by consecrated Christians. It will be done by no others. It can be done by no others.

The institution was founded for women only because it is believed that, under the present conditions, separate education is better; that it largely escapes certain difficulties and has more advantages than disadvantages.

The gifts of Mr. Hartshorn, including a bequest of fifteen thousand dollars, amounted to forty-one thousand dollars. The grounds and buildings are valued at forty-five thousand dollars. The bequest referred to, with the necessary additional contributions, is expected to be used for the erection of another large college building.

The policy of the management is not to multiply numbers, but to select and sift, in order that students may have the better advantages, and that the best results of education may be reached. For this reason, or for some other, the normal graduates have been remarkably successful. They have made reputation for themselves and for their school and have shown themselves especially devoted to the welfare of their people.

In the industrial department the young women receive such instruction and training as fits them to stand at the head of Christian homes—homes which shall be the nurseries of thrift, virtue and grace.

The charge for board, room and tuition is sixty-five dollars for the school year.

The engraving shown above does not now well represent the grounds of the institution. The grounds are fenced and are well set with thrifty ornamental and shade trees.

Thus far the institution has had the advantage of uniform management under the same administrative officers. The president and the lady-principal have been with the institution from the beginning.

The Board of Instruction at this time is as follows:

Rev. LYMAN B. TEFFT, A. M., President; MISS CARRIE V. DYER, Lady-Principal; MISS LIDA M. SUTHERLAND, Miss H. AMANDA MILLER, B. S., Mrs. CLARA F. WHITTEN, Mrs. Prof. J. E. JONES, MISS JENNIE S. CARO.

In May 1892, the first college class was graduated, receiving the degree of Bachelor of Science.

CHAPTER LXVI.

MRS. L. HUGHES BROWN.

The last quarter of a century has brought many changes in the condition of the American people. Indeed, it has been an epoch of great strides by the majority of the population, of all nationalities that have representatives among us. But in no case has the onward march of progress been more generally marked than that of the Afro-American people.

Young men and women have sprung up and taken the lead in the affairs of this people as teachers and benefactors, whose influence and works can scarcely be estimated. Among our strong, resolute young women is Mrs. L. Hughes Brown, who was born of poor parents in the town of Mebanesville, N. C. She had but little opportunity for schooling, her mother having been taken from her by death while she was yet quite young, and leaving seven children to be cared for by this young woman.

The responsibility, though a great one, was well met, while at the same time she pursued her studies at home as best she could under the circumstances, and so advanced as to 'become able to teach school at a very early age.

In 1881 she entered Scotia Seminary at Concord, N. C., from which she graduated in 1885; after this devoting four years to teaching, a part of which time she taught in her Alma Mater.

In 1889 she was married to Rev. David Brown, a graduate of Biddle University at Charlotte, N. C. In 1890 she matriculated in the Woman's Medical College of Philadelphia, where she still pursues her studies.

Her progress, as can be seen at a glance, has been steadily forward. She is one of our coining female physicians from whom we are to expect great things in the future.

CHAPTER LXVII.

VERINA H. MORTON, M. D.

This young physician, to say the least, has many good reasons to be proud of her accomplishments and hopeful for a bright future. It is quite probable yet that she, with her many professional sisters, will hush in silence the often and repeated statement that the practice of medicine "tends to destroy the womanly qualities" of females who enter the profession as regular practicing physicians. The statement is certainly without foundation when applied to all female physicians. There may be exceptions in the cases of both sexes. The exceptions on either side are rare in proportion as prejudice recedes and justice conies to the front.

The *Brooklyn Times,* June 27, 1891, had the following to say of our subject:

Brooklyn's youngest colored physician, Dr. Verina H. Morton, of Gold street, graduated in 1888 from the Woman's Medical College of Pennsylvania in Philadelphia, the best medical college for women in the country. She belongs to the regular school and has been practicing medicine, until recently, under her maiden name of Harris in Mississippi, where she was resident physician of Rust University at Holly Springs, and also gave talks on health topics to the industrial school connected with the university. She was the first woman physician of either color to register in that State.

She was married last August to Dr. W. A. Morton, also a young colored physician, who has been in practice a little over a year and came to Brooklyn and registered here this spring. She has made a good start already in this city, her very first patient being a German lady. She has been surprised at the number of calls she has received in the few weeks that have elapsed since she registered. Her husband also is doing well; they do not interfere with each other in the least. They are a handsome young couple, intelligent and refined looking.

As Dr. Harris she had good success in Mississippi, where she was welcomed by both races. The women of the South, she says, would flock to a woman physician. There is a pressing need for educated women in the South, not only to practice medicine, but to teach the laws of health, which are there sadly ignored. Even the Southern cities are not overstocked with practitioners of either sex.

CHAPTER LXVIII.

MRS. ROSETTA E. COAKLEY LAWSON.

The very acute little girl who grew to womanhood and by perseverance has come to the mark of distinction was born in King George County, Virginia, and was taken by her mother to Washington, D. C., in 1862 in the fifth year of her age, her father having fled for freedom when she was only two years old.

She attended the schools of the District until the plan of opening a public high school for colored children was completed, when she entered the highest grade in the public grammar schools in order to be eligible for admission into the high school. She pursued the studies of the preparatory high school for two years, and during the third year was made assistant to the principal of the grammar schools from which she had been transferred. Her services seemed to be satisfactory in this position, for in less than five months she was promoted to the charge of a school with an increase of $15 per month in salary. The work in the office of the General Superintendent being very burdensome, in reviewing each teacher's record-book for the year so as to insure accurate statistics, many of the best teachers were detailed at the end of each year to assist in this work.

In 1873, Miss Coakley was among the number thus chosen, and her efficiency and fondness for the work so pleased the Superintendent of Public Instruction that he asked the Board of Trustees to detail her *indefinitely for clerical work* in his office. His request was unhesitatingly granted, and she served in the Superintendent's office for twelve long years, and severed her connection with the public schools of the District of Columbia at the close of the school year in June 1885. The opportunity for meeting people from every land and clime while acting as assistant to the Superintendent of the Public Schools for twelve years was great and did much to broaden her ideas of life and of men as well as of *women*. The cares of a home to be maintained for an aged mother and a still more aged grandmother rendered it quite hard for her to let go the hold which she had upon the then incoming salary which she was then earning that she might continue her studies. Many a time she resolved to borrow sufficient money to keep herself in school and at the same time keep her home going. But Ben Franklin's "He who goes a borrowing goes a sorrowing" which she had been taught during her tender years, deterred her.

But the Chautauqua idea caught her attention, and from 1880 to the close of 1884 she pursued the course prescribed for the C. L. S. C. She went to Chautauqua, N. Y., and was graduated with the class of 1884, otherwise known as the *"Irrepressibles"*. During her single life she was active in both church and Sunday-school work. Since her marriage to Mr. Jesse Lawson, of Plainfield, N. J., she has devoted her time almost entirely to the domestic cares, which have left her no time for purely literary work. Nevertheless, she has ever been faithful to the cause of temperance, to which she still clings with a fondness and patience characteristic of a member of the Woman's Christian Temperance Union.

Mrs. Lawson may be regarded as one thoroughly alive to the needs of the race. She is full of *holy race pride,* and is ever ready to lend a helping hand to any effort that has in view the elevation of the Afro-American and the betterment of the condition of mankind. To say that she is liberal, wise, kind, prudent and just is to tell only a part of her good traits.

CHAPTER LXIX.

MRS. C.C. STUMM--MRS. LUCINDA BRAGG ADAMS--MRS LAVINIA B. SNEED.

M rs. C. C. STUMM, now of Philadelphia, Pa., was born in Boyle county, Ky., March 25, 1857, being the immediate descendant of Thomas and Elizabeth Penman. Having spent two years of hard study at Berea College, she has since taught as an employed teacher in Hearn Academy, in Texas, and Bowling Green Academy, in Kentucky, in both of which her efforts were successful. She has contributed to several of our Afro-American newspapers in the North and in the South. She is a good writer, producing such thoughts as are interesting and instructive. She has lived in Boston, and is now the wife of Rev. Mr. Stumm, of Philadelphia.

Mrs. LUCINDA BRAGG ADAMS is the very able daughter of Mr. and Mrs. George F. Bragg, of Petersburg, Va. Mrs. Lucinda B. Adams is on the editorial staff of the *Musical Messenger,* as assistant of Miss A. L. Tilghman. Mrs. Adams is well up in music and highly thought of and beloved in musical circles. She is able as a writer and has done considerable writing for the various Afro-American papers.

Mrs. LAVINIA B. SNEED is a lady of considerable power with the pen; an able and pleasing thinker. Born in New Orleans, La., May 15, 1867, but was educated in Kentucky, in the city of Louisville, where she graduated, as valedictorian of the class of 1887, from State University, receiving the degree of A. B.

In 1888 she became the efficient wife of Prof. Sneed, with whom she has since lived in much happiness.

She is an elocutionist of acknowledged ability and is also an attractive singer.

CHAPTER LXX.

MISS META E. PELHAM.

This young lady, though born in Virginia, went with her parents to Detroit and was there educated in the city schools, from which she graduated at the head of her class of more than fifty pupils, there being only four of Afro-American birth. This is certainly one instance in which co-education of the races was treated with fairness (at least in this respect) as is always a very noted feature of the management of the schools in Detroit. She then entered Fenton College, in Michigan also, and took a normal course. As her health was not robust she did not teach school very long, but entered upon a most encouraging and successful career in connection with the *Plain Dealer,* which marked the beginning of her newspaper work. Mr. Penn, in "Afro-American Press," says of her:

She is a woman of most excellent traits of character and has a prolific and productive brain. Miss Pelham is not so well known as many lady writers of less ability, because, in her entire writings, she has used no *nom de plume* or signature.

The *Plain Dealer* of May 1888, speaks of her in the following very complimentary terms:

Since the inception of the Plain Dealer the influence of woman has sustained it in adversity; the product of her mind bas given lustre to its columns, and now, more than ever, much of its success, in the character of its productions, is due to her. To Miss Meta Pelham is due the credit of this aid, who has always taken an active interest in the paper and often contributed to its columns. For the past two years she has become one of its essentials in the office, and she devotes her whole time to the work. She was among the first Afro-American graduates from our high school, and subsequently took a normal course at the Fenton Normal School. She also spent several years teaching in the South until newspaper allurements became more tempting. Her idea of a newspaper is that it should be metropolitan in character, deal in live issues, and be reliable.

Her career is worthy of consideration in this book.

CHAPTER LXXI.

MRS. RACHEL M. WASHINGTON.

This is one of the many ladies of whom Boston may well be proud. Graduating from the New England Conservatory of Music, she has ever been active as an instructor to the young with whom she came in contact, as well as an earnest searcher after knowledge in the line of her chosen profession. It is said that she has possibly done more to cultivate a love and admiration for music among the prominent citizens of Boston than any other one person.

The following lines are taken from a letter written by her to a friend:

As I read the lives of the great composers, and think of their sacred devotion to the art dearer to them than their own lives, I feel anxious for the time to come in our history when a child like Mozart shall be born with soul full of bright melodies; or a Beethoven, with his depth and tenderness of feeling; or a Handel, lifting us above this earth until we shall hear the multitude of voices joining in one vast song-- "Alleluia, for the Lord God omnipotent reigneth!" Nor is this impossible. Our history, it seems to me, has but just begun. All the past is but sorrow and gloom, and here and there a bright ray to bid us hope. * * * I hope they (the colored youth of the country) will early develop a love and taste for the beautiful in musical art; that soon we shall be proud to mention those whose names, through their works, shall be immortal.

This extract is sufficient proof of her strong, active mind and soul full of love for her race and the beautiful in musical art.

CHAPTER LXXII.

ARTISHIA GARCIA GILBERT, A. B., A. M.

Situated among the "foot-hills" of the Cumberland Mountains is the quaint little town of Manchester, Ky., where, in a little log cabin, was born, on the 2nd day of June 1868, the subject about whom we propose to write this sketch. Her parents, William and Amanda Gilbert, were farmers, and were, like many of their race in those days, poorly prepared to educate the little ones.

In Artishia Garcia was a growing inclination and love for books, and although too young to be enrolled as a pupil in the county school yet she daily went with the school-teacher to and from school, where she remembered much that she heard, and soon could spell and read; hence from her association she was given the name of "little teacher" by the pupils. In this way she was soon able to help the pupils prepare their lessons. father, having no settled pl, moved from one mining district to another for six ys. During this time this little girl learned all that she could from contact with the teachers wherever she went, and became so cautious that at four years of age she was often sent alone with a pocket-book two miles to purchase necessaries at store. In 1878 her parents moved to Louisville, Ky. Here this child entered the public schools, where she remained three years. In September 1881 she became a Christian, and entered the State University, then known as the Normal and Theological Institute, under the presidency of Rev. William J. Simmons, D. D. After spending four years in the normal department she graduated May 13, 1885.

During this time she worked in and out of school, at odd times, wherever she could get work, to earn something to help her mother pay school bills. In the meantime she had united with the Green Street Baptist Church, of Louisville, Ky. Artishia has always been faithful to the Sunday-school, to which she owes much of her spiritual strength. She taught a class when so small she had to stand upon the benches to see all of her class.

The temptations to lucrative positions kept her from entering the college department for awhile, but finally she decided and did so. In 1889 she graduated as valedictorian from the University proper, with the degree of A. B. She then became editor of a magazine, *Women and Children,* which position she gave up to take a chair as teacher in State University, her *Alma Mater,* as instructor in English and Greek grammar, and also acted as secretary of the faculty. She has traveled and lectured throughout the State, under the Woman's Baptist Educational Convention, as State agent and otherwise; has served several years on the Board of Directors of the Colored Orphans' Home and as assistant matron of State University. She has been upon the programmes of some of the largest meetings held in the South; is a good writer; is interested in both home and foreign missions. She is president of three large organizations in the State; has several times been a representative at the National Baptist meetings. She is now a member of the senior class in the Louisville National Medical College. She has saved her earnings and owns property. She advocates the right of woman to engage in any sphere of life. She has not forgotten her mother's help when in school. She is an example of piety and good works; a lover of her race; a coming power for a long neglected people as a leader and benefactor. She has recently received the degree of A. M. in course.

CHAPTER LXXIII.

MARY E. LEE, B. S.

Mrs. Mary E. Lee, *nee* Ashe, daughter of Simon S. and Adelia M. Ashe, was born in Mobile, Alabama, January 12, 1851. Her parents were in good circumstances and her father was and her father was prominent in business and benevolent colored people. In 1860 he purchased a farm in Ohio, in the Vicinity of Wilberforce University where he settled and schooled his children

The subject of this sketch graduated in the scientific department of said institution in 1873, with Misses Mary E. Davis, Julia Shorter, Hallie Q. Brown and Messrs. Alexander D. Delaney and Samuel T. Mitchell, receiving the degree of B. S. She distinguished herself on several occasions by displaying a more than ordinary mind in essays and poems during her course of studies at the university, and was appointed and wrote a class ode, the first in the history of Wilberforce graduating classes. After graduation she taught in the public schools of Galveston, Texas, having previously taught two years in the city of Mobile, Alabama.

Miss Ashe was a successful teacher in both secular and Sunday-schools. On the 30th of December 1873, she was married to Benjamin F. Lee, Professor of Pastoral Theology, Wilberforce University, afterward president of that institution, now Bishop of the A. M. E. Church. The severities of the life of the wife of a Methodist preacher, as well as that of a professor in a college, and the life of six children, have been great tests of the strong character of Mrs. Lee, but she has proven equal to the rigorous demands, and is rewarded by the pleasure of observing the steady development of an interesting family and being a college graduate wife of an African Methodist Bishop.

She has contributed several articles to the columns of the *Christian Recorder* and the *A. M. E. Quarterly Review,* and at present edits the "King's Daughters' Column" in *Ringwood's Journal,* a fashion paper, published by Mrs. Julia Ringwood Coston, Cleveland, Ohio.

Among the writings of Mrs. Lee may be mentioned "Afmerica," a poem that has been copied extensively. The following verses from the composition must take a creditable place in American verse:

Afmerica! her home is here!
She wants nor knows no other home;
No other lands, nor far nor near,
Can charm or tempt her thence to roam.
Her ancestors, like all the rest,
Came from the Eastern Hemisphere,
But she is native of the West;
She'll lend a hand to Africa,
And in her elevation aid,
But here in brave America,
Her home—her only home—is made;
No one has power to send her hence;
This home was planned by Providence.

From her "Voice of the Zephyrs," written while still in college and just in her teens, which, like her "Afmerica", is addressed to the African race, the following is quoted:

Hark! sweeping o'er spicy plains and streams
Of Africa's sunlit shores the balmy breath
Of zephyrs comes, all fragrant with glad,
A joyous song, like some Aeolian harp,
Whose strings are dripping with the sweets blown
From the bosom of a thousand flowers rare.
In deepest silence, low I how to catch

The blissful words wafted in these accents soft:
"Ethiopia shall stretch forth her hands to God,
Her wilderness shall bloom into the land,
The lovely bridal land of Beulah, fair
As Queen of Sheba shall she he adorned,
Her head shall he filled with the wisdom of
King Solomon, her heart shall overflow
With beauty to all humanity;
Then nations shall look up to see her face.
Amen! Blow on, ye winged zephyrs, blow!
Until you bring about the promised time.

Doubtless had fortune favored Mrs. Lee with requisite leisure and more robust health she would be reckoned one of the writers of this country.

In the city of Philadelphia Mrs. Lee is identified with the Ladies' Christian Union Association, the W. C. T. U., and the King's Daughters, also the Women's Mite Missionary Society. In the Afro-American Press Association meeting of 1892 Mrs. Lee represented the *Ringwood Journal* and was elected vice-president of the organization.

Were all the facts mentioned, here wanting, the peculiar womanly spirit, the elevated and the positive personal character of Mrs. Mary E. Lee, would constitute her a worthy subject for the study of young Afro-American women. Every one who knows her bears witness to her sterling qualities and fine sense of proprieties. By the request of her friends she expects to publish a book of poems. This book will, no doubt, be looked for and read with great interest by our aspiring young women.

WOMEN OF DISTINCTION

CHAPTER LXXIV.
MRS. VIRGINIA E. M. HUNT SCOTT.

The lady under whose name this narrative appears was born in New York City, August 26, 1861, the daughter of Holloway W. and Mary Rebecca Hunt, both of whom were born in Newark, N.J. and moved to New York some time prior to the advent of their daughter.

Her father has been entirely deprived of the use of both eyes for more than thirty years, and possibly has gazed but little, if at all, upon his child of whom we now write. He has been in the employment of Trinity Chapel twenty-six years notwithstanding his physical defect. When she was about fifteen years old, her mother, whose tender care a child most needs, was suddenly taken from her by death. Virginia was for some time a pupil under Prof. Charles L. Reason and was in the graduating class when her mother died.

Having to assume the duties of housekeeper for her father (who was blind), she was compelled to leave school before finishing, and was his only domes-tic dependence up to the time of her marriage, February 21, 1889. During this period she continued a fondness for music, having taken her first lessons at the age of nine years under Madam Magnan, who taught her with much success. Her second teacher was Miss Blanche D. Washington, whose instruction she received for seven or eight years, making most wonderful progress. There can be no question but that she owes much of her success to Miss Washington.

In 1881 she gave a concert of amateur performers which was a success in every way and greatly commented upon by the public, the proceeds of which were used in continuing her musical education. After this lengthy course of private instruction she entered the New York Conservatory of Music, where two years were devoted to the organ with much success; also received instruction upon the piano, and in the mean-time played for concerts and regularly for one church. She also taught music as early as her sixteenth year. She has been organist at Mt. Olivet Baptist Church for over ten years, where she plays a very fine and powerful organ of modern make for the largest colored congregation in New York City. The history of the church for which she plays, as well as that of herself, points out very remarkable instances of Afro-American progress. About eight years ago (1884) she entered a piano contest with Miss Minnie St. Clair and Miss Viola Townes (now Mrs. Pilkington) for a gold watch. All three of these ladies occupied high rank in musical circles and were well prepared for the contest. However, after mature consideration, judgment was rendered in favor of Miss Virginia E. M. Hunt (Scott), to whom was awarded the prize.

In 1885 she attended the renowned Dr. Palmer's Choral Union, where she was the only colored participant in a class of between two and three hundred singers.

She is still rising in eminence as a public performer and is doing much to el-evate her race by teaching others to skillfully manipulate instrumental keys.

Beginning life in humble circumstances, with all the discouragements that beset her pathway, she now stands high in the estimation of the very large church which she still serves and of which she is now a member, reflecting credit upon the race, and at the same time affording a living example of the possibil-ities for those upon whose childhood it may seem that fortune has not smiled.

WOMEN OF DISTINCTION.

CHAPTER LXXV.
MRS. ROSA D. BOWSER.

On their arrival in the South the teachers from the North found an almost impenetrable wilderness of ignorance. Only here and there could be found a colored family with a single member able to read. Wherever this was true it was a mark of superior natural intelligence, for with the stringent laws prohibiting the negro from reading he must be no ordinary man who would run the awful risk of being found with a book in his hand. Of such parents was the subject of our sketch born. Henry Dixon, a cabinet maker by trade and a native of Amelia County, was no ordinary man, and his daughter, Rosa, whom he brought with him to Richmond when only a wee tot, inherited from him in larger measure, perhaps, than from her noble mother the traits of character that have distinguished her career. Obedient, thoughtful and quick to understand, it was not long before her teachers were convinced that she would be no mean leader of her people. With systematic training it was not many years before she was thought competent to take charge of a school in her adopted city. Having passed creditable examinations and received her sheepskin from the Richmond Normal and High School, then in charge of Prof. R. M. Manly, she was elected by the Richmond School Board to teach in the Navy Hill group, of which Miss M. E. Knowles, of Massachusetts, was principal. This was at this time, and until 1883, the only group in which the teachers were colored. Her election was a special honor, for, although there were many more colored schools, the Board expressed the opinion that they could not secure competent teachers to fill them.

Possessing, as she did even in these youthful days, stern integrity, invincible purpose and a will strong to command, traits of character more frequently sought in the other sex, she has not been troubled with the question of discipline as most teachers are. But with this apparent sternness Mrs. Bowser possesses a tender heart, which always pulsates with sympathy for the anxious inquirer after knowledge and for the distressed of whatever creed or nationality. Her boys and girls, who can be numbered by the hundreds, would gladly unite in this testimonial to her ability as a teacher and to her warmth of heart as a friend. She did not, like many school-teachers, as soon as elected content herself with pursuing the rut of only her daily routine work in school, but each evening found her either learning more about her profession, reading for the sake of culture, pursuing some new art or perfecting herself in some new accomplishment. That same determination to succeed which characterized her early efforts has run through all her later attempts. Anyone who has conversed with Mrs. Bowser for half an hour will he convinced of the first and second statements, and you have only to spend an evening in her cultured home to be assured of the third and fourth. A well-selected and carefully read library graces her parlor. Specimens of her fine laces, fancy needle-work and wax flowers will be shown at your request, and the calls of a number of music pupils will evidence that she has a name as a musician.

From what has been said one might suppose that the subject of our sketch was so engrossed with her professional and other duties that there was no time for the exercise of the tender passion, but not so; she possesses a woman's heart which, like the lyre, answered to the gentle touch of James H. Bowser, Esq., a former schoolmate, a native of Richmond,scholarly, refined and worthy. Her industry, versatility and good sense, as witnessed by him on various occasions,commended her more highly than all the praises of her friends. Having taught school with marked success seven years, the knot which made them one was tied in the simplest possible style. Ostentation, so objectionable to them, was not indulged on this occasion, not because of inability (for they were both possessed of considerable means), but because their good judgment dictated otherwise. Though a happy one, their married life was short. Scarcely two years had passed before he was called to his reward, beloved by his friends and respected and honored by all who knew him for his bright intellect, sterling good qualities and Christian character.

I need not say that Mrs. Bowser was given up with reluctance when her resignation was handed in to the School Board. The following testimonial from her former teacher is, perhaps, not out of place at this point:

Mrs. Rosa D. Bowser graduated with honor from the Normal School while it was under my charge, and then, with others, was a member of an "ex-senior" class and pursued more advanced studies for one year under my own instruction. She was always a studious, faithful and intelligent scholar, her character always above criticism, and her deportment marked by a dignity, sobriety and respectfulness not common with girls of her age. She had a very successful experience as teacher in the service of the city, and should she wish to teach again I recommend her to you with entire confidence that she would do her work not only faithfully, but wisely and with the approval of yourself and School Board.

Very respectfully, R. M. MANLY.

Testimonials of a similar nature were written by the Superintendent of Schools, Col. E. M. Garnett, by his predecessor, Prof. J. H. Peay and by Miss M. E. Knowles and Messrs. H. G. Carlton and T. P. Crump, who had been her principals. With such indorsements as these it is not surprising that in a short while after the death of her husband she was again called to a teacher's place. She has since served nine years.

In all that concerns the best interests of her people Mrs. Bowser has taken an active part. She was an earnest member and supporter of the first colored educational society of Virginia, of which Prof. J. W. Cromwell, of Washington, was President. As teacher in the Peabody Normal Institute held at Lynchburg, Va. in 1887, under President J. H. Johnston, she added no little to its success by her excellent work as teacher of the model class. It is hardly necessary to say that she became a Christian in early childhood and that her life has been a true exponent of her profession. As a teacher in the Sunday-school she has on more than one occasion represented her school in the State Conventions. In the Ladies' Auxiliary of the Young Men's Christian Association, in missionary societies, in local literary societies, as president of the Woman's Educational Convention of Richmond, of the Normal School *alumni,* she has been ever active. To her ability as teacher and organizer may be attributed her election as president of the State Teachers' Association of Virginia, which she has held for two years, notwithstanding this has, perhaps, more active, progressive educators than any other in the State.

I should not fail to mention that as manager of the Woman's Department of the Colored Fairs held in 1891 and 1892 in Virginia and in 1892 in West Virginia she succeeded in making these not only the most attractive departments, but demon-strative of far more skill among our women than even they dreamed of.

Thus far a truly useful career. May she be spared many more years to help in these various progressive movements.

JAMES H. JOHNSTON

CHAPTER LXXVI.

MRS. M. R. RODGERS WEBB.

While we are searching this country for distinguished women of Afro-American descent we may also turn our eyes to the "islands of the sea," for out of them also there shall come some good material for this temple we are laboring to build.

Out of Jamaica, B. W. I., comes Mrs. Rodgers Webb, who has labored in America for many years, spending more than seventeen years in Texas alone. Born of English parentage mainly, she has labored among the women of the race as *lecturer, missionary, preacher and teacher;* has for a number of years been a newspaper correspondent, and is at present associate editor of the *Texas Reformer;* has traveled extensively in the State, lecturing and visiting more than one hundred and fifty towns, cities and villages. She is well known by leading Afro-American gentlemen of four States, who speak in praiseworthy terms of her work. Some of the subjects upon which she has spent much time, patience and energy, as a lecturer, are as follows: "An Eye-opener to the True Causes of the Unpleasant Condition of the Colored People," "What Best Helps to Character-making."

Mrs. Webb has, no doubt, done much good in her chosen field of labor. She seems to delight in presenting the truth from the public rostrum.

The following are some newspaper clippings and general notices of her, which we subjoin with pleasure:

Mrs. M. R. Rodgers Webb we found very intelligent, broad-gauged, liberal and thoroughly posted—a woman of literary attainments.— *Texarkana Daily Times, Texas, June 20, 1889.*

Mrs. Webb, of superior ability, has given great thought to the condition of the colored race ; means and methods to elevate it; presents valuable suggestions and arguments.— *The Southwestern Republican, Texarkana, Ark., June 29, 1889.*

More than ordinary literary ability.—*Interstate News, Texarkana, Texas.*

Hardly ever have we been more profitably entertained than in listening to this gifted woman—the most sensible and unique expositions; eloquent, earnest, pleasing talker.—*The Bulletin, Birmingham, Ala., December 29, 1889*

Greatly benefited by series of lectures here. Mrs. Webb has closely observed, has taken a keen insight into needs and hindrances of our people. They will certainly be greatly profited.—*Rev. 1. B. Scott, P. E. of the N. E. Church of Marshall, Texas, taken from Southwestern Christian Advocate of January 2, 1890.*

Mrs. Webb lectured in my church and others, to our great satisfaction. Talks interesting and full of valuable information. We recommend her as a lady of culture, worthy of acceptation.—*Fred. H. Wilkins, Pastor Bethesda Baptist Church, Marshall. Texas.*

Mrs. Webb's lectures are among the substantial philosophy of practical and common things; recommend her intellectual worth; will be found among continued and advanced thought to bless her memory.—*Rev. H. S. McMillan, Pastor Ebenezer M. E. Church, Marshall, Texas.*

Mrs. Webb has done effective work in all churches of this city for a month. Lecture expresses the real situation of the negro in a nutshell; awakens deepest thought.— *Rev. W. R. Pettiford, Sixteenth Street Baptist Church, Birmingham, Ala., and President of State Baptist Association.*

CHAPTER LXXVII.
MRS. ADA A. COOPER.

This acute little lady was born in Brooklyn, N. Y., February 6, 1861. She is the daughter of Rev. A. H. Newton and a granddaughter of Robert Hamilton, who was a strong Abolitionist. At a very early age she manifested a desire for books, and before she was five years old she could read and write a little. At the age of eight years she was astonish--ingly brilliant, both in her studies in school and in music; was always apt and could speak from the rostrum with much ease and readiness. At the age of fourteen she wrote a story that was much praised by her teacher. Her mother having died when Ada was only seven years old, she remained with her grandmother until fifteen, when she went to her father, who was then in charge of the A. M. E. Church at Little Rock, Ark. Still desiring to be somebody and to do something to help forward the cause of humanity and civilization, she continued in study with an earnestness that was simply surprising. She wrote another story, "The Bride of Death," when only fifteen years old. Remaining in Arkansas one and a half years, she went to New Orleans and spent one year; then going to Raleigh, N. C., with her father and stepmother, she entered Shaw University. Being a very *poor*,her department, and, as a result, she was often held in *ridicule* by those who could do better. They often referred to her shabby dress and plain clothing in such a way as to try her very *soul* with *vexation*. However, she was only stimulated to greater effort, knowing that a *well-cultivated brain was far more ornamental* and *useful* than fine dress. She pushed her way on and on until she was recognized as without an equal in her class in elocution and composition, being only seventeen. At the age of eighteen her story, "The Bride of Death," was published in the *North Carolina Republican,* edited by William V. Turner. This called forth many congratulations from the reading public. Owing to circumstances she did not remain in the institution to graduate, having spent three years there, during which she supported herself by teachings, etc.

Returning to Brooklyn, she remained a while and then went to Newbern, N. C. It was while at this town (last named) she was called upon by a committee to read the poem on emancipation celebration day. She accepted the invitation, but afterwards remembering that she had not a *decent dress to wear,* what to do was the question. Finally, she succeeded in borrowing a dress of a friend. This necessity so humiliated the girl of tender years that she resolved that since she was compelled by necessity to read in a *borrowed dress* she would not (as was the custom) read a *borrowed poem.* She set to work and made a poem from her own original brain and read it upon the occasion mentioned. It so stirred the people that it *yet lives* in the memory of many who heard it.

Some time was spent in teaching school throughout North Carolina at various points. She then came to Raleigh, N. C., and was married to Mr. William R. Harris, to whom she had been engaged for six or seven years, and who was, at the time of marriage, a teacher in St. Augustine Normal School. Just eight months after this happy union she was left a widow.

After the death of her husband she taught one year in St. Augustine Normal School, and from there accepted a position in the city graded schools of Raleigh, and at the same time edited the "Woman's Column" in the Outlook.. Now health at this time fails, and a hospital operation is the only very slight hope. Death stares her in the face, for the chances were that she might die ere the operation was completed. She decided to try and *did* withstand the keen blade of the surgeon; she conquered her disease and yet lives.

Mrs. Cooper is a brilliant scholar, a pleasant lecturer, a fine writer and an earnest, energetic Christian woman. Her speech on the 5th day of November 1891, at the North Carolina Industrial Fair, in connection with the Interstate Exposition, was, possibly, the best effort of her life.

She has recently joined the A. M. E. Conference and is now at work in that Church, and on the 13th day of January 1892, was married to Rev. A. B. Cooper, a young but rising A. M. E. minister.

Though her way has been beset by many an obstacle, often disappointed and discouraged, she has steadily passed forward, climbing higher each year. Young and accomplished as she is there can scarcely be any doubt about the brightness of her future.

She is accustomed to visiting the sick-room, jails and huts of the poor, and reading the Bible she kneels and offers a word of prayer with them. When leaving them she always, in a very comforting way, commends them to Jesus Christ, who alone can, at will, heal the sick, free the captive and provide for the poor. Who can estimate the good this woman may do in this way? Who will do likewise? Truly the call for such women in this special mission is indeed great!

CHAPTER LXXVIII.

MISS MARY JONES.

This young lady was born in Halifax county, North Carolia, May 1, 1869. When she was only seven years old her mother died, leaving her and five other children. Mary and the three younger ones were taken to Raleigh and divided among her mother's relatives. From this time Miss Jones has had to struggle for her own support. Her aunt, who had the oversight of her, very soon hired her out to make her self-supporting.

When she was fourteen or more years old she had been given only six months' schooling, her father having deserted her since the death of her mother; and desir-ing to go to school, she made her intentions known to her Church, of which Rev. W. A. Green was pastor. This kind and very benevolent minister at once advised the Church to help her, stating her circumstances; but despite his advice the ma-jority of the members declined to help her. Still determined to be "somebody," she made her way to the residence of the president of Shaw University. Having no money with which to pay expenses, she was there refused admission. Again, she thought to try her Church and, if possible, get the Church to help her just one year. She went before the body and pleaded with them, and they did agree so to do. She again went to Shaw University and was allowed to enter the school with the under-standing that her Church would help her one year. Here she remained two months, and the promised aid failing to come, she was notified to leave for non-payment of bills, as the school had no beneficiary fund. She asked for work to pay back the board of two months but at the time there was no place open to her. She found em-ployment as a domestic and was earning some money to refund to the institution. But before she had been at her new home two weeks, the president found employ-ment for her in the nursing of sick in Leonard Medical Hospital, where she could also attend a few classes in the literary branches at the same time. He thus went for her and she accepted this new work and at once entered upon duty. During the following three years she found work enough at the school to keep her going in some way, attending only a few classes daily and studying hard at night. She was in the meantime developing some talent as a songstress and began to attract much attention at the commencement exercises each year, at the same time standing first in two of her daily classes. At commencement of her third year she carried off the first prize in a recitation contest among the young ladies of the seminary.

When she left Shaw University, having worked and supported herself for three years, she began public life in reality. She taught one winter in the Greensboro Normal and Collegiate Institute, and then went North and took lessons in elocu-tion and music under a very popular and noted Italian professor of New York City. Since returning from the North, she has traveled extensively, singing and reading before the public in the large cities and towns. She speaks with freedom and ease. She sings with melody, pathos and a charm of voice that makes one who hears her once most sure to want to hear her again. Indeed, she is in some respects a remarkable young woman. Her mother died early and her father deserted her soon afterwards.

From that time she has been her own bread-winner and has made her way into prominence over many and great obstacles. Her voice is indeed a delightful chord of fine, mellow sweetness of song. She is temperate and is a consistent Christian. She has a bright future before her, and if she fails to make herself felt, it will cer-tainly be the fault of some one. Her steady onward progress from humble condi-tions to better in the past bespeak great things for her in the future.

CHAPTER LXXIX.

MISS ANNA HOLLAND JONES.

The subject of this narrative has been fortunate as to heredity and opportunities. Her father and five uncles were graduated from Oberlin College in the '40's and '50's when colored graduates were few. In those early days they were designated by Henry Highland Garnet as "the most educated colored family in America." She was born in Canada, and at an early day was sent to Oberlin. She graduated from the Oberlin High School, and later graduated also from Oberlin College in 1875. She was one of the youngest in a class of sixty students, among whom there was only one colored member beside herself. During her college course she rarely stood second to any in scholarship, and in her junior year was elected class essayist. After grad-uation she was made assistant principal of the Wilberforce Institute in Chatham, Canada. Severity of climate led her to seek employment in the States. She was appointed to a position in the city schools of Indianapolis, and afterwards in the schools of St. Louis. In these she taught with success and acceptance. She later accepted a position as head of the normal department and instructor in Latin and geography in Lincoln Institute, Jefferson City, Mo., where she labored for four years. In 1885 she accepted the position she now holds as lady-principal and in-structor in the English language, literature and history in Wilberforce University.

Though teaching especially these branches, she has been called upon at times to teach zoology, logic, German and elocution. The long time which she has been engaged in teaching, the branches she has taught and the length of time she has held important positions in one of our best schools, Wilberforce University, is sufficient evidence of her worth and success as a teacher. She regards her work in the classroom, in stimulating young men and women to take a high stand and live a pure and useful life, as of far more importance than a mere training in books for the sake of intellectual development alone. She regards it a mistake to seek mental development at the neglect of the moral and practical side of the student. Upon one occasion she said, "He is not a true teacher who is not both a true friend and teacher." Her class-room is said to be more characterized by enthusiasm and zeal than by military order. She is yet a hard student, working as hard as she ever did in college. She has written some articles and sketches for magazines and periodicals, but writing almost entirely under a *nom de plume.* The whole tenor of facts relative to her life and works present a clear proof not only of the ability and am-bition of this rising star of the West, but a forcible setting forth of her good traits of character as an educator. She is a scholar, a profound teacher, a race lover, a Christian lady, struggling hard to make practical leaders for an oppressed people.

MRS. WILLIE ANN SMITH.

CHAPTER LXXX.

MRS. WILLIE ANN SMITH.

Mrs. Willie Ann Smith, nee Burnett, was born in Goldsboro, N. C., of pious parents. She exhibited an early love for books and was a remarkably apt pupil. Her intellectual aspirations and moral endowments soon reached a degree of prominence in the school and community to call forth frequent commendations and gained for her the deepest interest of her teachers and the highest respect of her acquaintances.

When quite a child she read and re-read the Bible, "Pilgrim's Progress", "Uncle Tom's Cabin", and other publications which cultivated a taste and inspired an abiding love for the pure and the good.

After completing her education Miss Burnett was married to Mr. E. E. Smith, with whom she has lived happily, sharing alike with him life's bitters and sweets.

A faithful wife, a devoted mother and an accomplished lady render her a model of her sex and the fond idol other pleasant home, where she is wont to receive her large circle of admiring friends. As a teacher in the graded schools of her native city she has taken rank with the progressive and industrious instructors.

Mrs. Smith has written some essays and articles for the press of real merit. She is a cogent reasoner, a deep thinker, and always handles her subjects in a masterly manner, which never fails to fascinate and sway her hearers. She reads extensively, retains what she reads, and is, therefore, a lady of varied information on live issues. Mrs. Smith has traveled considerably in the United States as well as abroad. She has enjoyed the distinction of visiting many cities and settlements in Liberia and other sections of Africa. She presided as mistress of the United States Legation and Consulate General near the government of the Republic of Liberia with grace and dignity, in which capacity she was brought into contact with the 'most cultured, refined and prominent ladies of that country. She has from time to time been elected president of various organizations of the women of her State. She was at one time chosen Most Eminent Grand Matron of the M. E. G. C. of the Eastern Star of North Carolina, where she showed executive powers of no mean order. Mrs. Smith is a zealous and consistent temperance advocate, having been connected with temperance organizations from childhood. She is a modest, affable, benevolent, Christian lady whose hand of charity is never closed. She is an ardent lover of her race, and entertains high hopes for its future glory, for the achievement of which she is a persistent laborer.

CHAPTER LXXXI.

MISS NANCY JONES.

Nancy Jones was born January 28, 1860, on a farm near Hopkinsville, Christian county, Kentucky. She was the slave of Jack Edmonds and of purely African descent. About the close of the war of the rebellion Nancy and her mother drifted to Memphis, Tennessee, where the American Missionary Association early organized schools for the freedmen. The mother had two ambitions: to buy a home and educate her daughter. By industry, frugality and patience she accomplished both objects. She was familiar with all forms of domestic work, but excelled as a laundress, and for years took in large washings. Sometimes Nancy helped her mother, who assigned her certain pieces as her share of the work and pay. Sometimes she hired out to white families nights and mornings. In this way she attended school at Le Moyne Normal Institute for several years. During one of the revival meetings at this school she was converted and united with the Beal Street Baptist Church.

She early expressed the purpose of going to Africa as a missionary, but her friends regarded it as a youthful fancy. She was fond of visiting the sick and providing for the needy. Saturday afternoons she went around the neighborhood inviting children to Sabbath-school. Where they had no suitable clothing she begged half-worn garments from white families and made them over for the children upon condition of attending Sabbath-school. If any children failed to keep their promise, Nancy took away the clothing she had given them.

In 1881 she entered' Fisk University, and graduated from its normal course in 1886. Her summer vacations were spent in teaching country schools, where she stirred up the farmers to more thrifty ways of managing and their wives to better housekeeping.

In the fall of 1886, Miss Jones offered her services to the American Board of Commissioners for Foreign Missions and was accepted. Her mother generously assisted in preparations for the outfit. On the route from Memphis to Boston Miss

Jones spoke to several large gatherings of cultivated ladies and made many warm friends for herself and her work. She sailed from Boston the last of January. At Liverpool she took steamer for Natal by way of Cape Town and reached Inhambane in the spring. At Kambini she joined Mr. and Mrs. B. F. Ousley.

She lives by herself in a corrugated iron house (sent from Liverpool in sections) and receives children whom she can persuade to leave the kraals and make a home with her. These she teaches to work, to read, to sew. She also has a day school of forty or fifty children. At first it was difficult to keep them at lessons. If a boy proposed to go fishing, the whole band rushed off to the river. Now they are not so wild.

When Mr. and Mrs. Ousley were obliged to return to America for a year, Miss Jones bravely remained alone. Once she made an extended trip attended only by natives. Miss Jones has the honor of being the first unmarried colored woman to be commissioned by the American Board.

MRS. MARGARET HARRIS

MISS MARY E. BRITTON.

CHAPTER LXXXII.

MISS MARY E. BRITTON.

The subject of this sketch was born in Lexington, Ky., more than thirty-two years ago, where she still lives and teaches in the public schools. She was also educated in the schools of this thriving little city, and now seeks to help lift up others as she herself has been lifted up.

Miss Britton has done much in the field of primary education for the race. She stands high in her own city as a refined, intelligent, faithful leader and teacher. She has done much for the general public in the line of newspaper writing and agitation. Prominent among the papers in which her writings have appeared we mention the *American Citizen,* a Lexington weekly, *the Cincinnati Commercial,* the *Lexington Herald,* the *Daily Transcript,* Lexington, Ky., *the Indianapolis World,* Indiana, the *Cleveland Gazette, Ohio, The Courant,* Louisville, Ky., *The Ivy,* Baltimore, Md., the *American Catholic Tribune,* etc.

Mrs. A. E. Johnson said of her

She has an excellent talent for comparing, explaining, expounding and criticizing, and has made no small stir among the city officials and others for their unjust discriminations against worthy citizens.

Mrs. I. Garland Penn says of her:

Miss Britton claims to be neither a poet nor a fiction writer, but she is a prolific writer on many subjects of a solid, practical, forcible character. Teaching is her forte, and she prefers to perfect herself in both the science and art of the profession. As a teacher she is greatly respected and esteemed.

A friend in the *Indianapolis World* speaks of her in the following complimentary manner:

The city (Lexington, Ky.) officials are building the colored people a school-house on the corner of Fourth and Campbell streets, and Miss Mary E. Britton, the "Meb" of our literature, smiles even more pleasantly than usual. She has done a great deal to educate the youth here under the most vexing circumstances, and none can appreciate or rejoice more in better facilities than she.

Mr. I. Garland Penn also speaks of her as follows:

Miss Britton is a specialist. Recognizing the fact that one cannot satisfactorily take in the whole field, she wisely concludes to pursue and perfect herself in such branches of it as she feels confident are hers by adaptation. Such a course cannot fail to give success to the one pursuing it.

The *Lexington Herald* had the following to say of her when she was on its editorial staff:

The journalistic work seems to be the calling of Miss Britton. No other field would suit her so well. In manner and style her composition is equal to any of her sex, white or black. As an elocutionist she stands next in rank to the accomplished Hallie Q. Brown. No literary programme gotten up by the Lexingtonians is complete without the rendition of some choice selection by her —Miss Britton. She is a hard student, a great reader, and a lover of poetry. Miss Britton is an acknowledged teacher of high intellectual attainments.

The *American Catholic Tribune,* Cincinnati, says of her:

It is with pleasure that we call the attention of our readers to a paper read by that talented young woman and rising journalist, Miss Mary E. Britton, at the State Teachers' Institute held in Danville, Ky., last week. Without commenting on the terms it proposes, we give it to the public for careful perusal.

The *Christian Soldier* (Lexington, Ky.) also thus refers to her:

Miss Mary E. Britton is one of the brightest stars which shine in Dr. Simmons' great magazine, *Our Women and Children,* and the magnitude of those stars is national. Lexington never gets left when it comes to pure, good and sensible women.

Suffice it to say that we need among us more such staunch and invincible champions of the cause of right and equal justice to all men. Miss Britton well deserves the place she occupies in the hearts of her people at home as well as throughout this country, wherever she is known. Who can predict her future?

WOMEN OF DISTINCTION.

CHAPTER LXXXIII.
MRS. C. L. PURCE.
(MATRON SELMA UNIVERSITY).

The subject of this sketch is the honored wife of Rev. L. C. Purce, D.D. President of Selma University, Selma, Alabama. Her maiden name was Miss Charlotte Cooper Sinkler. She is the eldest daughter of Mr. Paris Cooper Sinkler and Mrs. Tina Sinkler and was born in Charleston, S. C., August 4, 1855. She attended public and private schools in Charleston. Her mother and father dying while she was quite young, she was not only sister to her younger brothers and sisters, but acted the parents' part as well. She was baptized into the fellowship of the Morris Street Baptist Church in 1874 by Rev. Jacob Legare.

In 1877 she went North and spent several years with relatives in Easton, Pennsylvania. On January I, 1885, she was married to Rev. C. L. Purce in Philadelphia by Rev. Dennis, pastor of Shiloh Baptist Church. The couple then went to Selma, Ala., where they have been engaged ever since in doing what good they can to educate and elevate their people. She is the happy mother of one child, John William, who is seven years old. Mrs. Purce has been the matron of Selma University ever since her husband accepted the presidency in December 1886. She is a devoted mother, an earnest wife and a perfect helpmate. Shoulder to shoulder with her husband she has done all in her power to lift up the moral tone and elevate the good name of the institution which has called out all her noble, womanly and queenly character. She has a strong personality, marked by those motherly qualities which are so essential to a successful matron. The young men and women love her and confide in her as in a loving mother. Mrs. Purce is under appointment of the New England Women's Society, who claim her as "a faithful worker". She seems born to fill the place she has filled so successfully for the last six years.

As a housekeeper she is abreast of the times, especially in Northern methods. Anyone entering her home or her department is struck by the method and system of her household duties. This is one of the most beneficial lessons to the young women. If the young women need anything in their school-life, it is proper instruction in regard to their home-life, their habits. and domestic duties. Many girls in boarding-schools are from rural districts, and as a general thing they need instruction as to the duties of home-life, hence when they attend school they must not only be taught in "books," but they must be taught how to use the broom, the dust-brush, the needle and the washboard. The work of the matron is very trying.

The girls are to be taught these duties, and it takes much time and patience. Mould these girls aright and when they return home they carry lessons into their homes that they could not have understood from reading books. Mrs. Purce tries to be practical and exact in her dealings with her pupils and finds much pleasure in visiting their rooms while in school and their homes in vacation to see the changes wrought therein. She is loved all over Alabama, and whoever have the pleasure of meeting and being with her confess that she is the equal of her companion.

CHAPTER LXXXIV.

MISS HATTIE K. GREEN.

This young lady, the daughter of Julia C. and Alfred Green; was born in Cleveland, Ohio, January 8, 1868. Her parents made many plans for her future, but before the object of their affections and labors was one year old, the father fell asleep in death, leaving the mother with three small children for which to provide. Brave and full of hope, the mother decided that she would give Hattie a chance, and if she showed any aptness, she would continue her efforts to help educate her. She started to school with this condition before her. She did indeed show aptness, and in June 1883, graduated from the grammar department of the city school at the age of fifteen years. The mother, encouraged by this, said, "Go to the high school." This meant a long, hard task for the mother, who, when her attention was called to this fact, still said, "Go on." Hattie went on, and January 27, 1888, graduated from the Central High School. Then the mother said, "Go to the normal school," but before she had been very long out of the high school ill health became her portion. Still determined she patiently endured sickness until able to enter the normal school, from which she graduated June 19, 1890.

Application was made to the School Board for a position as teacher; being colored the matter was delayed for some time, as the schools are mixed with both races. Finally, she was given a position, which she has held till now. She has been a member of the Congregational Church for seven or eight years; is a consecrated Christian and much loved at home and at school; kind-hearted, industrious, painstaking and faithful as a teacher.

While she is quite young, yet she is promising, and has in her the elements to make a great and noble woman.

CHAPTER LXXXV.

AFRO-AMERICAN WOMEN AS EDUCATORS.

Yet whirl the glowing wheels once more,
And mix the bowl again;
Seethe fate! the ancient elements,
Heat, cold, wet, dry, and peace, and pain.

Let war and trade and creeds and song
Blend, ripen race on race,
The sun-burnt world a man shall breed
Of all the zones and countless days.

No ray is dimmed, no atom worn,
My oldest force is good as new,
And the fresh rose on yonder thorn
Gives back the bending heavens in dew.

—Emerson.

The possibilities and general trend of social reforms and universal advancement largely depend, as society is now constructed, upon the co-operation of the feminine with the masculine element. The truth of the statement is perhaps nowhere more forcibly illustrated than in the various departments of the educational field, where the efforts of women have not only changed the entire atmosphere of the school-room, but also have produced many other changes in the right direction. "Large bodies move slowly", but one by one the States are falling in line and are employing women as teachers holding important positions, as directors, supervisors, superintendents, etc.

Woman is said to be especially strong in the details of an art. Teaching is a series of details out of which we finally develop a science—an art. This may in part explain the fact that woman is in some respects a greater success in the school-room than man, where, as in the home, she seems "to the manner born," and develops rare executive ability. Is it not possible also that it is easier for women as a class to "become as little children"? without which qualification it is difficult to enter the "Kingdom of Heaven"—the hearts of the little ones.

The elements which enter into the composition of true womanhood are not restricted, and when we point with pardonable pride to the achievements of our race in comparatively few years, we also feel that the noble women of the race have done their full share of this magnificent work.

As teachers they have shown that spirit of hardy endurance, combined with patient self-sacrifice, from which springs heroic deeds; and by it they have helped to lay the foundations of a harmonious race development deep and strong, upon which the youths of today and of succeeding generations must place the superstructure. Necessity is the mother of invention and applying the implied principle to the urgent necessities of our case "in equity", these teachers, instinctively, as it were, early adopted the tenets of the New Education as the most rational if not a royal road to knowledge.

The industrial idea in education has received their hearty co-operation, because in it they recognize the safest method of fitting youth for practical, productive citizenship; and from the kindergarten to the university, from the normal to the industrial school, as supervisors and as specialists, they have shown an aptitude for all-round honest work bounded only by the limitations of time and space. Often, out of slender salaries, they have laid the foundation of the school library, the kindergarten, or the industrial school. In fact, they seem to have considered no sacrifice of time or money too great which would in any way benefit the race. Thus, spending their lives for one single and unselfish end, they have put into the work their fullest and highest personality; and upon this more depends in the development of character, which is all that counts in the long run, than upon the use of the text-book.

Within the last decade we have had a flood of talk (small and otherwise) of articles and would-be legislation upon the so-called "Negro Problem," and its presumable solution; meanwhile our worthy teachers, many of whom are women, have patiently toiled on, in season and out of season, solving a knotty point here, correcting an error there, and really accomplishing more toward the final solution of the problem than all the articles, talk and legislation combined.

At the close of a recent gathering of colored teachers in a former slave State one of the prominent daily papers contained the following editorial:

The annual meeting of the State Colored Teachers' Association, which closed this evening, has been a most interesting event. Without personal observation it would be quite impossible to form an idea how interesting. The remarkable character of the gathering itself of two hundred colored teachers from all over the State; the visible evidences of culture and refinement; the excellence of the music, largely due to the development of a natural and God-given faculty; the brightness and proficiency of the model classes taken from the colored schools of our city; the high range of thought and knowledge covered by the speakers and essayists—all this had to be seen and heard to be appreciated.

There was something, too, which recalled the old saying that "One half of the world does not know how the other half lives". It is certain that the majority of white citizens have little real knowledge of the high attainment reached in the art of teaching and in scholarship by those who constitute the membership of the State Colored Teachers' Association.

While the magazinists are writing, and the orators are orating, and the directors of divinity are preaching over the "Race Problem," and even Henry Watterson is confessing that his own wisdom is inadequate and that he will be obliged to leave the matter in the hands of God, these teachers are solving it by acquiring and imparting to others that knowledge which is power and the best qualification for the lawful use of liberty.

Thus, throughout the land, in the midst of unyielding obstacles, to use the words of one of our most distinguished women, "We are rising", as all who are equal to the task of rising above their prejudices are willing to admit.

An estimate of the extent of the educational work, which is being accomplished by our women, can be drawn from the following statistics, issued by the Commissioner of Education for 1890 -'91, of the common schools in those States containing the highest per cent. of colored teachers:

1890—'91.

STATES	PUPILS ENROLLED IN THE COMMON SCHOOLS	TEACHERS, COLORED	
	COLORED.	MALE	FEMALE
Alabama	118,712	1,496	812
Arkansas	63,830	862	270
Delaware	5,602	54	45
District of Columbia	14,147	40	225
Florida	37,342	403	282
Georgia*_	150,702	1,290	1,208
Kentucky	54,125	586	650

Louisiana	49,671	500	301
Maryland	34,796	217	491
Mississippi	173,378	1,835	1,377
Missouri*	34,622	308	418
North Carolina	115,812	1,370	988
South Carolina	116,535	958	664
Tennessee	105,458	992	753
Texas	104,512	1,639	914
Virginia	123,579	928	1,080
West Virginia	6,428	93	91
Total	**1,309,251**	**13,567**	**10,497**

* Teachers in Florida, Georgia and Missouri classi ied according to U. S. census.

Out of the total 24,064 teachers in the common schools of these States, as given in the preceding table, 43 percent in round numbers, or about one-half of the entire teaching force, are women, and then we have not taken into account the private and denominational schools, which, founded and mainly supported by missionary benevolence, have so materially contributed to the development of the South; and when we consider that the majority of the women who make up this percentage work for less wages than skilled nurses receive, and that often they walk miles, through mud, wet and cold, to buildings called school-houses that will barely afford shelter to beasts of the field; when we find them continuing in this work year after year more from a desire to advance the race than from any pecuniary advantage derived from teaching; when we realize that the children who sit daily under their loving and watchful care have also often walked miles with scarcely any protection from the inclemency of the weather (for we do not find the South one long summer day during the Northern winter months), and with little food to satisfy the appetite of youths, we begin to know something of the innate heroism of our race.

The Rev. A. D. Mayo, that well-known benefactor of humanity, who in discussing any phase of educational work speaks from years of experience, has recently issued a book of three hundred pages, entitled "Southern Women in the Educational Movement in the South". Referring to the education of the colored race he says:

And especially is the colored woman teacher—competent in acquirement, character, professional ability, religious consecration, womanly tact and practical, patient industry—such a benediction to her people as nobody can understand unless, like myself, he has seen year after year the development of this class of the teaching body in the border cities and through all the Southern States.

There are probably 8,000 colored women teaching school, the great majority of them in the common schools. Of course, too many of them are every way incompetent, and too few thoroughly qualified for this greatest of all sorts of American woman's work. But a larger number every year are doing better service, and a considerable class are so good that I never spend an hour in the school-room with one of them without feeling that the colored woman has a natural aptitude for teaching not yet half understood by her own people, but certain to make her a most powerful influence in the future of both races in the South. * * * Here is the providential furnishing in this native, loving kindness, unselfishness, endless patience, overflowing humor and sympathetic insight into child-nature for the office of teacher, with the added qualification of suitable education, moral stamina and the social refinements that come so easily to the colored woman.

Perhaps you ask, *Cui Bono?* What are the results of this work on the part of our women? In reply we direct you to the Institute for Colored Youth in Philadelphia, where, for years, Mrs. Fannie Jackson Coppin, a woman known and honored on both sides of the Atlantic for nobility of character and scholarly attainments, has been the presiding genius, and where, as a result of her untiring efforts, successful preparatory, high, normal and industrial departments are conducted, the last mentioned having at least ten well-taught trades; to the Miner Normal School of Washington, D. C., which was for a long time very successfully managed by Miss Martha Briggs, and since by Miss Lucy Moten, under whose excellent guidance it has sustained its high reputation; to the Agassiz School of Cambridge, Mass., one of .the best managed and equipped schools of the State, of which Miss Maria Baldwin is principal; to the many schools of the South Atlantic and South Central Divisions, and to the increasing number in all divisions of the United States, which have well-educated women of our race at the head, upon the corps of instructors, or as supervisors; to the refining. influences which these women impart to the home, church and social life of the communities in which they work; and, finally, to the moral and intellectual development of character in the young people who have come under their tuition, who, in turn, have entered the various avenues of life and are there making for themselves and their race name and fame.

It has been well and wisely said that "A race no less than a nation is prosperous in proportion to the intelligence of its women". A race that can boast of a Briggs, a Coppin, a Moten, a Jones, a Baldwin, a Garnet, a Howard; of graduates of Oberlin, Ann Arbor, Wellesley and other famous institutions at home and abroad among its prominent educators, need have little fear of its future prosperity.

"Whatever you would have appear in a nation's life you must put into its schools" reads a Prussian motto. American civilization, with wise forethought, changes this to read, " Whatever you would have appear in a nation's life, you must *teach its women*." Following out this line of argument it follows that there are many ways outside of professional teaching by which women have become general educators, and our women have shown themselves to be capable of adopting all of the nineteenth century measures for the development of that which is best in humanity. The professions of law, medicine, dentistry, etc., have found in them able exponents. Among these may be mentioned Doctors McKinney of New York, Anderson of Philadelphia, Jones of St. Louis, Gray of Cincinnati.

In literature we have, among others, Mrs. Frances E. Harper, Mrs. A. J. Cooper, Miss Ida B. Wells, Mrs. Julia Ringwood Coston, editor of *Ringwood's*

Journal of Fashion; "Victoria Earle," Miss Lillian Lewis, a salaried writer for the *Boston Herald;* Miss Florence Lewis, who has won an enviable position as a journalist on some of the white periodicals of Philadelphia.

In music, Mesdames Selika, Sissieretta Jones and many other prominent queens of song. And it is not presuming too much to say that each of the fine arts is worthily represented by our women.

Sixty years ago, according to the United States Commissioner of Labor, there were but seven paying industrial occupations for American women. Now there are three hundred and forty-six. In each of these industries colored women are gradually pushing their way to the front, and wherever they take with them intelligence and refinement they become an educational factor whose value cannot be overestimated. Scattered throughout the cities, towns and villages are numerous colored women who are conducting some prosperous business enterprise which they have undertaken voluntarily, or that has been thrust. upon them by circumstance. One instance of which we have personal knowledge shows what can be accomplished under difficulties. Mrs. D —, a lady of much native genius, was born a slave and has never attended school, although by various means she has acquired a rudimentary education. Assisted by her husband she succeeded in acquiring a considerable amount of valuable property in one of the rapidly growing cities of the West. Besides rearing a large family of children this woman found time to do a great variety of church, Sunday-school and benevolent work, and was one of the founders of the Colored Orphans' Home of that city.

A few years ago the husband died; the children were leaving the parental roof to form homes of their own; and feeling that she would soon be compelled to take entire charge of her business affairs or employ an agent, at the age of fifty-two she secured private instruction and applying herself with zeal to the intricacies of arithmetic and English prose composition is, at the time of writing, ably illustrating that " Labor conquers all things."

Every community furnishes brilliant examples of what our women accomplish in church and Sunday-school work, while Mrs. Harper and Mrs. Amanda Smith have gained national reputation in a combination of temperance and evangelical work. In that urgent necessity—prison reform—Mrs. Alice Dugged Cary has made a brave struggle to better the conditions of life among the colored convicts of Georgia, and in other States women are making the convict system, with all which that system implies as now conducted, the subject of careful study and attention. Thus, in their work for the prevention and cure of intemperance, poverty and crime, our women are learning to deal with the most difficult problem which sociology affords us, and the longer they grapple with these problems the more fully is it forced upon them that the home must be the corner-stone of our social structure, and that here—where education should and does begin, let its tendencies be true or false, elevating or pernicious—woman's influence is the strongest for good or for evil.

As wives and mothers, as elder daughter or sister, as friend or counselor, our women have made heroic sacrifices to educate children and establish refined Christian homes—sacrifices that the world at large will never be able to appreciate--- and as the great body of mothers becomes more liberally educated their work will be yet more effective. Looking around at the result of the efforts of a past generation of mothers, and bearing in mind the fearful odds against which they had to con-tend, it would seem that even ordinary respect for the dead demands that in some suitable place a monument shall be erected to their memory, bearing the simple inscription, "To the Noble Mothers of the Negro Race," or words to that effect, which shall properly testify to the nobility of their lives and deeds.

Home, school and society—these three act and react one upon the other in such way that whatever affects one affects the other; together, they are the triple forces which shape a race and make for its eternal weal or woe. Give us, then, in every sense of the expression, truly educated mothers, earnest educators and wise leaders of society, and not only is our race development, in a general way,. secured, but also that perfection of character or broad culture, which Matthew Arnold defines as "a *harmonious perfection*", developing all sides of our nature, a *general perfection,* developing all parts of our society."

MRS. J. SILONE-YATES.

Atlanta University

CHAPTER LXXXVI.

ATLANTA UNIVERSITY.

L ocated in Atlanta, Ga., was one of the pioneer schools for the freedmen and their children.

Scarcely had the last guns of the late war ceased firing when the founders of this institution began the work from which has developed what now answers to the name of the Atlanta University, said by many to be the foremost and best equipped school in the South attended by the youth of the freedmen.

About a mile out from the center of the busy city, but connected with it by electric cars, are its seventy acres of land, four large brick buildings, a large barn and three cottages, two of which are the homes of the president and one of the professors.

The following clipping from the Atlanta University's leaflet, No.4, will give some idea of the character of the school:

The broad nature, however, which the work of the school almost from the first assumed, together with its relations to the State and public, made it desirable that it should avoid an exclusively denominational connection and develop an independent life under the guidance of its own self-perpetuating board of trustees, after the well-approved pattern of the great colleges and universities of the country.

Besides a full college course based upon the best New England models there is a college preparatory course of three years, a normal course of four years, a grammar course, a model school of primary scholars, serving as a practice school for the normal students, and a mechanical course. Moreover, instruction in wood-working, turning, iron-working and mechanical drawing is given to all boys; and instruction in cooking, sewing, dress-making, nursing and housekeeping duties to girls; and instruction in printing and newspaper and job work to optional classes of both boys and girls.

The last issue of the catalogue shows a record of 244 boys and 317 girls. Of that number 233 are boarders, 328 are day pupils.

The number of States represented is eleven; the total number of pupils is 561. The number of teachers and officers is thirty.

There are 235 graduates from the college and normal courses, nearly all of whom, together with hundreds of-post undergraduates, are engaged in teaching and other useful work in Georgia and surrounding States.

The real estate together with the library of 7,000 volumes, apparatus and other equipment are valued at not less than a quarter of a million dollars.

In former years it has received aid from the Freedman's Bureau, the Slater Fund, the American Missionary Association, together with an annual appropriation of $8,000 from the State of Georgia. But now it stands, as it were, in its own strength, with bright prospects and justifiable assurances for continued progress and sure development.

It has been and is still the purpose of the Atlanta University to send out men and women of any race or nationality who may have gained admittance within its walls, rounded and well-equipped in mind and character to uplift their fellow-men, to give. Special service helpful to those with whom they must come in immediate contact in life.

The past and present assure us that its labors are not in vain, and that ere long this whole. Southland will feel more effectually than now its influence for developing *true worth in men* and *women*.

343

CHAPTER LXXXVII.

MARY E. HARPER, B. E.

This lady of the rostrum was born in Zanesville, Ohio, and remained in that State till two and a half years of age, when her. father died and her mother, Mrs. F. E. W. Harper, moved to the East, where Mary spent most of her early life: She received her early primary training in the public schools of 'Baltimore and Philadelphia. Sometime later they moved into the State of Massachusetts, where Mary finished her education, graduating with honors. Afterwards she taught school in Virginia for several years, and, also, in Maryland. She had previously shown some taste for elocution by converting a chair into a rostrum, the family and visitors at the same time composing her audience to which she would speak from this very modern platform, addressing herself to the question of slavery. Her speech was in the following words: "The negroes shall be free". At this time she was quite a child of three or four years.

She had evidently imbibed these thoughts from her mother, who had been a champion of the cause of abolition.

Mary's fondness for the public rostrum finally induced her mother to send her to the National School of Elocution and Oratory at Philadelphia from which she graduated as Bachelor of Elocution.

After this she took a course in Boston under the instruction of the well-known actress, Miss Rachel Naah, and later took lessons (under Miss Julia Thomas) in " Psycho-Physical Culture."

She has read in the principal churches of Boston; has traveled extensively in America, reading to the cultured people throughout the East, West and South. Many of the largest and best churches and halls have been opened to her.

The following are some of her press notices, and are very complimentary to her as well, as they bespeak much for her possibilities as an elocutionist. Miss Harper partakes of many of her mother's good traits as a public speaker, and is destined to do much good for her country and especially her race:

The poem was recited in an excellent style.—*Brooklyn Eagle.*

Miss Mary E. Harper, the well-known elocutionist, adding much to the general enjoyment by her fine recitations and readings.--*Sunday Item, Brooklyn.*

Having had the rare pleasure of hearing Miss Harper render a number of selections, we are free to say she is well fitted by nature and preparations to make a success as public reader. She has a commanding presence, a graceful carriage, a rich, pleasant voice, and her gestures are natural and effective.—*New York Freeman.*

Miss Mary Harper recited several fine selections and did exceedingly well. She has a fine stage presence, and possesses elocutionary talent of a high degree.—*Carlisle Evening Sentinel.*

The elocutionary entertainment given last evening at the A. M. E. Zion Church by Miss Mary E. Harper, of Philadelphia, was all that could be desired. The selections rendered were from standard authors, consisting of pathos and humor, all of which were produced in the highest style of elocutionary art. All present were more than pleased with the entertainment, and Miss Harper can feel well flattered with her success as an elocutionist.— *York Daily.*

The elocutionary entertainment given at the A. M. E. Church last evening by Miss Mary E. Harper, of Philadelphia, was a complete elocutionary success. The selections were from standard authors, and rendered in the best of style. Miss Harper justly lays claims as an elocutionist possessing all the requisites of the art.— *York Democratic Age.*

A much larger audience than usually assembles in the A. M. E. Church to witness intellectual efforts complimented last evening Miss Mary Harper, the elocutionist, who gave a series of select readings. The selections were mostly new, which made the task to interest the audience more difficult, but the elocutionist proved herself equal to the occasion. Miss Harper has undoubted talent of a dramatic order, which she pleasingly and effectively utilizes. Miss Harper's gestures are applicable to the sentiment, and a voice of much volume, which is under artistic control.—*Harrisburg Morning Call.*

Miss Harper possesses sensibility of high order. She will please and move her audience more by her naturalness, pathos and earnestness. She is a lover of the art of elocution, and destined to achieve success.—*National School of Elocution and Oratory, Mrs. J. W. Shoemaker, Vice-President.*

An entertainment was given last evening at the Berean Presbyterian Church, South College Avenue and Nineteenth street, by Miss Mary E. Harper and the Stevens Family Parlor Orchestra. Miss Harper, who is a graduate of the National School of Elocution and Oratory, gave some excellent readings, while the Stevens family rendered choruses, a musical sketch, and other numbers in excellent style. - *Philadelphia Press.*

The features of the entertainment at the Berean Presbyterian Church last evening were music by the Stevens Parlor Orchestra and Miss Mary E. Harper's reading. Miss Harper has a fine stage presence, a good voice, and recited with much expression. She gives promise of success. Altogether the entertainment was unusually good of the sort. -- *News.*

Miss Mary E. Harper's reading was the feature of a very pleasant entertainment at the Berean Presbyterian Church last evening. Her stage presence is fine, both nature and training have done much for her voice, and with perseverance her success as a reader is insured. The Stevens Family Orchestra contributed the music, which was very good - *Philadelphia Times.*

Miss Harper, a graduate of National School of Elocution and Oratory, gave some excellent readings.--*Philadelphia Press.*

CHAPTER LXXXVIII.

MRS. SISSIERETTA JONES

("THE BLACK PATTI").

Perhaps one of the marvels of the nineteenth century is to be found in the person of Mrs. Sissieretta Jones, who has been well styled "the great colored *prima donna,"* and has been often called "The Black Patti". It may not be going too far to say that she might more appropriately be called the great *American prima donna*. This most wonderful product of the negro race needs no special introduction at our hands to the reading and inquisitive people in the larger cities of Central and South America. As popular as she is, however, there are a great many thousands of all races who, quite naturally, know nothing of her. In this particular case we shall leave it to the press of the country to speak of her more knowingly and, therefore, more strongly than the author can possibly. do. Up to our going to press we have been able to learn but little of her early life and education, but clip the following from an advertising sheet, which we offer upon its. merit, since it is over the name of Major J. B. Pond, who was her manager in the great Madison Square Garden Concert in New York City:

Sissieretta Jones was born on January 5, 1868, at Portsmouth, Virginia, being twenty-four years of age at present writing, and in her fourth year her father and mother, Jerry and Henrietta Joyner, left Virginia and settled down in Providence, R. I., where they are still living. When a mere girl, Mrs. Jones evinced a great taste for music, and at the age of fifteen years she commenced her instrumental lessons at the Academy of Music, Providence, R. I., of which Mr. Monros and Baroness Lacombe, the latter an eminent Italian musician, were tutors.

At eighteen she commenced vocal training at the New England Conservatorium in Boston. She made such rapid strides in her studies that those who heard her sing at some private entertainments pronounced her as America's future colored Queen of Song, and in 1887 she was asked to sing at a grand concert in aid of the Parnell Defense Fund, on which occasion the audience numbered upwards of 5,000; she sang next in the Boston Music Hall, where she received the highest encomiums from her hearers. A grand star concert was next given by Mr. J. G. Burgeon, at which all of the best American colored singers took part; on this occasion she again distinguished herself, from which time she has been considered the brightest singer of her race in America. In 1888 she commenced her professional career at Wallack's Theatre, a place where no other 'colored singer had been privileged to shine. It was here that Mr. William Riesen, a famous musical director in New York, hearing of her wonderful voice, called to hear her sing; after doing so he telegraphed to Mr. Henry Abbey, of the firm of Abbey and Schoeffel Grau, managers to Adelina Patti, Henry Irving, Ellen Terry, and all the greatest notables, when on American tours, telling that he had found a "phenomenal singer," and instantly Abbey sent an agent to secure her for a West Indian tour. Before proceeding on her mission, she sang in New York before all the newspaper critics. The *Times* said she was a phenomenal singer and that she had no equal in her race; the *Sun* said she was a great singer, who in a few years would surpass some of the world's greatest singers; the *Herald* predicted a great future for her; and the *Providence Journal* said she would be a credit to her race and would do honor to any stage on which she sung. The *New York Clipper* gave a glowing account of her and was the first paper that described her as the " Black Patti".

On 29th July, 1888, she started on her West Indian tour, paying a visit to Jamaica, where she commanded two months of great success in Kingston. It was here that Mrs. Jones received her first decoration—a gold medal inlaid with pearls and rubies. The tour lasted eight months, during which time she sang in all the principal colonies, being recognized as the greatest lyric star of her race and was the recipient of several other beautiful decorations. On her return home at Providence she was feted in a grand style by her numerous friends. She returned to Madame Lacombe for further study. Then came an Australian manager, who offered her great prices to go to Australia, but she declined his offers, as she had promised to return to the West Indies, where she was greatly delighted with her success. Mrs. Jones has received more presents and testimonials in the various places in which she has sung than any other *prima donna* was ever honored with, and whenever she appears in public her breast is seen brilliantly illuminated with some of the most chaste medals extant. The following are the cities where she received gold medals, with the dates: Kingston, Jamaica (with pearls and rubies), September 2, 1888; Colon, November 3, 1888; Barbadoes, November 26, 1888; Port of Spain, Trinidad, December 18, 1888; San Fernando, Trinidad, December 15, 1888; Demerara, December 28, 1888; Surinam, January 7, 1889; French Society, Port au Prince, December 10, 1890; Citizens of Cape Haytien, January 5, 1891 and presented by the

President,before whom she sung, a purse of gold of $500; St. Thomas, January, 1891, four pearls one emerald, one ruby and one large diamond; G.U.O. Odd Fellows of St. Thomas January 9, 1891. A medal from the citizens of Grenada is in course of preparation against her return to that island.

Mrs. Jones is an American girl, reared and educated in Providence, R. I. She returned from South America in February last, and has since given five concerts in New York, five in Brooklyn, seven in Baltimore, two in Washington (one in the White House, for the President of the United States, his household, members of the Cabinet and members of the foreign legation), two in Jersey City, two in Philadelphia. Invariably the houses have been packed to their fullest capacity. The following press testimonials tell the true story of her wonderful success. The printed reports that Mrs. Jones has sting in Europe, Australia and California are untrue. She is but twenty-four years of age, and has never traveled or been heard anywhere except in Central and South American countries, the West Indies and the American cities above quoted. --- *J. B. Pond.*

The richness of the negro's singing voice has long been recognized, and the belief has been expressed that were such a voice cultivated and trained an artist of exceptional worth would be the result. The only doubt as to the success of such an undertaking has arisen from the fear that the process of schooling the voice might rob it of those natural qualities which lend it a peculiar charm.

A singer appeared in Central Music Hall last night, however, who set at rest all such doubt and confirmed the belief in no slight measure. The singer was Mrs. Sissieretta Jones, a colored woman, whose work upon the concert stage has won for her the title "The Black Patti." She was heard in the Page's song from "The Huguenots," an aria from "L'Africaine" and as encores "Comin' Thro' the Rye," "Bobolink Song," "The Cows are in the Clover," and "Every Rose Has Its Thorn".

The first aria sufficed to show that her voice is indeed phenomenal of extended range of great volume and of wonderful richness. The peculiar plaintive quality that is ever present in the negro voice is still there, and it exerted a charm in every number sung by Mrs. Jones last evening.—*Chicago Tribune, Friday, January 6, 1893.*

The second concert of Mrs. Sissieretta Jones, the "Black Patti," attracted a large and enthusiastic audience at Central Music Hall last night. The great richness and sympathetic quality of the voice of this singer grows upon one.

Her selections were "Robert, toi que j'aime," from Meyerbeer's "Robert le Diable," and Gelli's " Farfella Waltz." She sang the aria with so much feeling and expression that one can overlook deficiencies in vocalization and method. In the encore numbers she made a great success. She sang "Comin' Thro' the Rye," "Bobolink," and " Suwanee River." She carried her audience fairly by storm with the latter. She sang with a wonderful depth of feeling, and the exquisite quality of her voice is admirably suited to the plaintive melody. This simple song has been sung in Chicago many times by the greatest artists, and it is but justice to Mrs. Jones to say that she excels them all in this one song. — *Chicago Times, Saturday, January 7, 1893.*

Another incident of interest in the week of music was the appearance of Mrs. Sissieretta Jones, the "Black Patti." this woman comes as the first vocalist of her race to whom a place in the ranks of artistic singers may be accorded. She has been endowed by nature with a voice that in any throat would he remarkable for its great range and volume, but which, with her, possesses even greater attractiveness by reason of its having also the wonderful richness and fullness and the peculiar timbre that lend the negro singing voice its individuality. The tones in the lower and middle registers are of surpassing beauty, and those of the upper are remarkable for their clear, bell-like quality. Another striking element of the voice is its plaintiveness. In every note Mrs. Jones sang in her concerts here that one quality was unfailingly present. In the arias, in ballads, comic or sentimental, it was noticeable, and it soon became evident that it was the most individualizing element in the voice, and that no amount of schooling or training could eradicate it. Not that one would desire to have it eradicated. It is the heritage the singer has received from her race, and it alone tells not only of the sorrows of a single life, but the cruelly sad story of a whole people. It lends to her singing of ballads an irresistible charm, making her work in this kind of music as artistically satisfactory as it is enjoyable.— *Chicago Tribune, Sunday, January 8, 1893.*

Mrs. Jones possesses a wonderful vocal organ of extraordinary compass and distinct in enunciation.—*New York Evening Telegram.*

Mrs. Jones has taken New York by storm, and showed she is a great singer. — *New York Clipper.*

She is the greatest singer that ever sung in Jersey City. The applause that greeted her would make even the great Patti happy.—*Evening Journal, Jersey City.*

She sings like Patti without the slightest visible effort her voice is well cultivated, her high notes enable her to effectually render the most difficult compositions, and her low tone is peculiarly deep, intense and masculine.—*New York World.*

It has been truly said that the great colored soprano stands without equal in her race, and few in any race.—*New York Times.*

Recalled again and again she sang "The Cows. are in the Clover" very effectively,. her upper notes being especially sweet. She received an ovation. —*New York Herald, April 27, 1892.*

Her voice coming from a skin as white as her teeth would he counted the wonder of all lands—it is a strong and beautiful voice, that sounds with the steadiness of a trumpet. Though it does not ring with passion it shakes your heart.— *The Sun, Friday, April 29, 1892.*

It is an indisputable fact that she possesses a most wonderful vocal organ of extraordinary compass, exceeding sweetness and a delightfully perfect, distinct enunciation. "Black Patti" was given an enthusiastic reception when she appeared. She sang a cavatina by Meyerbeer smoothly and well. Her voice is sweet and tender, and has a pleasing mezzo strain in it.—*Cleveland Plain Dealer, November 15, 1892.*

She appeared and sang as only she can, and her reception was one continuous round of applause, stilled only as her voice was heard.—*Buffalo Courier, Monday, November 1892.*

Mrs. Jones is quite a marvel as a colored cantatrice. Her upper notes are phenomenally clear and pure, and she has many of the arts of the leading She was received with great cordiality. —*The Syracuse Standard, Syracuse, November 12, 1892.*

Her voice is a fine soprano, particularly full, and, sweet in the upper register. She possesses a good presence, and as "Aida" or as "Selika " in " L.'Africaine " would undoubtedly create a sensation.—*The Philadelphia Press, Saturday, December 3, 1892*

She has a musical voice. of extraordinary compass and even power and of really remarkable quality, and she sings with ease and fluency and with a distinct English enunciation, and with a repose of manner that inspires confidence.-*The Times, Philadelphia, December 1892,*

Sissieretta Jones may truly he called "The Black Queen of Song". Her voice, so rich, resonant, powerful, yet sweet, held her delighted listeners, who demanded repeated encores.—*Boston Post, Monday Morning, November 28, 1892.*

Sissieretta Jones possesses a remarkable degree of talent. Her enunciation is excellent and hr voice one of much brilliancy and power. She was tendered an ovation at the close of her first number. --*Boston Journal, Monday, November 28, 1892*

She sings with artistic taste and feeling.---*Public Ledger, Philadelphia, .Saturday, December 3, 1892.*

The wide range and power of her voice were noticeable.—P*hiladelphia Public Ledger, Monday Morning, December 5, 1892.*

MRS. LUCIE JOHNSON SCRUGGS.

CHAPTER LXXXIX

MRS. LUCIE JOHNSON SCRUGGS.

All persons are, to some extent, the products of their environments. The majority of people, measured by their usefulness, reach in society only a mediocre position; some fall below the middle point; while others, despite unfavorable surroundings and straitened circumstances, reach in life positions of worth, honor and usefulness. Many persons born in slavery are examples of the last named class. Not the least among them was Mrs. Lucie Johnson Scruggs, the wife of L. A. Scruggs, M. D. She was the youngest of four children, and was born a slave in Richmond, Va., October 14, 1864. As a child she was somewhat timid, therefore did not easily become attached to every one with whom she came in contact; showing also in a marked degree the infusion of Indian blood in her veins by the strong manifestation of like or dislike for person or persons. Until she was nine years old she had known very little of any association or companionship outside of the grandchildren of the family whose slave her mother formerly was and with whom she lived until 1873. She was noted during childhood for her clear conception of things and received unusual care from the white family.

She entered the public schools of the city at the age of nine years. The first year's work was very thoroughly done by the aid of her sister, a few years her senior, who was then in the fourth grammar grade. Lucie was promoted twice every session, always showing an unusual talent for mathematics. Having been kept out of school a part of two winters by illness attributed to too rapid growth, it was thought expedient to try a change of climate. Consequently, after having been in the high school only one session, she left Richmond highly recommended for Shaw University at Raleigh, N. C. She graduated from this institution in May 1883, and went to New York City, where her mother then resided. While in school she won many friends by her sweetness of disposition and ready sympathy, and Lucie Johnson (as she was then known) was a favorite with all her school-mates .

In October of the same year, shortly after the death of her only brother, she went to Chatham, Va., to teach school. In May 7884, she returned to her home in New York, and she and her sister opened a private school for little girls, which they managed very successfully for four years, Lucie taking charge principally of the musical part. Several white girls were among the pupils, one of whom married a noted professor of music.

It was during these four years that she wrote many articles for the *Richmond Planet* and other race journals. In 1886 she published a grammar designed for beginners, entitled "Grammar-Land". This work in itself would have placed her name high among the literary fraternity, being her original method as a teacher. It was at once comprehensive and simple, enabling the child to grasp the lesson to be learned, and placing before it such examples that the most stupid could not fail to receive some information.

On the evening of February 22, 1888, she was married to Dr. L A. Scruggs, of Raleigh, N. C., who had won her heart while she was yet a school-girl. They were married at St. Mark's M. E. Church, New York, by Rev. H. L. Morehouse, D. D., assisted by the pastor, Rev. Dr. Monroe. Their union proved a happy one, and was blessed with two children.

Soon after her marriage she wrote a drama, "Farmer Fox," which was played in Blount Street Hall. Her attention being taken by housekeeping and other duties, she gave very little time to literary work. Mrs. Scruggs was always admired for her unfeigned modesty. She became a Christian when she was fourteen years of age and joined the First Baptist Church of Richmond, Va. After her marriage and removal to Raleigh she united with the Blount Street Baptist Church of that city. She died November 24, 1892, after a brief but severe illness.

When a child Mrs. Scruggs was called "The Flower of the House" and in after years she proved herself a veritable "Flower." Cheery of disposition and extremely entertaining she was the most charming of hostesses, while as president of the Ladies' Pansy Literary Club, which was organized by her, she blended firmness with gentleness. Those with whom she associated felt the influence for good which emanated from her. Nor did it stop there, but extended to all with whom she came in contact. It may truly be said of her that:

"None knew her but to love her,
None named her but to praise."

The following is a notice of her death which appeared in the *New York Age* and was copied by the *Ringwood Journal:*

RALEIGH, N. C., November 28, 1892.—On the evening of the 24th inst. the soul of Mrs. Lucie T. Scruggs, beloved wife of Dr. L. A. Scruggs, fled to the God who gave it. Her illness, which was of short duration, but exceedingly painful, was borne with sweetest patience and calm resignation. To her husband she was a devoted wife, a loving companion and a most efficient manager of his business affairs. She was a tender and fond mother to her children. Mrs. Scruggs was a member of the Second Baptist Church and the King's Daughters' Missionary Society. She organized and was twice elected president of the Pansy Literary Society, and at the time of her death had planned to organize a Sewing Circle for the purpose of teaching the industry to such girls as were ignorant of it.

The following taken from the *Gazette,* Raleigh, N. C. shows the esteem in which she was held in that city:

The news of Mrs. Scruggs' demise carried consternation all through the city. While many knew she was sick but few thought that death was so near, and at this writing our beautiful city is buried in sorrow and tears, and our community loses one of its purest and brightest characters and society its purest gem. Not within the writer's memory has the death of a lady cast such gloom and left so many sad hearts. The Church loses one of its most valuable members, society its most earnest worker, and the poor their dearest friend. Wherever one went in the city the name of Mrs. Scruggs was held in high esteem. In fact, everybody loved her for her purity of character and personal charms.

For many years Mrs. Scruggs worked incessantly to create a high moral sphere among the people and occupied for a long time the chief place in many social and literary societies of the city, and not an effort was made without receiving her support for the amelioration of the poor.

As a wife she was true, as a mother loving, and as a neighbor kind. As a housekeeper she was a model, and as to her business qualities, the stricken husband owes much of his success, and to repeat his own words, "Her place can never be supplied". The citizens of Raleigh, regardless of race or sex, who knew Mrs. Scruggs regret her death while yet in the bloom of life.

The following in reference to the funeral of Mrs. Scruggs is clipped from the *Richmond Planet* of December 3, 1892:

Her funeral was very largely attended. Several ministers of other denominations spoke in praise of her lovely Christian life, and also offered consolation to the bereaved family. The two institutions, Shaw University and St. Augustine Normal and Collegiate Institute, suspended studies that the students might attend in a body the funeral. This was never before known in the history of Raleigh—the closing of two schools to allow their students to attend the funeral of a private citizen.

Thus passed away a most beautiful life in the morning of its usefulness, and in the quiet shades of evening the tortured, pain-racked body was laid to rest.

"Precious in the sight of the Lord is the death of His saints."

"Earth's sweetest flowers bloom but to decay."

The following lines which- we subjoin are the last expressions of her pen, and in full harmony with her genial disposition as a mother.

Mother! How much that word means; how much care, trust, responsibility, power and self-sacrifice are involved in those six letters of the alphabet, m-o-t-h-e-r. Yet so many of our mothers regard that position in life as a mere trifle, as irksome, never giving one thought to the many duties resting upon them as the laying of the true foundations upon which their little innocent ones are to build. Did I say innocent? Yes, because they are truly pure and innocent when given to our care and keeping. How can you consider them irksome? Have you a mother? Then remember the pang it gave your young heart when by a look or a word your mother seemed tired of you. If you have not one (a mother), how much worse, because as you look back upon your childhood you can see how much your young heart yearned for a mother's love, a mother's care and a mother's interest. How can you expect your child to be sweet and loving if you yourself are not the embodiment of those true and noble principles? Many mothers foster the idea that being patient only spoils the child, but can you not be patient and yet be positive?

Some mothers sigh over the great responsibility, as they term it, of rearing girls, while the rearing of their boys is a pleasure, but if they were to look on the other side of the picture would they not see that if the proper care and pains were used to keep the boys' minds pure and innocent as is taken for the girls, how much less would be the shedding of tears over fallen girls ?

Look at the temptations your boys are throwing in the paths of your neighbor's girls, or the temptations your neighbor's boys are throwing in the pathway of your own girls. Is this not sufficient proof that the reins should be drawn with equal force on the boys as well as on the girls? How many mothers care so much for pleasure and society that they entirely neglect the training of their little ones! Oh, mother! Remember that upon you depends the future of your children; upon you in after years will they shower blessings which will be a comfort to you in your old age if you have tried in every respect to carry into effect the meaning of the word mother. Why look upon this position so lightly? Can you find one in which you would have the power to do more, be of more real value to your neighbor, your friends and to the world than by rearing your children with such pains and care as to make them real examples to others?

It should be a pleasure as it is your duty to sacrifice, toil and study for the well-being of your children.

Look at the noble men and women we have among us today. Ask many of them where the power lies that prompted them to such positions in life, and the answer will he, "I owe it all to my loving, patient, self-sacrificing, forbearing mother" - *Ringwood's Journal*.

MRS. ELLA C. PEGUES.

MRS. ROSA KINCKLE JONES

CHAPTER XC.

MRS. ROSA KINCKLE JONES.

I n the onward march of progress of any people there is no one thing that can do more to make or mar than the disposition and tendencies of its women. Just as surely as water can only rise to its own level so surely can a race hope only to rise to the height of its women. If they are noble, pure and good, we may confidently expect their influence to bring about the characteristics in the sterner sex, for

> "The hand that rocks the cradle
> Is the hand that rules the world."

The negro race is peculiarly fortunate in having among it good, noble, pious, refined and cultured women, and none of them are more deserving of a niche in the temple of fame than the subject of this sketch.

Lynchburg, Va., the "City of Hills," that has had the honor of sending out so many distinguished sons, was the place at which she first saw the light of day, and where the better portion of her life was spent.

She attended the public school of that city, making an excellent record, until 1877, when she left for Howard University, from which she graduated with honor in 1880. As is usually the case with gifted women she devoted the first years of her public services to teaching, having taught with great success in the State of Virginia and city of Lynchburg for two years.

Mrs. Jones is a well-read and cultured lady, having a voice of unusual compass, and is an excellent teacher of vocal music; but it is as a pianist that she is especially distinguished. Her execution of the most difficult of classical music is indeed marvelous.

Possessed of a touch of rare sweetness she can give the most excellent interpretation of the great masters, delineating every passion and emotion with a most delicate finish.

Mrs. Jones is undoubtedly possessed of natural ability in the musical line, but in addition to this she has been blessed with the best of instruction from competent teachers from early childhood, continuing the study in the city of Washington, finally taking a course in harmony at the New England Conservatory of Music.

Since residing in the city of Richmond she has been considered one of its most prominent, if not the most prominent and successful teacher of music, having taught some who are now successful teachers themselves.

For the past five years she has been the highly accomplished teacher at the Hartshorn Memorial College, and hundreds of pupils in and out of the State testify to her great ability.

In 1882 she married Rev. Dr. J. E. Jones, of the Richmond Theological Seminary, and is thus the eminent wife of an eminent man.

Their married life is an ideal one, and the union has been blessed with two bright and interesting boys.

Mrs. Jones is an indefatigable worker, and yet finds time to give her services free to every worthy enterprise.

Pleasant, affable, kind, loving, she is loved by all who know her, and is an ideal woman, wife and mother.

G. W. HAYES.

CHAPTER XCI.

OTHER DISTINGUISHED WOMEN.

With a desire to be impartial as far as possible, the author has found it necessary to devote one chapter to the consideration of those distinguished persons to whom he could not at this late day give special separate chapters, having already reached the prescribed limits volume. It is pleasant, however, to make *honorable mention* of the following ladies of distinction, to whom we hope, in the future, to do greater justice.

MRS. DR. G. F. GRANT, of Boston, was a pupil at the New England Conservatory of Music, and was for quite awhile the very popular and accomplished organist at the North Russell Street Church.

The *Boston Globe* said of her:

A fine-looking young lady; achieved a like success in all her numbers, and in fine presence on the stage and in her simple, unobtrusive manner winning the sympathics of the audience.

MRS. DR. C. N. MILLER, also of Boston, was for a long time the leading soprano singer of Rev. L. Grimes church, a very valuable and favorite member of the great Tremont Temple Choir, so well noted for its good music.

The *Boston Globe* said of her:

She is the possessor of a well-cultivated voice of natural sweetness.

MRS. P. A. GLOVER and MRS. H. JEFFREYS are both of high rank in musical circles of Boston and possess voices of rare and natural beauty—wonderful in their power to thrill the very souls of their hearers with the melody of their songs.

MISS SARAH SEDGWICK BROWN, a lady of most charming voice as well as possessing a most wonderfully well-developed musical talent, fine interpretations and renditions of operatic and classical music. She has been quite often called the "Colored Nightingale."

The *Daily Pennsylvanian* of May 3, 1856, said of her:

We have never been called upon to record a more brilliant and instantaneous success than has thus far attended this talented young aspirant to musical honors. From obscurity she has risen to popularity, She has not been through the regular routine of advancement, but, as it were, in a moment endowed by nature with the wonderful power of song, she delighted the circle in which she moved, and is now enchanting the public. Last evening the hall was thronged at an early hour. In every song she was unanimously encored.

She has always stood high in Philadelphia, where she has quietly lived and acted well her part.

MISS CELESTINE O. BROWNE, a very prominent citizen of Jamestown, New York, has made much prestige as a pianist.

The *Boston Folio* of December 1876, said of her:

She is a fine pianist, very brilliant and showy as soloist and accompanist.

She was at one time a member of the Hyers Sisters' Concert.

MADAM ALBERT WILSON, of Brooklyn, New York, is among our foremost pianists and has been highly spoken of by the press—having accompanied some of our best singers. She was prominent with Madam Sissieretta Jones ("Black Patti" on several very noted occasions.

MADAM EMMA SAVAILE JONES, of Brooklyn, N. Y., possesses one of those *well-cultivated voices.* In this she is not so richly endowed with the gifts of nature as some others of her sisters, while on the other hand she is a *well-trained and highly cultured vocalist.* She furnishes a living and striking example of what a young woman may do for herself and her race, even though Nature may not have so richly endowed her as it has some others of her companions.

MADAM ADELE V. MONTGOMERY, of New York City, has been by many very competent critics regarded as the colored pianist of America. She is certainly an expert at the piano. She has accompanied Madam Bergen in many of her concerts in the Eastern and Middle States.

MISS EMMA MAGNAN, of New York City, is sister of Madam Montgomery, and is quite a noted pianist, and at the same time sings very sweetly.

MRS. JOSIE D. HEARD. We very much regret that somehow we failed to get any response to repeated efforts to obtain the facts of this very excellent lady's history. However, suffice it to say that she is a valuable part of the best society in Philadelphia, not only from a strictly social stand-point of view, but as a talented, faithful woman; popular not only at home, but throughout the country, because of her sterling worth as a woman in the full sense of the word —ambitious,'learned and true.

We take pleasure in quoting the following poem, "I Love Thee," as a specimen of some of her many and varied writings ;

> Thou art not near me, but I see thine eyes
> Shine through the gloom like stars in winter skies,
> Pointing the way my longing steps would go,
> To come to thee because I love thee so.
>
> Thou art not near me, but I feel thine arm,
> Soft folded round me, shielding me from harm,
> Guiding me on as in days of old—
> Sometimes life seems so dark, so dreary and so cold.
>
> Thou art not near me, but I hear thee speak,
> Sweet as the breath of June upon my cheek,
> And as thou speakest I forget my fears,
> And all the darkness, and my lonely tears.

O love, my love, whatever our fate may be,
Close to thy side, or never more with thee,
Absent or present, near or far apart
Thou hast my love and fillest all my heart

MRS. DR. A. M. CURTIS was born in San Francisco, Cal., on the 10th day of July 1871. Having been deprived of her parents by death when she was quite young, she was cared for by an aunt, who encouraged and fostered her education. She, in after years, married Dr. A. M. Curtis, with whom she went to Chicago to begin life's work. Dr. Curtis is now enjoying a large and lucrative practice; to this energetic lady, doubtless, he owes some of his success. Mrs. Curtis has recently been made Secretary of the Colored Department of the World's Fair at Chicago. Mrs. Curtis is an energetic, faithful, pleasant woman of inure than ordinary gifts. She is educated and refined—a great race lover.

MARY ANN SHADD CAREY. This remarkable person was born in Delaware. She did much to educate herself, and far outran many of her sisters who were also free during those dark days of *American Slavery*. As a lecturer, debater and shrewd speech-maker she was indeed a most wonderful member of the *Dark Race.*

MISS H. CORDELIA RAY is the daughter of the late Charles B. Ray. She has reached a high point of reputation as both an excellent poetical and prose writer. Having received her education in the very excellent schools of New York City, the place of her birth, she quite naturally ranks high in literary circles. She began to write verse as early as ten years old. Her works are very numerous in both prose and poetry and would do her credit if published in one volume. Miss Ray has the distinctive honor of being a graduate of the School of Pedagogy, which is one of the departments of the University of the City of New York, from which she received the degree of "Master of Pedagogy" in 1891.

MISS M. L. BALDWIN, of Cambridge, Mass., is doing a most excellent work in her native State. She is principal of the Agassiz School in that noted city of letters. A strong advocate of equal justice to all men, a strong opponent of the separation of Americanized races into classes, she believes that the idea of "fencing off is equally harmful" to all concerned. In matters of country and the country's welfare and best interests she thinks there should be one common standard by which all should be judged. As we understand her position, we heartily indorse the idea of equality of rights, in law and government, to all.

MISS EDWINA BLANCHE KRUSE is an example of good works, and well establishes the fact of Afro-American possibilities. When matters of negro education were enshrouded in gross darkness in Wilmington, Del., this woman of the Mosaic type came to the front, and, like a well-skilled warrior, as she is, she pushed the fight for schools in which her people could be educated to some degree of satisfaction. Her work succeeded and now in Delaware there are several well-equipped schools. Miss Kruse is principal of one of these three schools. To her belongs the credit of this great work, which it has taken her years to accomplish.

Although we failed to obtain the facts, we so much desired concerning the lives of the following named ladies, yet we take great pleasure in placing them upon the list of " Women of Distinction" by giving, as near as we can, their names and addresses. They deserve even more than honorable mention, but "such" as we have we "give unto" them, with the hope of doing them full justice when the facts in their history are at our command: Miss Lucy Moten, Washington, D. C.; Miss Frazelia Campbell, Philadelphia, Pa.; Miss Julia Wormley, Washington, D. C.; Miss Addie Wait, Normal, Ala.; Mrs. Frances Preston, Detroit, Mich.; Mrs. Lucy Hereford, Montgomery, Ala.; Mrs. Mary Shadd Carey, Washington, D. C.; Mrs. Carrie L. Steele, Atlanta, Ga.; Mrs. Bertha B. Cook, Wilmington, Del.; Mrs. R. H. Long, Columbus, Mo.; Mrs. E. L. Boone, Columbus, Mo.; Mrs. Sarah Mitchell, Cleveland, Ohio; Mrs. M. C. Terrell, Washington, D. C.; Miss Lucy Laney, Mrs. Alice Vassar, Lynchburg, Va.

Miss Martha B. Briggs

CHAPTER LCII.

MISS MARTHA B. BRIGGS.

Martha Bailey Briggs was born in New Bedford, Massachusetts, March 31, 1838. She was the only child of John Briggs, of Tiverton, R. I., and Fanny (Bassett) Briggs, of Vineyard Haven, Martha's Vineyard, Massachusetts. Her father is reputed to have been a man of uncommon intelligence for the limited opportunities afforded him. During his early life, like most poor country boys, he was permitted to attend school only during the winter. He was quick to accept and utilize every advantage in the way of learning which presented itself, and thereby acquired a great deal of knowledge. When but twelve years old he went to New Bedford. to live in the family of a Quaker, George Howland, who had two sons—one the age of John Briggs, the other younger. From these boys he obtained much help in his studies, and so faithful to duty did he prove that he was retained in the employ of the Howlands, father and sons, up to the time of his death, which covered a period of more than fifty years. He had an insatiable appetite for reading, was extremely fond of politics, and, being a rampant anti-slavery character, enjoyed the close friendship of Hon. Frederick Douglass during much of his lifetime. His wife having died when his daughter was quite young, he entrusted the rearing of his child to an aunt, Mrs. Bailey, whose motherly care and guidance did much to develop the strong character of the woman whose destiny it was to play so important a part in the education of her race.

Upon his only child Mr. Briggs bestowed every facility for an education which the private and public schools of New Bedford afforded.

At the age of twelve years she was prepared to enter the New Bedford High School. The rules would not allow children under thirteen to enter, and she was compelled to wait for some time before admission could be gained for her. Through the influence of friends she was admitted in September, 1850, when but twelve and a half years old. She completed the course with honors and was the first colored girl graduated from this high school.

HER CHOSEN PROFESSION.

Her earliest experience at teaching was at home in her father's house. There she opened a private school with ten or twelve pupils, and at different times had evening pupils, whom she taught to read and write. These evening pupils were most largely men and women who came from slavery. To such fugitives her father, out of the largeness of his heart, often gave refuge and aid. Subsequently she taught at Christiantown, Martha's Vineyard, in the private and public schools of Newport, R. I., and acted as governess in the family of Mr. George T. Downing, of said city, for several years. Because of his loyalty to manhood and justice Mr. Downing repudiated the idea of fastening upon his posterity the notion of their inferiority, by permitting them to submit to attendance upon public schools for colored children, separate and apart from those for white children, when the conditions were such that both teacher-ships and pupils might have been mixed without detriment to either race. He therefore gave the use of one of his houses as a school and paid for the private tuition of his children, Miss Briggs being one of the three teachers employed. She lived with his family and enjoyed their warmest friendship.

In 1859, while teaching at Newport, she was invited by Myrtilla Miner to go to Washington, D. C., and assist her in teaching a school which Miss Miner had established for the education of colored girls. She did not, however, accept the invitation, because her father was not willing that she should brave the bitter feeling existing between the North and South. Miss Miner was thus left to combat her perilous attempt all alone, but victory crowned her efforts, and it was the result of her struggles that the Miner fund was created, through which Miss Briggs came to the public colored schools of Washington and Georgetown, D. C., as principal of the Miner Normal School, twenty years later.

LATER SUPPLEMENTARY STUDIES

She began the study of medicine at Boston before she went South to teach, but did not complete the course, a taste of the subject having convinced her that she was better adapted to teaching than for becoming a mere nurse, the purpose for which she entered the Boston Medical College.

It is said by good authority that she was specially trained for teaching at the Bridgewater Normal School, but her immediate relatives now living are not sure that such was true. She was away from home quite awhile, taking a special course in Latin and French, and it may be that during this time she took the normal course. Be this as it may, she was pre-eminently master of whatever she attempted to teach, and so well equipped was she in every direction that her capability and aptitude for teaching seemed unbounded. She did good and thorough work wherever placed.

She added to her mental store a knowledge of German during her career in Washington.

IN SOUTHERN FIELDS.

As early as 1867 she went to Easton, Md., where she taught two years. No facts are available to tell of her work there.

Two years later she received encouragement through the persuasion of friends at Washington, D. C., to go to said city and teach. Her application for the position of teacher in the public colored schools of Washington and Georgetown was favorably considered, and the date of her first appointment to a school in said District was during the autumn of 1869.

CAREER IN WASHINGTON.

It was in this city, and through the schools of its vicinity, that the widest range was opened to develop all that was sterling in this woman. She was now in the employ of the largest and best system for public instruction for the race in this country, and rapidly grew in favor as teacher and disciplinarian, being made principal of one of the largest school buildings then under the public school management.

Having attained the highest position within the gift of the Board of Trustees, outside of the High School principalship, she was, in 1873, offered a position to teach at Howard University, which she accepted and filled creditably for six years.

In 1879 she was invited to return to the public schools as principal of the Miner Normal School, through which teacherships were supplied to the public schools of the District of Columbia. She accepted said position, held it for four years, having graduated during said time about eighty teachers.

The work of the Normal School increased during the four years to such an extent that the tax to carry out the excellent system she had inaugurated, with the limited assistance allowed, wore heavily upon her. Always sought after by the Howard University management, she returned there where the work was not so arduous and was teaching there at the time of her death, having been out of school but a few days.

She was principal of the Howard University Normal School at the time of her death and enjoyed the confidence and respect of the faculty and trustees to the highest extent.

IN SOCIETY.

Socially she will ever be missed at Washington. Much was due to her tenacity of purpose and innate love for literature that the admirably organized Monday Night Literary Club was kept intact for so many years, which has since "fallen to pieces" much to the detriment of many whose literary tastes were stimulated through it, and to that of Washington society, which had for so many years maintained as its pride this most admirably select organization. It seemed to be her hobby to have our boys and girls taught in industrial lines as well as otherwise, and through her efforts many were instructed through the means afforded by the Industrial Institute Association of Washington, D. C., to which she was elected president just prior to her death.

Miss Briggs was liberal with her means. While principal of Miner Normal School her salary was $1,350 per annum. She went about doing good to the needy, and withal accumulated some property, and was owner of the house in which she was born until she died.

Exercises "In Memoriam" were held by the Bethel Historical and Literary Society, Washington, D. C., May 14,1889. At said meeting addresses were made and appropriate resolutions eulogistic of her worth were passed. A committee of nine citizens was appointed to wait upon the District Commissioners and ask that one of the school buildings then in process of erection be called the "Martha B. Briggs Building," as appreciative of her work in the community. The request was cheerfully acceded to by the honorable Commissioners, and the large building at the intersection of Virginia into and Twenty-second and E streets, N. W., now principled by one of Miss Briggs' normal graduates, Miss M. E. Gibbs, bears that name.

Appropriate exercises to her memory were also held in Howard University Chapel, where eulogies were delivered by her friends and pupils, Prof. G. W. Cook and Miss E. A. Cook. A marble tablet has been inserted in the wall of the chapel bearing the inscription, "Her works do follow her."

MRS. R. E. LAWSON.

MRS. DINAH WATTS PACE

CHAPTER XCIII.

MRS. DINAH WATTS PACE.

Dinah Watts Pace was born in Athens, Ga. She attended school at Atlanta University in Atlanta, Ga., and graduated from the normal department in June 1883.

During the summer of the same year she began her work as teacher in Covington, Ga. She took two little orphan girls to care for and rear. This resulted in the founding of an Orphan Home, where orphans and other needy children are cared for. She has reared six children and has at present twenty-two in the home. The work has grown gradually each year.

During the past ten years her greatest aid has been from a brother, Lewis G. Watts, who has given her regularly a part of his earnings toward the support of the work, otherwise the work is mainly supported by her own earnings.

She has received some aid from Northern friends. Mrs. A. C. Reed, of Manchester, Vt., donated at one time the money for the erection of the present Home building, a large two-story frame structure. She has also given other aid. Friends in and near Boston have also contributed to the work.

The work is nothing like completed, but it is gradually growing.

The mission is known as the Reed Home and School for Colored Children, and, although yet in its infancy, the enterprise is a striking illustration of what a consecrated heart with well-defined purposes and sufficient energy and will to do can accomplish at the hands of an Afro-American woman of small means.

MISS GEORGIA MABEL DEBAPTISTE.

CHAPTER XCIV.

MISS GEORGIA MABEL DEBAPTISTE.

Miss DeBaptiste's native home is Chicago, Ill., where she received most of her education, completing her course of study in Evanston, Ill. She also took a musical course.

When very young she was much interested in literary work, and when she became an advanced student she accepted the offer of being a regular correspondent of several papers and a magazine. She continued to write for some time after she completed her school course.

Her father, Rev. R. DeBaptiste, D. D., of Chicago, Ill., is her only living parent, her mother having died when she was five years old.

Miss DeBaptiste served as private secretary to the president of the State University, Louisville, Ky., and Dr. Simmons wrote the following compliment, which she appreciates very highly:

With her strict application to duty, her untiring perseverance, and her sweet, lady-like demeanor, she cannot do otherwise than win the hearts of those with whom she comes in contact. Her determination to overcome difficulties and her ambition to accomplish great good attract all whom she meets.

She was instructor in music in the Selma University, Selma, Ala., one year, was re-elected, but owing to a failure in health, because of the change of climate, she could not return. She was then summoned to a position in Lincoln Institute, Jefferson City, Mo., as assistant teacher in language and instructor in music, and after two years' work she resigned and received the following compliment from the faculty:

During Miss DeBaptiste's stay of two years we have found her to be earnest, zealous, upright and amiable, desiring at all times the good of those around her, and ever working for that good, often at the sacrifice of self.

As a teacher she has given thorough satisfaction to all concerned, both in respect to ability and to character. She is scholarly, talented and refined, and is held in the highest esteem by all the students and her co-workers in Lincoln Institute.

Prof. Page said the following:

Miss DeBaptiste has made an excellent record as a faithful and conscientious teacher. By her moral character, as well as her work as a teacher in the class-room, she has left a lasting impression upon all who have been associated with her.

The President of the Board of Regents said:

We cheerfully speak of the faithfulness of Miss DeBaptiste as a teacher and of her lady-like deportment.

The secretary of the board said:

We accept Miss DeBaptiste's resignation with regret, but with full confidence and respect. She has given evidence of excellent training, clear discernment, upright character, irreproachable demeanor, earnestness and ability, and I cheerfully speak of her as a lady and a teacher.

It was the intention of Miss DeBaptiste, when resigning, to rest from her very taxing labors of teaching for a time and assist her father in his work, but the Baptist College, located at Macon City, Mo., was in need of teachers, and urged her acceptance of a position. Being desirous of doing all that she could for her race and her denomination, which she dearly loves, she went there and is earnestly striving to do all that she can.

This is a young field, but prospects are most encouraging.

Miss DeBaptiste loves literary pursuits, and, although she has many pressing duties, she has not given up this work. She aims to be one of real power of mind and character, with true dignity of soul, not for mere social attainments, but that such might only be the outward expression of inward grace and courtesy. Miss DeBaptiste is one of the progressive young women of the race. She is not only at home in the school-room, but also in social and literary circles as well as at the musical instrument.

Courteous, sweet in temper, and yet of a decided and commanding bearing, charitable, devoted and true.

MISS RUTH LOWERY.

CHAPTER XCV.

MISS RUTH LOWERY.

As strange as it may appear, and equally as contrary to what was at first hoped for or expected, it is none the less an important and well established fact connected with the history of American slavery that many of the now paying industries of the South were born in crude negro huts, as were also many of the modern and improved implements now so useful in the agricultural and domestic arts. In many cases, however, the idea was seized by the stronger and more active element, who only carried into practical execution what had already been conceived and made known by his less favored contemporary, to whom but little if any public credit was ever given for the suggestion. Like all normal human beings, he had a mind and used it in such a way as to accomplish the *most possible* with expenditure of the *least* amount of energy. And, thus, there was proven to be a real and true inventive and ever active genius running through the very being of this enslaved. people.

And now with the opportunities which many of them are well using to improve both their mental and material condition the present is only a positive index to the disclosure of much of this latent force in the near future.

Still more strange and amusing is the fact that it was left for a negro female to pave the way and *introduce* the *silk culture* into the great and wealthy State of Alabama.

As it is the custom of many of our more favored friends to attribute any of our important accomplishments to the "white blood infused into the veins of some of us" we take pleasure in calling attention to her portrait, which proves to be that of a pure African.

This woman was Ruth Lowery, of Huntsville, Alabama. While we are thus musing with a mind filled with more facts than we have either space or ability to write we are pleased to quote the following from *Frank Leslie's Newspaper* of August 17, 1878, which is quite convincing:

In the "New South " there is neither room for drones nor brainless people; capital finds ready and profitable investment; labor, skilled and conscientious, reasonable employment. In looking over the new industries, either in the full tide of success or in encouraging progress, it is really singular that it has been left for poor colored people to inaugurate an enterprise that capital and experience have long tried in vain to establish in this country. The story of the inception of silk culture in Alabama possesses elements of a highly romantic character, and the condition to which Mr. Samuel Lowery has brought the industry at Huntsville shows that the State may become the peer of France in this great business.

Mr. Lowery was born in Nashville, Tenn., December 9, 1832, his father her being Elder Peter Lowery, a slave, who purchased the freedom of himself, his mother, three brothers, two sisters and a nephew, and became the first colored pastor of a church in the South, preaching in the Second Christian Church at Nashville from 1849 to 1866. Ruth Mitchell—afterward the wife of the "Elder"—was a free woman, who devoted the results of her energy to the funds Peter had accumulated for the purchase of his freedom. The amount, $1,000, was paid over forty-five years ago. The couple were married, and Samuel was the only child. At the age of twelve he was placed at Franklin College, Tenn., where, in spite of his color, he commanded the respect of the faculty and pupils. At the close of the war Samuel began reading law, and was the first colored man ever admitted to the Supreme Court of Tennessee and the courts of Northern Alabama. In due time he married, and in 1875 he was directed, by curiosity, to call upon Mr. and Mrs. Theobold, at Nashville, who had brought some silk-worm eggs from England. His daughters, Ruth and Anna, accompanied him. Upon hearing Mrs. Theobold describe the methods of raising the worm Ruth became so deeply interested that she begged her father to purchase some of the eggs and give her leave to try the experiment of hatching them. To this he consented, and shortly after the family removed to Huntsville, where he opened a school. His daughters introduced sewing, knitting and needle-work among the poor girls, and began preparations for hatching the eggs. Having no books to advise her, Ruth received all her knowledge of the subject from that stern but thorough teacher, experience.

During the first season the Corporation of Huntsville granted her a large white mulberry in the midst of the city, upon the leaves of which her first worms were fed. This tree is perennial in Southern Alabama, but drops its leaves in from four to six weeks in the latitude of Huntsville. It is not troubled with parasites, and the worms fed upon it have proved unusually healthy. She made sixteen spools of strong silk, spun some with a device of her own, and saved about one thousand good eggs for the second season. For the spools she received premiums from the Huntsville Mechanical and Agricultural Fair. Having become satisfied of the ultimate success of the enterprise, the Lowery family and the boys and girls in the school devoted all their time not required by the curriculum of the institution to the eggs and worms. This first success attracted considerable attention among the prominent citizens, and generous offers of assistance were made by some of the large landed proprietors, who saw in the introduction of the new cultivation a source of wealth capable of well-nigh indefinite development. Among those who take an active interest in .the introduction of the silk-worm culture is one of the *ante-bellum* Governors of the State, Reuben Chapman, on whose estate Mr. Lowery's Industrial Academy is situated.

CHAPTER XCVI.

MADAM SELIKA.

A s Afro-Americans there are many conditions and circumstances that tend to make life dreary and discouraging. Some of these difficulties are the results of our own life and thoughts and constitute the foe within us; some are also due to circumstances over which we have but little, or no control, and constitute the foe from without.

After all that seems dark and burdensome along our pathway we should feel that our condition today is far In advance of our condition one quarter of a century ago. We suffer, as a matter of course, much more than some other races at present, and yet possibly not more than others who have occupied a similar position.

Let us look up and look forward, patiently laboring and waiting and praying for a better day with greater and more lasting blessings.

To do this one must grasp every opportunity for making a step forward.

As the years roll on, and as we ripen with the experience we shall gather, we may do our part in giving prestige to this race by economy and thrift and watchfulness.

Among those womanly characters that have done so much along this line is to be mentioned Madam Selika, who has well been called the "charming, enchanting singer". This lady seems to have achieved a victory in the beginning of her career as a public musical artist. We commend her achievements as worthy inspirations to many of our young women who already possess great and wonderful talents, who have many opportunities for improvement of same, and who seem to be greatly favored by nature in the distribution of certain special gifts. Each of you can do something to bless your race and country.

While you cannot be a Selika, a Batson, a Harper, a Weatley or a Brown in their special callings, you can be equally as great and as good in some other important calling. While we much regret that we cannot at this time present to our readers a full and just account of this great woman as an incentive, yet we are not to be blamed, as the facts were *sought* and *promised,* but never reached us.

However, we give the following from the *Colored American* as to her study, travels and accomplishments:

RENOWNED IN EUROPE AND AMERICA

Just sixteen years ago there appeared on the stage in San Francisco a young colored woman who had spent three years in musical study under the great artist, Signora G. Bianchi. So great was the success of her *debut* that it became an ovation. This young woman was no other than Madam Selika.

Beginning her career at this time, she has continued winning triumph after triumph over all the world, until now she holds the distinguished honor of being the most skilled and most renowned of her race among the music-loving public. The *Boston Herald*, after complimenting Madam Selika in high terms, says: "Especially sweet are her upper tones".

Madam Selika has not only won triumphs in this country, but she traveled five years in Europe, winning laurels in Germany, France, Russia, Italy, Belgium, and England. A little over a year ago she made a triumphant tour over Norway and Sweden, receiving marked honors at Christiana. In London our distinguished race woman appeared on the stage of St. James Hall in a concert given under the patronage of the Spanish Minister. The others of the programme were the renowned Madam Carlotta Patti, Madam Norwich, Messrs. Percy Blandford, Joseph Lynde, and Signor Vigara.

Madam Selika is erecting a beautiful home in Cleveland, Ohio, and will soon retire from the stage to take a well-earned retirement. All who have not heard her should not lose another opportunity. Those who have listened to her charming voice will not fail to hear her on her last appearance.

CHAPTER XCVII.

GEORGIA ESTHER LEE PATTON, M. D.

Born in Grundy county, Tenn., April 15, 1864, she attended the primary school in the town of Coffee in all about twenty-five months. In 1882 she entered the Central Tennessee College at Nashville. Beginning quite low in her classes, she pushed her way upwards from lower to higher until graduating from the higher normal department in 1890. Then she entered the medical department (Meharry Medical College), and from the first took a high stand in her studies, making ninety her standard. At first her thirty or more class-mates did not receive this new addition to their number with satisfaction, but sought to discourage her. Unmoved by their efforts she pushed her way to the top, and no doubt by her constancy some of them at times feared they might have to take a lower seat.

However, she gained them (as a shrewd woman will most always do), and, unlike former ones of her sex, she stuck to her work like the ever "busy bee" and graduated with honors in a class of thirty-six persons, she being the only female. This is the more remarkable when it is remembered that she had to remain out of school much of her time to earn her bread, having to depend upon her own *will* and *strength* for support as a student. It is again remarkable, yes simply wonderful, when we who have traveled that road learn that her general average was ninety or thereabouts, and she spending only a part of her time at study. She sails for the "Dark Continent" of Africa sometimes during this spring, 1893. May her example serve as a stimulus to others of her race and sex that they may make similar marks of *distinction* in this *noble profession!* She carries with her our hearty good wishes and our "God- speed" in the good work of her mission. She will, no doubt, join in with the large number of her brethren (who are successfully practicing medicine all over this Southland) in sustaining the reputation of her *Alma Mater,* which has done so much for the negro in medicine. We again assert that the practice of medicine by woman does not necessarily rob her of any of those good feminine traits of character.

CHAPTER XCVIII.

HIGHER EDUCATION FOR WOMEN.

The dense darkness which for six thousand years has enveloped woman's intellectual life is rapidly disappearing before the rays of modern civilization. Advanced public sentiment says, "Let there be light" and there is light, but it is not that of a brilliant noonday; rather is it the brightness of a rising sun, destined to flood the world with glory.

There are still many who, while advocating female education to a certain point, decry the necessity and the propriety of giving to woman what is known as the higher education. By this term we mean that education involving the same head-training, having for its basis the same general studies deemed essential-to our brothers, that education acquired only at the college and the university.

The very fact that woman has a mind capable of infinite expansion is, in itself, an argument that she should receive the highest possible development. Man is placed here to grow. It is his duty to make the most of the powers within him. Has anyone a right to thwart him in these efforts, to shut him out from the means to this end, to say to him as concerns his educational training, "Thus far thou shalt go and no further"? This being true of man specifically, is no less true of man generically. Poets and novelists all agree in according to woman a heart, but in the practical treatment of subjects the fact should not be overlooked that she has also a head. The Martineaus, Hemans, Hannah Mores, George Eliots and Mrs. Brownings have not failed to make this demonstration. Admitting, for the sake of argument, that most women are intellectually inferior to most men, still, in the words of Plato, "Many women are in many things superior to many men". Should not those who have capacity and inclination be allowed to receive this higher education? Should not those who have a gift be allowed to develop and to exercise it? If a woman has a message for the world, must she remain dumb? Notwithstanding woman has been hedged in by certain artificial limitations from time almost immemorial, the effort to repress powerful intellect, magnificent genius, because found in her person, has not always been successful. What a loss to the world had not Mrs. Stowe taken up her pen to depict the horrors of slave life, yet probably she would have darned a greater number of stockings and sewed on more buttons had she desisted from such labors. Nor would we have had Lucretia Mott withhold herself from public life, from her platform efforts as temperance reformer and anti-slavery agitator. "Something God had to say to her" and through her to an erring people.

Woman moulds and fashions society. Man's chivalrous deference gives her a pre-eminence and an influence here which carry with them a proportionally great responsibility. The better the training she has received the better enabled will she be to perform the social duties devolving upon her. The more effectual the intellectual armor in which she encases herself the more prepared will she be to engage in the skirmishes of mind. Men adapt themselves to their company, and conversation in society does not rise above the level of its women. It is necessary, then, that woman be ready to meet man upon equal intellectual ground, that her mental equipment be not inferior to his own. We would not have social converse composed exclusively of discussions on the "ologies" or made up of quotations from the "little Latin and less Greek" learned in the schools, but the discipline gained by such scholastic training makes one undeniably brighter, wittier, more entertaining, capable of wielding a greater influence for good. The *salons* of the intellectual women of France afford numerous examples of what may be accomplished by woman in society. Who has not heard of Madames Recamier and Roland, of Madame de Sevigne, hated by Louis XIV because of her wit; of Madame de Stag, persecuted by Napoleon, who could not forgive her for being more clever than himself? These women, when old and faded, still charmed by grace and cultivation of mind. Loveliness of person is a rare gift, a precious boon to be duly appreciated, but only mind is truly beautiful.

"Mind, mind alone, bear witness, earth and heaven;
The living fountain in itself contains of beauteous and sublime ! Here
 hand in hand
Sit paramount the graces."

The possession of a higher education multiplies woman's bread-winning opportunities. This is a most important consideration. All women do not enter the domestic state, and even many who do are afterwards so situated as to require a resort to some means of earning their own living and that of others dependent upon them. What shall these women do? It is true that sewing is considered a very respectable occupation and nursing is certainly a most feminine employment, but some women have no desire to sing the song of the shirt and possess no taste for minding babies, least of all those of other people; besides, both of these avenues of female labor, as others of similar character, are overcrowded and but slightly remunerative.

I repeat it, what is to be done with these women, seeking the means by which to earn their daily bread? Will you give them this higher education, and thereby open doors to congenial and paying pursuits; or will you frown them down, and tempt to dishonor by refusing the means of self-support? Quoting Plato again: "Neither a woman as a woman nor a man as a man has any special function, but the gifts of nature are equally diffused in both sexes; all the pursuits of men are the pursuits of women also". While I do not agree with the ancient sage in his comprehensive statement I do believe that if a woman has a gift for a particular calling and she is not debarred from that calling by the natural barrier of sex, it is both presumptuous and unjust for man to attempt to restrain her, on the plea that the work for which nature has evidently designed her is unfeminine. Even men with wise and statesman-like views upon other subjects turn fanatics upon this. They would not have a woman lecture, because it would make her too public; as if publicity could harm one whose only desire is to do good work in a good cause. Nor would they have her a physician, because she must study "indelicate" subjects; as if to a pure-minded person the contemplation of the workmanship of these bodies, wondrously and divinely wrought, could be indelicate.

Woman is for a helpmeet unto man. She is meant to be his assistant in every good work and his companion in the fullest sense of the word. Properly to sustain this relation she must needs have equal educational advantages. There can be no perfect companionship between two people one of whom is by far the intellectual superior of the other. The one will have thoughts, feelings and aspirations which the other can neither sympathize with nor understand. That wife whose mind has been equally broadened and deepened, who is capable of giving wise counsels and judgments, and of intelligently aiding in the furtherance of their mutual aims, can alone be truly a helpmeet to her husband. "Verily, two cannot walk together except they be agreed." Many an eminent man attributes greatly his success to the clear head, as well as the loving heart, of the woman who is his wife. She is the power behind the throne, often more powerful than the monarch himself; hers may be the hand at the helm, moving noiselessly but most effectually. There are many unknown Caroline Herschels, quietly aiding a brother or a husband on to fame.

It is even more necessary that women be well educated than men, for they are to be the mothers of future generations. Men make laws and institutions, but women make men. The child in the hands of its mother is as clay in the hands of the potter. It is hers to "rear the tender mind", to direct the infant thought, to impress the growing character. There can be no higher mission than this, no more responsible position, no calling requiring greater knowledge and wisdom.

An ancient philosopher says: "The most important part of education is right training in nursery. The soul of the child, in his play, should trained in that sort of excellence in which, when he grows up into manhood, he will have to be perfected." The learned Bacon and the great Washington were equally indebted to their mothers, because of the studiousness of the one and the broad culture of the other. No one can direct the early training of the child as can the mother herself; she gives a bias to the youthful mind which it is more than likely to retain

> "'Tis education forms the common mind,
> Just as the twig is bent the tree's inclined."

Ought not women to have broad and full and able minds to perform aright the duties of motherhood? Is it not to the interest of society, of the state, of the nation, that women be liberally educated? To have the mothers ignorant would be through them to weaken the sons, and finally the commonwealth.

"The hand that rocks the cradle,
Is the hand that rules the world."

Fear not to lend your influence for the higher education of woman. She will be none the less a woman when she has received such an education; she will have lost none of that grace and sweetness of character which men admire. Woman asks not of education to make her a man; she asks that herself be given back to her, but herself awakened, strengthened, elevated. Would you open new avenues of employment for her, would you render her a useful and independent member of society? Then give her a higher education. Would you develop the hidden resources of her mind, would you fit her to raise the tone and character of society? Give her a higher education. Would you have her assist her husband in his vexed problems of thought? Would you have her his companion in intellectual and spiritual life? Would you have her train her children aright and be a fountain of knowledge to her family? Then give her a higher education.

MRS. JOSEPHINE TURPIN WASHINGTON.

CHAPTER XCIX.
INFLUENCE OF NEGRO WOMEN IN THE HOME.

That a large part of the great NEGRO POPULATION in America is yet in a condition of *ignorance, superstition* and *poverty* is evident, and that this present condition is a natural sequence of a former and more wretched condition, no one who is well acquainted with the real circumstances can truthfully deny; and that *another* large part of the race has made unparalleled advancement far in excess of what was naturally expected at the close of the late war, and that as an American citizen the negro has already been a success in every avenue and avocation in which he has been permitted to freely operate and compete, cannot be truthfully denied.

Now let us for a moment assume that he is *ignorant, superstitious* and *poor*. Is that any more than could have been naturally expected of a people who have been from under the yoke of bondage only thirty years, and who came into citizenship in one day more than four millions in number without a dollar and without an established credit for one dollar's worth, or is it possible that the world has so little of the sense of justice or charity for an oppressed people as to expect them *en masse* to become a perfect people in one-quarter of a century—a thing that no race has ever done? To expect this of the negro is simply to acknowledge that he possesses ability far superior to that of other races, which is not true.

It is amazingly strange to note the scrutiny that some of our friends bring into use at times to avoid .giving the negro due credit for many of his good deeds, and at the same time to note their willingness to magnify and publish to the world his mistakes. Can our friends in America not afford to be just?

After all, it would seem that somehow, and certainly without good reason, the negro is the American bone of contention." He is discussed and abused by a large part of the public press and upon the stump and public platform in almost every conceivable and unfair manner. Conventions are called in the *North* and in the *South* in which they discuss *the what to do with him* and *what to do for him* without ever asking him or his representatives to meet them and discuss *the how to let him alone,* other than to help him become a man like all other good men. Some Legislatures pass discriminating laws against him, some (and many) courts of justice pass upon him and his case without regard to his rights before the law of the just.

Mob violence hunts him by day and by night like the fierce lion of the forest in search of his prey. In the name of our glorious American flag we ask, Why is this so? He is not responsible as yet for his condition. He is in no way responsible for his presence in America, being brought here against his own will.

And surely, he is a human being, created in the image of a just God, who made alike the *black man,* the *white man,* the *red man and* the *Chinaman* in *His own image.*

Surely the God who rules in *heaven* and in *earth* without error, and who is void of partiality in any form, would not be partial in dealing with the highest order of His created beings.

In 2 Samuel, 14:14, we read: "Neither doth God respect any person." In .1 Peter, .1:17, we read: "Who, without respect of persons, judgeth according to every man's work." We read in Acts 17:26: "Hath made of one blood all nations of men for to dwell on all the face of the earth." In addition to these references the whole account of redemption through Jesus Christ shows beyond all question that God has not only been just in *creating all men equal,* but has further manifested that justice by His provisions for the redemption of *all men* through the *one medium, the blood* of His crucified Son, Jesus Christ.

It would seem to the writer that to charge God with partiality in the *creation* or *redemption* of man is simply to deny that He is just, which is to deny Him of an important attribute. In addition to this the great Alexander Von Humboldt has truthfully said, "There is no typical sharpness of division among men, all being interfusible." His well-known and able brother, William, has said, "There is no real inferiority of race." The scholarly J. L. M. Curry, D. D., LL. D., has said, "There is no caste in mind." The distinguished and philosophic Dr. Thomas has said also, "The whole drift of scientific reasoning tends to the conclusion that there is really but one race modified and modifiable by environments."

Upon the above evidence, gathered from the Book of books and the writings of wise and scholarly men in recent days, we submit as a reasonable conclusion:

(1) THAT ALL MEN ARE BY CREATION EQUALLY ENDOWED;
(2) THAT UNDER SIMILAR CONDITIONS ALL MEN ARE, TO THE SAME EXTENT, CAPABLE OF INTELLECTUAL DEVELOPMENT.

Whatever, therefore, has been said above as applicable to man in his high calling is equally and to the same extent applicable to woman in her equally high sphere.

Whatever one woman has done in the development of home and home-life among her fellow-creatures others of her sex can also do.

Whatever of good qualities are applicable to American or English women are also applicable to Afro-American women under similar circumstances.

In fact, we need to lay more stress upon our capabilities to do whatever God has enjoined upon us.

Let us not be too easily discouraged, but let us learn more to *labor* and to wait for results.

It seems to be quite true that our noble women possess more of this quality than our men, and I am not certain if our women in the home are not the *most powerful* and *progressive* and *substantial agencies* of the race.

In their quiet and often unseen work of building up, preserving, maintaining and purifying the home they are certainly *"the power behind the throne"* in many instances; and although often kept back, discouraged and haltered, so to speak, by the jealousy and tyranny of the *would-be* and *so-called lords of creation*, still they push forward.

The author has taken special pains to inquire of a great many successful business and professional men. of both races as to the causes of either their *success* or *failure,* and the reply has come as expected from both.

Whenever one of our race has freely and willingly stated the cause of his success it has been attributed to the influence of a *mother* or *sister or wife,* while on the other hand, they have almost invariably attributed the causes of their *failures* to their *refusal t*o be advised by *mother* or *sister or wife.*

Now while we do not intend to underrate the importance of man's work in the betterment of his own condition, and while we do not desire to be understood as advocating what is often called an apron-string government nor the subjugation of man by woman, yet we do desire to emphatically teach (and to urge) that a hearty co-operation of man and woman in all worthy undertakings whenever possible is the most hopeful means of success.

We believe that man and woman are created equal. He seems to be *refined* and *encouraged* and *purified* only as she herself is refined and purified and encouraged to look high and labor for the betterment of man. She does not seem to be created as man's slave. She is certainly not his beast of burden. She is not created to follow, necessarily, in all things, but seems to be rather his equal, and therefore belongs at his side, and is his companion in the truest sense.

We have only to recall to mind the nations and individuals of ancient, mediaeval and modern times to remind ourselves of a chain of testimony clearly proving that man has scarcely ever risen higher as a matter of fact, nor has had even higher ideals than the corresponding position which woman has occupied as his immediate associate.

Man's estimation of woman seems to be a true index to his own worth and condition. Now, then, if she is his equal, an associate and companion, then surely she is capable at least of helping and encouraging him to become whatever God has intended that he should be. In no place is she a more necessary power than in the home:

I. *As a mother* she may, to a great extent, assist in shaping our destiny. (1). *The child's physical development* will largely depend upon the *condition of the home* and the *care and conduct* of the mother. If the moral and hygienic surroundings have been good, then we may expect a good physical development. These she may greatly modify. Let the home be attractive, neat, pleasant and pure. (2). *The child's moral development* is greatly modified by the condition of the home. Suffice it to say that the home, as far as possible, should be a model Christian home, presided over by gentle,

400

loving mother, whose influence for good falls as *constantly* and as *gently* and as *effectually* upon the child as do the dews of night upon the tender plant. Kindness, with sufficient restraining positiveness, may often command a loving and willing obedience when all other powers may fail so to do. Who knows but that in this or that Christian home is being trained some great character, possibly a philosopher, a historian, a scholar, the president or queen of some great nation, a great reformer or conqueror? Who can tell what the extent of that home's influence shall be?

One thing is certain, however, that the influences of the home will be just what the home is, and the home will be largely what the woman of the home makes it. If the queen of a great and good home, then there will radiate therefrom great and good influences.

(3). *Intellectual development.* Children are great imitators, both by inheritance and by acquisition of the habit. It is quite possible that even the acts of childish imitation serve as little whetstones, so to speak, to the little mind in giving it sharpness, and at the same time as an exercise may do much by assisting in the development of the same. Whether true or not, it does seem that the more intelligently the powers of the mind are brought into play in early life, the more readily that mind will acquire knowledge, all things else being equal. The more intelligent the home and home surroundings the more intelligent, as a rule, are the offspring of that home. It is here the child gets an idea of its own intellectual powers. It is in the home it seems to get its first ideas of becoming what it seems to see in others of its surroundings, whether good or evil. It is generally true that a child reared in an intelligent home has a more tenacious memory than one of opposite situation, yet this may not always prove true. The fact that one child at some time, or at all times in its history, shows more aptness and acquires more readily than another is no argument in favor of the superiority of one mind, by creation, over the other; no more than the fact that one organ in the same body, or a set of organs in the same body, is created superior to the other, simply because one organ or one set of organs in that body is better developed than the other; nor is it any more so than the fact that the muscles of one arm are better developed than those of the other arm, because one arm has had the advantage of a more complete development. Suffice it to say, however, that the home should be as intelligent as circumstances will allow, and yet there are many good homes that are not so brilliant as those some would call intelligent, and yet they are intelligent; they are full of good sense, wisdom, virtue, piety and thrift.

From these homes have come many of our best men and women. Such homes are practical and greatly beneficial.

II. *As a sister* she may wield an influence at times more powerful than the mother, for many times she can find out the tendencies of a brother or sister long before the mother observes them. She is often taken more into confidence (and yet no friend should be regarded more confidential than mother), but somehow it is true that they, as children, talk of their desires and inclinations so that even in early childhood an older sister may do much good in assisting the mother in the care and well-being of the children. When her influence is combined with that of the mother, she may be even more powerful. The two constitute possibly the greatest power of the home, and especially so in giving counsel to those who are approaching womanhood and manhood and are formulating their plans for the future. The restraining influence of a sister is far-reaching in its effects. It may haunt even an older brother in the midst of his wildest deeds and reclaim him therefrom.

How many young men, talented young men, have been saved by the tears and pleadings of an affectionate sister even when the fleecy locks of a tender mother were of no effect. She has often led to the mercy-seat a way-ward brother whom God has greatly blessed and used as a means of saving thousands of souls. III. *As a wife.* Possibly woman is never so powerful as when queen of her own home—the wife of a faithful husband. Here she may reign in the fullness of her power and to the fullest extent of her love and sympathies, with almost unlimited interest and a never dying satisfaction. She is indeed a queen in the full sense of the word; the ideal of a fond husband whom she serves and loves and obeys as a part of the joys of her life and the aspirations of her soul. Here her influence upon the community is most powerful as a neighbor and a sympathizer with the afflicted and unfortunate, a model of good works, a teacher of faithfulness and an administrator of impartial justice.

Presiding over a quiet home with dignity, and at the same time with almost unlimited love and interest, is truly a condition of a home that is a most wisely bestowed blessing upon any people or community.

All these positions of trust and great responsibility have been well filled by our women for more than' a quarter of a century.

Beginning life as they did, *without a home* and without the means with which to buy a home, yet, as determined as if Spartan soldiers, they placed homes where there were no homes, and at once became the queens thereof. Negro women have done more for the peculiar growth and development of their race than the women of any other people. In fact, negro women have been the life of nearly every negro enterprise now in existence. Without her the Church would be a mere name, and the ministry would scarcely eat bread.

They have been the life of the schools, and, indeed, many of our great men and women have been educated by the money earned by the hard and unceasing efforts of our women. By the sweat of their brow and by the powers of their brain and muscle our women have made statesmen, lawyers, preachers, doctors, teachers, artists and mechanics, many of whom have coped with the best brain of America. The negro has successfully operated in every avocation in which it has been his privilege to enter, in both State and national affairs. By what power was he impelled and sustained if not by the constancy of Afro-American women?

As our women have been great in the past, they may be even more in the future. The race needs men, not only educated and scholarly, but men with will-power, and, if possible, with a *steel backbone;* men who once seeing the right will maintain the same in the protection of home and home's dearest interests. We need man in some of our men; and most naturally we need men and money.

To our own true women alone we must look largely for these necessities. They preside over the home, they train the children of the home, and they will development and women in the home.

APPENDIX

WOMEN OF DISTINCTION:

REMARKABLE IN WORKS AND INVINCIBLE IN CHARACTER.

BY

L. A. SCRUGGS, A. M., M. D.,

Former Resident Physician at Leonard Medical Hospital, former Professor of
Physiology and Resident Physician at Shaw University, present Visiting
Physician and Lecturer on Physiology and Hygiene at
St. Augustine Normal and Collegiate institute.

INTRODUCTION BY MRS. JOSEPHINE TURPIN WASHIN3TON.

SPECIAL CONTRIBUTIONS By

T. THOMAS FORTUNE, WILLIAM STILL, J. HUGO JOHNSTON, E. E. SMITH,
MISS IDA B. WELLS, MISS MARY V. COOK, MRS. ROSETTA E.
LAWSON, MISS L. C. FLEMING, MRS. SARAH J. W. EARLY,

MRS. J. SILONE—YATES, MISS LENA JACKSON,
MRS. E. C. PEGIIF.14, G. W. HAYRS,
W. B. HOLLAND.

"Cod that made the world, and all things therein, ...bath

ctsmade of one blood all nations of men for to dwell on all The fare of the earth."—*Acts* xvii: (part of) 24-26.

ILLUSTRATED.

RALEIGH, N. C.:

L. A. SCRUGGS, PI7BLISHER, 21 EAST WORTH STREET.

1893.

DEDICATION

TO THE AFRO—AMERICAN MOTHER.; AND DAUGHTERS WHO, IN THOSE

DARK DAYS OF OUR HISTORY, ENDEAVORED 'TO BE FAITHFUL TO

WHAT THEY UNDERSTOOD TO BE THE PRINCIPLES OF TRUTH

AND VIRTUE; AND ALSO TO THE NOBLE WOMEN OF

THE RACE WHO, IN THESE BRIGHTER DAYS

HAVE ASSIDUOUSLY LABORED, AS BEST

THEY COULD, TO ESTABLISH AN I'N

IMPEACHABLE CHARACTER IN

THE WOMANHOD; OF

THE RACE;

AND TO THE PHILANTHROPIC MEN AND WOMEN OF THE COUNTRY

WHO HAVE DONE AND ARE DOING MUCH TO ELEVATE THIS PEOPLE

BY PROVIDING FOR THEM A CHRISTIAN EDUCA-

TION, AND HAVE NOT IN CONSEQUENCE THEREOF

DEMANDED ANY SACRIFICE OF THEIR

MANHOOD AND WOMANHOOD;

To CHARLES J. PICKFORD, THE AUTHOR'S EARLY FRIEND AND

BENEFACTOR;

AND TO THE SACRED MEMORY OF A LOVING AND SAINTED WIFE,

LUCIE J. SCRUGGS, A MOST VALUABLE HELPER, WHO REN

DERED MUCH ASSISTANCE, EVEN IN THE

PREPARATION OF THESE PAGES ;

THIS VOLUME IS SINCERELY. DEDICATED

BY THE AUTHOR.

PRESSES OF E. M. UZELL,
RALEIGH, N. C.

SCRUGGS FAMILY PHOTO.

Scruggs Family Picture 1955 – Left to Right:
Leonard Andrew Scruggs, Jr., Yvonne Scruggs, Leonard Andrew Scruggs, Sr.,
Geneva Byrd Scruggs.
Seated on the floor:
Roslyn Elizabeth Scruggs, Harriet Alva Scruggs
and Jackie, the family dog.

NOTES

NOTES

NOTES

NOTES

NOTES

NOTES